Georgia's Ghostly Getaways

Kathleen Walls

Georgia's Ghostly Getaways

ISBN: 978-0-9845926-2-3

First published in print in 2003 by Global Authors Publications

Current edition 2024

Global Authors Publications

Filling the GAP in publishing

Cover Design by Kathleen Walls

All photos on cover and interior are by Kathleen Walls

Printed in USA for Global Authors Publications

Dedication and Acknowledgment

This book is dedicated to all the helpful Convention and Visitors Bureau people and all the Chamber of Commerce folks who helped set me up with visits to these wonderful places.

Without you this book would not exist.

Table of Contents

Introduction

Come with me on a visit to Georgia's ghostly getaways. They offer spirited excitement and haunting beauty. From the seaport of Savannah to the Appalachian Mountains, the Peach State has its share of spooky spots. The spirits come in both sexes and all races. You can even find animal ghosts. Join me as we look behind all the creaky doors and eerie mansions at Georgia's most spectral sites.

It's probably just coincidence that these spooks choose to abide in some of the most interesting places in all of Georgia. It would be an awful shame to visit these haunted sites and miss out on some other fascinating places just around the block. So, in order to get the most enjoyment out of each place with a haunted site, Georgia's Ghostly Getaways will also recommend other places of interest in the area. After all, the title says "Getaways."

Since, unlike the spirits we seek, travelers have bodily needs; this book will also give helpful hints about food and lodging. Whether your choice is a rustic campground or a historic bed and breakfast, you will find suggestions to please every weary traveler. Likewise, fine food gourmets and fans of home style cooking will also find something to please each taste.

This edition has been updated since many places go out of business and now are just a fond memory in the author's mind. On the bright side, many new and exciting places come into being and are worth a visit.

Section 1 Georgia's Turbulent Coast

Georgia's coast was the gateway to the state for the English settlers. They thronged to this last of the thirteen colonies to make a new life. Most were hardworking and honest, some adventurers with an eye for gold and excitement. For some of these, their fortunes lay on the bounding main.

From the 1700s to the early 1800s, pirates ruled the oceans. They lived and died with legends far larger than reality. Wherever they landed along Georgia's coasts, they left their mark. Some say their spirits still roam this area.

Chapter 1 Savannah, Georgia's Hostess City

Savannah is a place where past and present mingles. Its turbulent history created one of the most haunted cities in America. In fact, it is the home of what many consider the most haunted house in the country. To everyone who has read the book or seen the movie, Midnight in the Garden of Good and Evil–and who hasn't–Jim Williams name is forever associated with the infamous murder in Savannah.

However, he is remembered by others as the former owner of the only house in the city to be the site of an official exorcism. Unlike his more famous Mercer House, this one is just a simple New England style home, The Hampton Lillibridge House. It is located near Washington Square on Julian Street. Built originally by Hampton Lillibridge, it and the similar house next door were saved from the demolition ball when Williams bought it in the 1960s. Both houses were to be moved from the original site.

Problems began at once. The neighboring house collapsed and killed a workman. As the work progressed, workers reported inexplicable sounds coming from the empty house. One man, investigating strange noises on an upper floor, felt himself being dragged towards the steep drop of a chimney shaft. Others described the sounds of a party and music coming from the top floor. Williams experienced several occurrences while he occupied the house. Many people reported seeing different apparitions, ranging from an elderly man, a younger man and a woman.

The causes are obscure. When Williams was moving the house, the remains of an ancient tabby crypt were found underneath. He didn't investigate at the time and later the site had been filled in and the crypt destroyed. Another possible cause was the sailor who hanged himself from a bedpost in one of the upstairs bedrooms.

On December 7, 1963, the Right Reverend Albert Rhett Stewart, Episcopal Bishop of the Diocese of Georgia, preformed an exorcism in the house. It is the only house in Savannah to have been the scene of an official exorcism. Perhaps the more malevolent spirits are gone or just dormant but some eerie phenomena continue to this day. It is currently a private residence.

To enjoy Savannah to its fullest, you must consider its past. Step back to 1733. In Savannah, that's easy. Maybe it's the multitude of historical buildings. Or perhaps, rumors that James Oglethorpe himself dabbled in mysticism. The many tours aimed at unraveling the mysteries from beyond the grave all agree that tourists aren't the only strange creatures roaming the streets, inns and stately buildings of historic Savannah. Haunted Savannah Walking Tour is a good way to explore. There are no theatrics or make believe spooky stuff in her tour.

When you look in just the right places, the past is still very much present. Dappled sunshine filters through the canopy of live oaks attired in flowing drapes of Spanish moss. A few rays strike the life-sized bronze statue of James Edward Oglethorpe. The General reigns supreme over Chippewa Square. He stands, facing south towards his enemies in Florida, ever vigilant against Spanish attack. It's oh so easy to imagine him as he was in life.

When General Oglethorpe stepped off the deck of the tiny ship "Anne" in 1733, he was a man with a plan. He had been commissioned by King George 11 to found the thirteenth English colony here as a buffer between the thriving South Carolina settlements and the Spanish enemy in St. Augustine. His Savannah was to be a planned city, laid out around 24 squares. Visitors ever since have been singing his praises. His foresight has made Savannah one of the easiest cities in the country to navigate. However, some historians hint that Oglethorpe may have had other motives besides ease of navigating the city. There are rumors that he dabbled in the occult.

The city squares may have had a more sinister basis. The design may have originated in a desire to copy Solomon's Temple. By a common measure of the day, cubits, the original city was a square 1,000 cubits per side, mimicking the ancient temple. Squares are an important pattern in occult symbolism. Could Oglethorpe have been trying to create some type of mystical gate into another dimension? Whatever his motives, the bonus was Savannah's location. It sits near the Atlantic coast with the broad Savannah River separating it from South Carolina.

Savannah has so many haunted spots it's almost easier to say "what's not haunted?" In 1733 when the Yamacraw chief, Tomochichi, befriended George Oglethorp and suggested a good place to built Savannah, he neglected to mention this spot was on top of an Indian burial ground. One possible reason Savannah has been called "America's most haunted city."

The residents created a cemetery for their dead right in the heart of the small settlement. About half of the original 114 settlers had died by the first year. One of the first deaths was the only doctor which was not a good omen. But the town grew and the settlers repeated the initial problem about 17 years later. They wanted to the site of the cemetery for town growth. They called on all the loved ones to come move their dead to the new cemetery. The problem was many of the dead had no family left to move them, so they stayed behind under what is today The Collins Quarter, a popular bistro.

The Visitors Center, located in a restored railway station of the Central Georgia Railroad, can help you get oriented. Here you can find maps and brochures. Also here is the Savannah History Museum. The exhibits and movie will bring you up to date on Savannah history since Oglethorpe and his 124 settlers arrived.

Even here, history intertwines with modern events. The train that left that station daily was the "Nancy Hanks," named for Lincoln's mother. Tom Hanks, who came to Savannah to film Forrest Gump, is quite proud to be a descendant of Nancy Hanks. Savannah History Museum displays the bench where Forrest Gump sat to tell his life story. Just look for the one with the box of chocolates.

In the Railway Museum one passenger car is believed to be haunted by the spirit of man dressed "old fashioned" attire.

The car that was President Warren G. Harding's personal Pullman sleeper, The Superb, also is the home of a restless spirit.

All of the trolley tours depart from the Visitor Center parking lot. This is a great way to orient yourself. The Old Town Trolley offers "off and on" privileges so you can stop and sightsee wherever you wish. They give an excellent commentary. The Gray Line and other tours give an overview of the city history and events. Some of these let you get off and on. Each tour has a slightly different slant and route. Of course, there are several "Ghost Tours" both by trolley and on foot.

Savannah's newest museum shows you gangsters, moonshine makers, flappers, anti-saloon leagues, rum runners, and a hatchet-wielding Carrie Nation. You learn what the three Xs on moonshine mean. It's America's only prohibition museum. There are exhibits on catching rum runners and the gangsters and moonshiners who made fortunes during prohibition. It tells of its effect on women's fashion. For the first time, women cut their hair short, wore short skirts and danced the Charleston to Jazz.

After you are admitted to the museum by a 1920s era flapper, the first exhibit is a Budweiser deliver driver in a Model T Ford Truck trying to deliver booze to McCurdy's Saloon while two ladies protest holding signs saying "Alcohol is poison" and "Bread not Beer." The Independent Presbyterian Church is located next to Chippewa Square. It is from its sky-piercing steeple the feather dropped at the beginning of the movie. Incidentally, the bus is actually going up a one-way street the wrong way in the movie.

It's too new to have discovered any resident ghosts but with all the gangster era artifacts there, I'm betting at least one spirit surfaces here.

Bull Street begins at Savannah's gold-domed city hall (Isn't that appropriate?) It's the main thoroughfare and leads you to Savannah's first square, Johnson Square. Picture that early settlement filled with wooden houses. The danger of fire was rampant. Thus, communal ovens were set up here. At baking time, the entire settlement must have smelled like the inside of a bakery. In the center is a monument to Revolutionary War hero, General Nathaniel Greene. Again, like most of the city, huge oak trees with ever present Spanish Moss offer shade.

Wright Square was named for Georgia's third and last royal governor, Sir James Wright. Tomochichi, the Yamacraw Indian chief who greeted the settlers as they disembarked is buried here. His grave marked by a simple boulder. If he hovers nearby, his visage would be frightening. Tomochichi was reputed to be seven feet tall, with one eye and bear claws tattooed on his chest. In spite of his fierce appearance, the elderly chief befriended the young English general and was so helpful that many consider him a co-founder of Georgia.

There is a phantom in the square that is far less fearsome looking than Tomochichi. Alice Riley, a young Irish indentured servant, was the first woman to be hanged in Georgia. She was executed here on January 19, 1735 for the murder of her master, William Wise. She and her boyfriend, Richard White, were accused of drowning Wise in his bath water. She was pregnant at the time of her trial and was allowed to deliver the baby before her execution. Legend says she was immediately dragged to the gallows after the birth and hanged. She claimed that Wise had raped her and that the child was his. However, since she helped kill Wise on March 1734, it is impossible that this part is true. White was hanged on the same gallows.

Visitors to the square have seen a young woman dressed in blood-soaked rags in Wright Square searching for her baby. Sometimes she is sitting under the tree where the gallows once stood. If you approach her she will vanish.

Supposedly, Spanish Moss will not grow where innocent blood was spilled. While Alice was in jail she repeatedly told many people that William Wise had raped and beaten her. Scientists have tried to prove why no Spanish Moss will grow on the trees of Wright Square but no one had found a reason.

Wright Square's central monument is dedicated to William Washington Gordon, an early mayor and founder of the Central Georgia Railroad. However, he is more remembered as the father of Juliette Gordon Low, founder of the Girl Scouts. Her birthplace, on this square, is open to the public as a museum. Beyond the stately façade of the magnificent home, there is a love story. One that hints of a love stronger than death.

Willie and Nellie Gordon, Juliette's parents lived here during the turbulent times of the Civil War and on into the nineteenth century. Perhaps they still abide within. Willie died first in 1912. Family members feared for Nellie's sanity because they had been so deeply in love throughout their lives, but she lived out her days peacefully until her death in 1917 secure in the belief she would one day be reunited with Willie. Moments after her death, both her daughter-in-law, Margaret Gordon, and a family butler saw Willie in his Confederate general's uniform coming to meet his beloved. Staff at the museum reports sightings of Nellie to this day.

Lafayette Square is named in honor of the French nobleman who fought so valiantly for the American cause during the Revolution. The Cathedral of St. John the Baptist towers over the square and its fountain centerpiece. The Hamilton-Turner Mansion, built in 1873, is now an inn. It is considered one of the best examples of Second French Empire Victorian in the country.

Here, too, is The Andrew Low House, where Juliette Gordon Low held the first Girl Scout meeting on March 12, 1912. The home is open as a museum and has a gift shop in the carriage house.

The place where Lafayette stayed, on his visit to Savannah in 1825, was the Owen-Thomas House located on Oglethorpe Square. The Regency style house, described as "the most beautiful house in America," has a charming white balcony on the side where the Marquise addressed the local citizens in French for hours. They had no idea what he said but, true Savannahians, they were polite to a guest. Whenever he paused, they nodded their agreement. (Sometimes, Savannah gets a little confusing. Lafayette didn't stay near Lafayette Square. Oglethorpe's statue isn't in Oglethorpe Square. Nathaniel Greene's monument and tomb is not on Greene Square. But, that's all part of Savannah's charm.)

History, architecture, and more merge at 1819 Owens Thomas House and Slave Quarters. You start your tour in the slave quarters and learn things like why enslaved people painted their windows and ceiling "Haint Blue." You see how the enslaved people lived and worked.

Moving through the garden into the main house, the furnishings are beautiful and authentic but there is more here. The architectural details like a floating bridge over a hall at the top of the staircase, a serving table inset into a curved space in the dining room, and the ice chamber downstairs in the basement. The ice chamber was a state-of-the-art feature in homes built by architect William Jay for wealthy clients that allowed them to have ice shipped in 50 pound blocks from up north and stored in this chamber located next to the cistern. Another remarkable feature was the plumbing system. Three differ-ent-level cisterns on the roof allowed them to use three marble bath-tubs, a shower, multiple sinks, and even two flushing water closets, or toilets as we know them today, in the 1800s.

Downstairs there is a section devoted to documents relating the history of the families that lived in the home and the enslaved peo-ple, who are identified by name not just as a group. Much is known and told about these people's lives.

For specter seekers, the house-museum has other charms; the reported presence of deceased owner, Miss Margaret Thomas has been known to make an appearance at her former home turned museum. Margaret was known for throwing elaborate costume par-ties where everyone dressed in 19th century costumes. She died in the 1950 and left the house to the Telfair Museum. Many people in the house at night have seen the Lady in Gray, believed to be the spirit of Margaret Thomas. This spirit strolls around the garden, which Margaret loved in life, wearing a large hat and a gray shawl.

Another spirit often seen wandering the house is the ghost of the man from the 1830s.

Telfair Square's commanding presence is the Telfair Academy. The building is a superb example of English Regency Architecture. William Jay built it. It houses the oldest art museum in the Southeast. And something else, Mary Telfair's presence!

Mary had inherited the home from her father. Rumors imply that Mary and her more attractive sister, Margaret, loved the same man. Margaret won the matrimonial sweepstakes and Mary never married. Upon her death in 1875, she deeded the magnificent mansion to the city for an art museum with the stipulation that there be no eating, drinking or smoking within. Occasionally, if this prohibition is violated, Mary admonishes the culprit with rattling windows and the sound of distant voices. Mary is a lady who likes things to stay just as they were. Our trolley driver told us of an occasion when workman were remolding the dining room where her huge oil portrait hangs. When workers removed her portrait, a portion of the rotunda ceiling fell. Needless to say, her portrait was replaced in its accustomed position.

Until the Civil War, (politely called The War of Northern Aggression here) cotton was king. It was the wealth derived from this "white gold" that created the gracious homes. John Norris built the Green-Meldrim House, located on Madison Square for wealthy cotton merchant, Charles Green. It played its reluctant part in the abdication of King Cotton.

December of 1864 saw General Sherman sweeping towards Savannah. Almost everything on his path had gone up in flames. Savannahians did not want to see their beautiful city torched. They devised an ingenious strategy to captivate Sherman and save their city. Green, who was technically English though he had a son fighting for the South, along with several prudent city fathers, met Sherman and presented him with the keys to the city. They treated him like an honored guest. In turn they hoped he would consider them hosts not firewood.

Green offered the General the hospitality of his home. It worked! Sherman, like other visitors before and since, was charmed with his "Hostess City." Instead of putting Savannah to the torch, he offered it to President Lincoln as a Christmas present. Sherman had no idea he had been outflanked for once.

The house next came into the possession of Judge Peter Meldrim. The Judge and his large family were outgoing and loved parties and music. An old family retainer, Joe, the butler, loved to eavesdrop on the festivities. When Mrs. Meldrim began playing the piano, he would quietly open the door from the servant's quarter to enjoy the music. He is reported to have taken such pride in the old home that he never wanted to leave it. Some believe his specter still resides there.

Today, the home is the rectory for the neighboring St. John's Episcopal Church. Several of the rectors have been accomplished pianists. One noted that frequently when he was playing, the back door inexplicably opened. Residents tell of hearing male footsteps in the old servant's quarters.

Colombia Square was the rallying point for another war. Lady Aster, who visited Savannah in the early 1900s, described the city as "a beautiful lady with a dirty face." Since the decline of the city's wealth after the Civil War, decay had set in and many historic buildings had been destroyed. In 1955, the wrecker's ball took aim at the Isaiah Davenport House on Colombia Square. The tiny forces of the Historic Savannah Foundation took a stand. Seven stalwart ladies mounted a campaign to stop the Federal Style home from becoming one more parking lot. In a dramatic last minute rescue, the home was purchased by the Foundation just 24 hours before its date with destruction. They restored it to the former glory and thanks to their efforts, you can now visit this beautifully restored house museum. As so often happens, victory brought reinforcements rallying to the cause. Today, Savannah has the nation's largest registered historic district. Over 1,200 buildings have been restored.

Colombia Square is also the site of another of Savannah's charming contradictions, The Kehoe House, built by William Kehoe as a testament to his business, Kehoe Ironworks, has some rather unique features. He boasted that anything made of wood would be better in iron. As proof, he had all the detail, staircases, railings, columns, windowsills and anything that is not brick, built of cast iron. Today, it is an inn that has been featured on television as one of "America's Most Romantic Inns."

In its earlier life, it has not always been romantic. It once served as a funeral parlor which might account for its reports of a female presence in room 201. If you choose to stay in that room you may smell the scent of roses and catch a glimpse of a woman wearing a luminous white gown.

The Massie School, located on Calhoun Square, offers an insight into Savannah's architectural and cultural past. This Greek Revival building is the only remaining structure left of Georgia's oldest chartered school system. During Sherman's occupation of Savannah, it operated as a Federal hospital for a short time.

It was a Freedman's School for a few months. Then in 1866, it became part of Savannah's public school system and operated until 1974. There is an exhibit of two real-life schoolrooms from the past. There is lots of information about emancipation and education of the former enslaved people in Savannah.

The Massie School offers a glimpse of Savannah's architectural and cultural past. There is a lot of exhibits related to the different styles you see in Savannah. Some objects from building no longer standing. There are other things left over from the past.

In the early 2000s, a local gas company was digging up the sidewalk in front of the Massie Heritage Center. The workers soon began digging up bones. Construction shut down, and it was yellow-taped off as a crime scene. Forensic experts determined that the bones were of African-American slaves who had been buried and forgotten here for 200 years. So, when you approach Massie Center, you are walking on the largest slave graveyard in Savannah.

The most recognizable house in Savannah faces Monterey Square. The Mercer House housed the infamous Jim Williams. The facts that he may, or may not, have murdered his young companion, created fodder for the bestselling book ever penned about Savannah. This is the home where Jim Williams of "Midnight in the Garden" lived and died.

It has a long history preceding this. It was begun in 1860 as the home of Confederate General Hugh Weedon Mercer, but construction stopped due to the start of the Civil War. It remained unfinished until 1868. Mercer was now broke and unable to finish the home. No Mercer ever lived in the house. It passed through different owners and was the site of the Shriner's headquarters when Williams purchased it.

The home is now owned by William's sister. There is a home tour about the history of the house, the antiques, and how Jim Williams contributions to Savannah's historic preservation. The guide is knowledgeable and explains the significance and architectural aspects in each room. His office is furnished much as it was when he died. There are his antiques and pictures of Williams and his guests at his many famous parties.

It has several ghost stories. One relates to the fact that Jim Williams died in the same room where he shot his young lover shortly after he was acquitted at his forth trial. Many say the dead young man would not rest when his killer was at large and living well. People have reported mysterious lights going on and off in the home at night when no one is in the rooms.

When you take the tour be aware his sister forbids guides discussing paranormal occurrences or any reference to her brother's trials.

The reigning centerpiece of Pulaski square is a tall pedestal bearing a statue of Count Casmir Pulaski, the Polish nobleman who gave his life for America's freedom during the Siege of Savannah in 1779. He is interred beneath the monument. The FBI performed a DNA test to settle conflicting reports that he was buried at sea. One legend claims he died and is buried near Bonadventure Cemetery. The rumors were so insistent that the grave was exhumed in 1854 in an effort to bring peace to the restless Polish nobleman who died for America's freedom. Incidentally, he is honored with his own Pulaski Square several blocks away.

Have you ever dined with a pirate's ghost? The Pirates' House in Savannah is reputed to have some lurking in its attic and in the old tunnel once used to shanghai drugged sailors. If you ask, the staff will show you the entrance to a tunnel from the restaurant that ran underground to the nearby river. Almost as old as the city itself, The Pirates' House began its career as an inn in 1853. It catered to the seafaring men who frequented the port city. The line between honest seaman and bloodthirsty pirate was thin in those times. Blackbeard, himself may have visited the inn on one of his forays into Savannah. Robert Louis Stevenson enjoyed the inn. He is said to have modeled the infamous Captain Flint of Treasure Island on one of the habitués.

In 1992 and again in 1996, reporters and photographers from the Georgia Guardian and several psychics remained in The Pirates' House overnight. They experienced cold spots, a strong feeling of a presence, the sound of footsteps. Some saw a black cloud-like mass floating about.

Mysterious lights and noises often emanate from both the upstairs and the seamen's old quarters. A few years ago, the ghosts have been a party to a new kind of fundraising. Several years ago Greg Proffitt, the owner of one of Savannah's tours, and his friend Richard Cross, spent the night in The Pirates' House attic as a fundraiser for Leukemia. "Things happened that were rather strange and totally inexplicable," Cross said.

A glass of rum left out for Captain Flint disappeared, the glass right along with the rum. They reported hearing knocks even though the restaurant was locked and empty. Whether or not you spot the ghost of the infamous Flint searching for his bottle of rum, you are sure to discover treasure at today's The Pirates' House. However, today the treasure is culinary not pieces of eight. Their daily luncheon buffet is a great way to sample their extremely varied menu.

Cross and Proffitt raised about $6,000 and the following year, 1999 moved their fundraiser to the 17Hundred90 Inn. The ghost here is supposedly Anna Powers who was married to the home's original owner but also had a lover. The lover was a sailor who either died or abandoned Anna. The heartbroken Anna leaped to her death from the second-floor balcony. Anna and her sailor have been sighted hanging around the inn's kitchen frequently causing instruments to fly through the air. Perhaps it's just a lover's quarrel about his overlong absence.

Troup Square is known as the Jingle Bells Square in honor of song's composer, James Lord Pierpont. His brother, John, was the minister of the Unitarian Church located at the corner of Troup Square. He also wrote many Confederate songs such as "Strike for the South," "Our Battle Flag" and "We Conquer or Die" while serving in the Confederate Army.

Ellis Square, once the City Market then transformed into a parking lot, has regained its former glory. With the parking moved underground, the square now boasts a visitor center, restrooms, an interactive fountain, a variety tables and benches for picnicking or just relaxing, and space for concerts or other performances. The park includes a bronze statue of Savannah native and popular songwriter. Johnny Mercer. The City Market next to it is a thriving series of shops, dining establishments and art galleries.

The brick cotton warehouses and brokerages along the Savannah River which sat abandoned and deserted since King Cotton was ousted, thrive again. River Street and Factors Walk stretch for over nine blocks. Today, they house restaurants, shops, pubs, inns and hotels. Several of these boast a resident ghost.

Shrimp Factory is one of the riverfront eateries with a mysterious presence. Workers there dread going alone into a storeroom in the attic. The dark airless room was used at night to chain the newly arrived slaves who worked at unloading the cotton all day. There is a story of one slave who died there of pneumonia, alone and untended. Staff who have had to go into the area at night tell of pitiful moans and shadows drifting along the walls.

If you wander into Churchill's Pub, it's easy to believe you are back in Merry Olde England. Located in the Historic District, the bar, built in England in 1860, is the oldest in Savannah. The food is typical British fare. You can order a chip butty (French fries on toasted French bread), Bubble and Squeak, (mashed potatoes with boiled cabbage seasoned with ham, beef and turkey), Bangers and Mash, (mashed potatoes and peas with sausage) or Toad in the Hole (Yorkshire pudding with sausage). Fortunately, the menu contains a dictionary to help you discover the American equivalent of the dishes. The atmosphere here is the biggest attraction. Here too, there is a dark side. The building was once used as a boxing arena. One of the fighters killed another, and was in turn hanged in the building right over part of the dining area.

Colleges always seem to attract restless spirits. Perhaps because of the youthful exuberance present there. Savannah College of Art and Design's Oglethorpe House, one of the student residences, has at least one haunt. Students have reported water being turned on mysteriously, whispering noises, and the sound of marbles rolling. The story is that a small boy was playing marbles on the upper balcony when he chased a marble and fell to his death. Another presence that has been reported there is that of a caretaker.

Naturally, you will find ghosts at three of Savannah's most famous theaters. The Lucas Theater was built in 1921 for Colonel Arthur Lewis by C. K. Howell as a theater and degenerated after the advent of television. It shut down for a time and was later restored in 2000 by The Lucas Theater for the Arts Foundation. Ironically the last film shown before it shut down was *The Exorcist*.

A few blocks from the Juliet Gordon Low House, what was once the York Lane Theatre was built above an old cemetery. Once during a play, the actors witnessed a group of Confederate soldiers materialize and then disappear.

The Savannah Theater, built in 1818, is the nation's oldest theater. It has been remodeled due to decay and fire and today sports an art Deco look. Edwin booth, brother of Lincoln's assassin appeared n its stage. It is believed that John Wilkes Booth acted there but is not proven.

All three of these theaters are known to be haunted.

Marshall House, now a hotel, is the scene of a Union Soldier hunting his arm. It was used as a hospital when Sherman arrived in town on his march to the sea. It served as a hospital during one of the many yellow fever epidemics. Sure enough when they began excavating and working on building the hotel, the crew discovered many bones of arms and legs. Today, many guests awake finding their arm outstretched with a hand on their wrist and their forehead. Monica, out ghost tour guide, told us, "Today, it's not a really pricy hotel but back in the old days, it cost and arm and a leg to stay there."

A great way to see the city in a new light is on one of the cruises offered along the docks. A dining cruise on the Savannah Riverboat Cruises allow you to glimpse the lights of the city from the water while enjoying a buffet style meal and dancing.

Savannah's most beloved ghost guards the riverfront. The Waving Girl in life was Florence Martus. In life she lived on the tiny island of Elba a few miles downriver from Savannah with her brother, the lighthouse keeper. When Florence fell in love with a sailor she promised him she would be the first thing he saw when he returned. He sailed away and for 50 years Florence waved to each returning ship. Her lover never returned and Florence died in 1943, still waiting. For her 50 years as unofficial ambassador of good will, the city honored her with a statue on the riverfront. Perhaps, Florence's spirit still lives on because witnesses have reported seeing the stone cloth she holds waving in the breeze

For Savannah's seagoing history in a nutshell visit Ships of the Sea Museum. It is located near the river in the William Scarbrough House. While you are there, keep a sharp eye out for the spirit of

Julia Scarbrough. The home was once her proud showplace. Her husband invested heavily in the *Savannah*, the first steam powered ship to cross the Atlantic. However, the ship was not a financial success and the Scarbroughs had to sell their home. Ever headstrong, Julia may have returned to her home after death. Later residents have reported seeing her rocking on the porch.

Savannah boasts some unusual spirits. Nearby Fort McAllister witnesses frequent appearances of Tom Cat. He was a black cat adopted by the fort's Confederate defenders. Tom Cat was killed during the battle's heaviest shelling. Strangely enough, Tom was the day's only casualty. His human companions erected a plaque to him and dutifully reported his death as if he were any other soldier.

Fort Pulaski was the key to Savannah during the Civil War. Lee had been stationed there earlier and proclaimed it unbreachable. Unfortunately for the city, he was wrong. In April 1862, twenty-five-year-old Colonel Charles Olmstead surrendered the fort and his sword with the historic comment, "I yield my sword. I trust I have not disgraced it."

The fort became the prison of over 500 Confederate officers held there during the bitter cold winter of 1864-65. In retaliation for the treatment of Union prisoners, they were kept in the most inhumane conditions. The casements were damp and unheated and food was scarce. After the war, Confederate cabinet officers and political prisoners were kept there. It is only natural that the fort retains a feeling of despair. The prison area and a stairway where a young Confederate defender died are especially psychically charged. The tragic history of the fort explains the presence, so often seen by nighttime observers, of soldiers marching along the ramparts and through the bushes.

Twice a year, at Christmas and in the summer, the fort holds a candlelight tour. The Christmas party, a reenactment of a Confederate Christmas in 1861, when the defenders believed the fort impregnable, is a moving experience. The uniformed re-enactors stand guard at the watch fires. Within, gaiety reigns as antebellum beauties and gallant Confederate soldiers observe Christmas festivities. Perhaps some of the former prisoners feel right at home during the performance. If you note a soldier that seems too authentic to be a re-enactor, maybe he isn't.

Fort Jackson began life as a Revolutionary fort. It saw the most action during the Civil War. Its live-in dead person is known by name. He is Private Gerighty who suddenly attacked his commanding officer for no apparent reason. The deranged soldier then jumped into the moat and drowned himself. Oddly enough, the water level is rarely over five feet deep. The officer recovered and is no longer anywhere around but Gerighty is still here.

According to an attendant at the fort, Daniel Grisette, "Visitors have frequently seen a man walking across the parade ground then he just disappears. Maybe it's Private Gerighty. Another strange thing happens with regard to an award given as a joke. Each year, the outstanding re-enactor is given an award called the 'Gerighty Award'. It's a trophy shaped like a musket. The first year, a piece of the musket broke off. It was later found on the drawbridge. The following year, a different piece of the musket was mysteriously broken off. It, too, was later found on the drawbridge."

Of course, cemeteries are always a logical place to find the deceased. However, you don't always find them as lively as at Savannah's Bonadventure Cemetery. This moss-draped site on the banks of the river is a natural setting for the unnatural. It was here that the famous Bonadventure Plantation was located. Famous for its hospitality, its last and most famous dinner party occurred around 1800. The guests were wining and dining in the extreme elegance for which the host, Governor Josiah Tattnall, was famous. Upon being informed that the hose was on fire, Governor Tattnall requested the party move outdoors and continue. As the house was engulfed in flames, one of the merrymakers proposed a toast, "May the joy of this occasion never end and may we always be as we are tonight."

Many visitors to the cemetery report the sounds of merrymakers and the clink of toasting glasses in the night. Perhaps the party continues uninterrupted to this day. The Bird Girl stature made famous in "Midnight in the Garden of Good and Evil" is no longer here. It is now at the Telfair Museum for protection against vandals.

An unusual one of Savannah's ghosts began his afterlife career in 1998. The tale began when Al Cobb, who owns Cobb's Galleries, bought a honey-oak antique bed for $120 at the Savannah Auction for his teenage son, Jason. Within several nights a presence began manifesting himself to the Cobb family and particularly Jason. He claimed to be Danny, a seven-year-old boy who died in the bed in 1899. Danny wrote notes with crayons and answered some of the Cobb's questions in this way. However, soon the presence became violent. Jason's mother, Lila, insisted the bed had to go. End of story? Not quite. The occurrences in the Cobb house continued after the bed was sold.

48 Hours did a program on "The Danny Phenomenon" and Al Cobb has written a book but no one has yet explained what caused Danny to manifest himself at the Cobb home and remain there.

Perhaps the reason for Savannah's many spirits are the result of a curse placed on the city by a former newspaper publisher who left the city in 1820. He had become disillusioned with Savannah and wrote, in his final issue, a poem called A Curse on Savannah. It expressed his most evil wish for the city thusly,

"Now to finish my curses upon your ill city, and express in few words all the sum of my ditty I leave you, Savannah, a curse that is far the worst of all curses – to remain as you are!"

Chapter 2 St. Simons Island

There is something ethereal about the light on St. Simons Island. Perhaps the way it reflects through the curving branches of the giant moss covered oaks that bewitch the visitor into seeing it as a magic place. One of its most visited attractions is the Christ Church Cemetery. Drive past it on a dark night and look for the ghost light. Stories tell of a wife who feared the dark. In life, she always maintained a good supply of candles to keep it at bay. When she died, her husband was aghast at the thought of her sleeping in the dark graveyard. At night, he would place a lit candle over her grave. Is this the light that hundreds of people have seen flickering among the tombs?

Christ Church presides over the ancient cemetery, many of its stones dating back to the 1700s. The families that made the island's history were members of this church and now lie entombed in its yard. The existing church was built .in 1884 to replace the original one destroyed by Union troops during the War Between the States.

The earlier church was constructed in 1820. It came to be known as the "BeeHive Church" due to a strange event that occurred in 1836. The church was in sad need of repairs. The rector was just about to request donations when a swarm of bees was seen around the belfry. When the members investigated, they found a store of honey large enough to fund the repairs and add a vestry room as well. The church and lighthouse are the two most photographed sites on the island.

St Simons Light is one of the oldest working lighthouses in the nation. Its story is told in Eugenia Price's Lighthouse Trilogy. Incidentally, Ms. Price herself rests peacefully in the Christ Church Cemetery not far from those she immortalized

The lighthouse began in the mind of a dreamer, James Gould. He came to the island in the late 1700s and in 1807 won the bid to build the lighthouse. In 1810 President Madison appointed him the first keeper. Since there was no money for an assistant, Gould trained some of his slaves for this position.

Confederate soldiers blew up the original lighthouse in 1861 to keep it from falling into Union hands. It was rebuilt in 1872 and now houses the St. Simons Island Lighthouse Museum. By day visitors can tour it. By night it is the domain of its resident ghost.

Some believe it is the spirit of lighthouse keeper. Fredrick Osborn, killed in March 1880, during an argument with his assistant, John Stevens, who had fallen in love with Osborn's wife. Another version of the story states that Osborn was a chronic faultfinder with everything Stevens did. Whichever the case, the two men fought. Osborn had a pistol; Stevens a shotgun. Stevens was later acquitted and the killing deemed self-defense. Stevens left his job shortly after the killing. Perhaps he could not stand being in the old building after what he had done.

Since then there have been legends that Osborn's ghost still haunts the majestic lighthouse. One occurrence happened in 1907. At that time the keeper was a man named Carl Svendsen. One night Mrs. Svendsen had prepared dinner. As was her custom, she began placing the dishes on the table when she heard Carl's footsteps in the lighthouse stairs, But this night, the footsteps stopped and her husband did not appear. At the same time, the family dog, Jinx began barking and acting as if someone was coming on the property. Mrs. Svendsen went to the tower and found her husband still working on the light. He told her he had not left the room and felt she was hearing things. Just a few nights later, he heard the same ghostly footsteps. Was it Osborn come back to attend his light?

The island, with its moss-draped oaks is a great place for horseback riding. However, if you ride at twilight, you may come face to face with Mary the Wanderer. Mary rides a white stallion searching for her lost lover who drowned during a storm when his boat capsized in the Frederica River more than a century ago. The story goes that Mary was an orphan who fell in love with her guardian's son. The guardian had designs on Mary himself in spite of the fact he was married and twice her age. When he learned about the romance, he was furious and sent his son out in a storm in a small boat. Of course, the young man drowned and Mary took her own life rather than surrender to her evil guardian.

Mary is sometimes seen through the window of the restaurant at the King and Prince Resort. This is a wonderful place to stay. The history of the hotel goes back to 1935. During WWII, it housed the operation center that sent out the radar signals. It's on the National Register of Historic Places.

For history buffs, you'll want to visit St. Simons newest museum, WWII Home Front Museum. Most WWII museums deal with the war in Europe; D- Day on Normandy Beach or battles in far-away Belgium. We all know the war impacted this country, but this museum shows how close it came to our own shores.

The island's history goes back over two and a half centuries to the time when England and Spain were locked in a bitter struggle for dominion over these new lands. In 1736, James Oglethorpe began the construction of Fort Frederica on St. Simons to defend England's' southern colonies from Spanish invasion. The fort was the largest and most costly British fort in North America. The prosperous town of Frederica grew around it by 1743, dependent on the soldiers for their livelihood. This fort played a major part in the rout of the Spanish at the Battle of Bloody Marsh, six miles to the south. The outcome of the battle drove the Spanish forces back to St. Augustine, ending the Spanish threat to the English colonies. Designed for war, Fort Frederica could withstand anything except peace. As the Spanish threat faded, the soldiers withdrew leaving the village economy crippled. The town quickly crumbled, unable to survive. Today, you can view the site. Much of the fort and the barracks remain. Other home and business sites foundations are carefully preserved allowing you a glimpse of what this thriving military town looked like in its heyday. The Visitors Center there has books and exhibits and an entertaining film about the founding of Frederica.

However, there may be something else still at the old fort. If you wander about you may hear a ghostly voice warning you to "Get out." He may speak in Spanish, German, French, English or even Latin. This multilingual spirit is believed to be a German immigrant, Christian Gottlieb Priber. Priber immigrated first to South Carolina.

Here he married the daughter of a Cherokee chief. He advocated the founding of a utopia based on natural law. He founded his "Kingdom of Paradise" for the Native Americans only and warned the settlers to leave. He became such a nuisance to the English that they had him arrested and imprisoned at Fort Frederica. He died there in

1742 and is buried on the site. Perhaps he is still trying to get rid of settlers.

If you view the site of the Battle of Bloody Marsh, after dark you might meet the earthbound spirit of Thomas Cater. Thomas built the prosperous plantation of Kelvin Grove in the 1790s. His home was a beautiful pink tabby house set among the live oaks and magnolia with a view of the ocean from its wide balconies. Thomas had a wife, Elizabeth, and a young son, Benjamin Franklin.

There was a hidden serpent in this colonial paradise. Thomas's wife was carrying on a clandestine affair with the overseer. Her jealous lover killed Thomas. The loyal butler, Benbow, fearing for the child's life, fled to Retreat with the young Benjamin who was raised by the master of that plantation, Major William Page. Retreat today is the site of the Sea Island Golf Club. Thomas was buried standing upright on the grounds of his beloved plantation.

Kelvin Grove has long since been divided unto subdivisions, one of which bears the name of the old plantation. Part of the grounds included the site of Bloody Marsh. Thomas still reputedly roams after dark, seeking revenge against the overseer.

Interestingly, there may be many more spirits in the area to accompany him. When a portion of the tract was sold to the county for an airport in 1936, remains of an ancient Indian burial ground were found on the site.

No institute more evil than slavery ever existed in the America. Ironically it brought out the best in mankind as well as the worst. Examples of both exist on St. Simon.

In May 1803, a group of Ebo captives were being transported to a life of slavery at St Simons. Rather than submit, the proud tribesmen revolted the only way left open to them. They marched into the waters of Dunbar Creek and drowned themselves rather than live in chains. To this day, their mournful chants and clanging chains are sometimes heard, an eternal reminder of man's inhumanity to man.

On the other side of the coin is the reason behind the name of the popular beachfront spot, Neptune Park. It stands at the end of Mallery Street, between the pier and the lighthouse. Its sculpture of a mother whale and her baby remind visitors of the right whales that visit this coast. These whales were named "right" by the whalers who considered them the right whales to hunt and succeeded in driving them to the verge of extinction. If you are lucky, you may spot one of the few remanding whales that use this area for a calving ground from December to late March.

The park is named for Neptune Small. Neptune was a slave during the Civil War. He accompanied his young master, Lord King, into battle and when Lord fell at Fredericksburg, Neptune dragged his body from the battlefield back to Retreat Plantation for burial.

Then the loyal Neptune returned to watch over the younger King son, Cuyler. After the war, a grateful Thomas King, gave Neptune the beachfront land to build his home. The small family remained on this land into the twentieth century. Thus a former slave became the owner of what would become one of the most valuable pieces of real estate in St. Simons.

The visitor's center is located in the park in the Old Casino Building. The Casino hosts the Island Players Theater and the public library. That most often overlooked but very important facility, public restrooms are located here.

The several blocks leading to the park is called the Pier Village and is home to specialty shops and restaurants. A cozy bookstore and many unique craft shops are found here. This is a boarding spot for the St. Simons Trolley Historical Island Tours. This tour is a great way to get an overview of the island and much of its history.

Dining options abound. Besides the fantastic ECHO Restaurant at King and Prince, here a few favorites.

Georgia Sea Grill owner Zack Gowen and Chef Tim Lensch specialize in seafood. They were named as one of the "Top Five Best Local Restaurants in Georgia," by *Southern Living* magazine.

Gnat's Landing, originally founded in 1999 and still owned and run by the Pope Family, is a place for beach goers to relax in a Beach Dress Code that allows flip flops and swimsuits. They serve standard American fare.

Southern Soul BBQ is the traditional barbecue joint.

Golden Isles Olive Oil is a different kind of treat. Owner Donna MacPherson will show you the benefits of olive oil. Her shop is a magical place where you learn how to taste olive oils and can find lots of cooking must-haves. Plus, there is a restaurant and wine bar as well where a culinary delight can be a healthy lunch.

If you begin to see faces peering at you from the gnarled oaks, you have not lost it. You are just seeing the Tree Spirits of St. Simons. These weathered images have been lovingly carved into the bark of the trees by local artists memorializing the countless sailors who lost their lives at sea as they sailed aboard the mighty ships once made from St. Simons Oaks.

One way to experience the ghostly side of St. Simons is to take the History & Mystery Tours. Captain Fendig has tours of both land and sea with his Lighthouse Tours and a terrific ghost tour.

Chapter 3 Jekyll Island, Blackbeard's Haunt

Whether or not you believe the legend that Blackbeard's treasure is hidden on Jekyll Island, it's a great spot to enjoy the bounty nature offers on its golden beach.

Embedded in a live oak tree deep in Jekyll's thick woods, a copper hook supposedly points to the spot where the ancient chest lies buried. While it's true, the notorious Edward Teach did roam the area, it's not necessary to search far to find treasure on this golden isle. Jekyll Island is a historical treasure trove. It abounds in the riches of nature, both plant and animal. Its location, just off the South Georgia coast, blesses it with a mellow climate.

The Creeks were the first to cherish this golden isle. They had no concept of "ownership." They and the land were one. The land where the golden sun rose from the depth of the wave crested blue sea and set behind the murky Marshes of Glynn, was their home for hundreds of years. They shared it in harmony with the animals. The deer, raccoon, possum, pheasant, wild turkey, and alligator inhabited the land with them and provided all the necessities of life.

The creatures of the sea provided food and tools. Then in the late 1500's, a new breed of man arrived on the island. The Spanish were seeking treasure of a different kind. They wanted gold. However, they recognized the richness of the land and established a mission to force the natives to their beliefs, and steal their land for Spain. Their enjoyment of the island was short lived.

The English were the next guardians of the island. Major William Horton, one of Oglethorpe's officers and later successor as commander of the military force in Georgia, built the first English residence on Jekyll in 1736. The gray tabby walls still stand near the northern end of the island on the marsh side. Tabby is a building material made from sand, lime, oyster shell, and water. The fact that many tabby buildings still remain bears witness to the durability of the material.

After the Revolution, Christophe Poulain du Bignon purchased Jekyll. He enlarged the Horton house and used it for his residence until 1825.The du Bignons were the leaders of the area's plantation families until the Civil War put an end to that lifestyle.

It was during this era that an event occurred that would live forever in the annals of infamy. It was on a stormy night in 1858, long after importing of slaves was made illegal, that the *Wanderer* landed on Jekyll's shore. The ill fated ship carried the last cargo of slaves ever brought from Africa. To this day, when the night is dark and the thunder rolls, people claim to see the glimmer of ghostly fires amid the sheltering trees where so many years ago they were lit to dry the huddled cargo and crew of the *Wanderer*.

Across the street from the Horton house, stands the du Bignon Family Cemetery, its weathered tombstones silent sentinels to the five generations of du Bignon's who cultivated the island plantation until 1886 when John Eugene du Bignon sold the island to a group of millionaires searching for a playground

With the sale to the Jekyll Island Club Resort, the island entered a new era of prosperity. Its members were rumored to control a seventh of the wealth of this country among its one hundred members. Men like Rockefeller, Morgan, Astor and Gould built "cottages" here for their families' winter home. These twelve to twenty room mansions contained every convenience money could buy.

Today as a state park, many of these homes are open for your inspection. Although they differ in style, they all have one thing in common; they reflect the feel of the gilded era when people flaunted their wealth

The Crane Cottage upstairs is guest rooms for the Jekyll Island Club Resort but the first floor is open to the public. The cottage was built in the Renaissance Revival style, many of its features copied from 16th century Italian Villas. From its double door arched entry to its red tile roof, it speaks of elegant simplicity. You can visualize Richard Crane's family sedately dining at the massive mahogany table, one of the children fingering the carved rungs of his chair as he waited to be allowed to go and play in the huge enclosed courtyard while his parents observed from the arched walkway or the upper veranda.

One thing is sure; the fidgeting child would never have to wait his turn to use the bathroom. Crane was the owner of the Crane Company, an international plumbing fixture company that was first to produce colored plumbing fixtures. His home boasted twenty rooms and seventeen bathrooms. Where the Crane family once relaxed is today a restaurant, the Courtyard at Crane. The menu features an array of salads and entrees with a Northern California wine country flair.

Indian Mound, originally built for Gordon Mckay and later purchased by William Rockefeller, is typical of the extravagant opulence of the Victorian age. A three-story shingle structure, it has a vine covered wraparound porch and large bay windows on each floor. One of the first floor bays is a massive semicircle of glass looking out over the Jekyll River. Its twenty-five rooms are furnished luxuriously. It has a stained-glass window on the stair landing, a dumb waiter, a cedar-lined walk in safe, and taps for hot and cold salt water in the master bath. It proudly displays countless antiques and art objects. Rumors have it that Mrs. Rockefeller's spirit is sometimes seen in the mansion.

The Goodyear Cottage now serves as a center for creative arts, housing the Jekyll Island Arts Association and is open to the public at no charge.

The Moss Cottage, a two-story green cypress shingle dwelling with a roofed porch that runs the length of the house, was once owned by George Macy, the owner of the Atlantic and Pacific Tea Company. You can tour the du Bignon House, Indian Mound and Mistletoe Cottage by taking the tram tours. The tours depart daily from the Jekyll Island Museum, which is housed in the former stable.

The museum presents an informative film about the history on the island to 1930. It has artifacts, pictures, and memorabilia of that era. Even if you don't plan on taking the tram tour, the museum and film deserve your attention.

Along with the private homes, there are many other buildings worthy of a visit. The Faith Chapel was the site of most of the island's religious functions. As you sit in the chapel beneath its two stained glass windows— the western one is a signed Tiffany— imagine yourself a guest at a 1920's wedding. Marcellus Dodge, heir to the Remington fortune, is marrying Geraldine Rockefeller. The union was rumored to make them the richest couple in the world. The chapel is open daily.

All of the romances on the island did not end well. At least one of the millionaires found that money couldn't buy happiness. Wealthy New York banker McEvers Bayard Brown's legacy is a chimney, the last remnant of his magnificent cottage. He built the cottage, stables, and a bridge to reach the isolated marsh spot for his intended bride. However, the wedding never took place and at thirty-seven, Brown left America for England. He renounced his native land and for 36 years, he lived aboard his yacht, *Valfreyia*, off the Essex Coast in England. His yacht engines were kept in readiness for a voyage that never occurred until his death. His 18-man crew waited in vain for the order to put to sea. It finally came. He died in 1926 and on his deathbed, he requested his body be returned to America aboard his yacht.

Although his personal fortune included an income of over a million dollars a year, he had such a little regard for money that he was known to frequently toss gold coins to harbor visitors. In life he became known as the Hermit of Essex. It is not too hard to believe that in death he haunts the scene of his greatest happiness and worst despair.

San Souci was the world's first condominium. Some of the club members, desiring more privacy than the clubhouse offered, built the huge green shingled apartment house. It contained six apartments and is still in use today as accommodations for the Jekyll Island Club Resort. You can walk through the halls and public areas.

The piece de la resistance of Millionaires' Row is the Clubhouse. Its turret stands head and shoulders above the other structures on the island. Here you can bask in the luxury that once was accorded only the millionaires and their chosen guests. You can spend the night, or as many nights as you can afford being pampered in the Victorian elegance of the clubhouse.

Dine in the Grand Dining Room. Could that be a Vanderbilt or a Morgan at the next table? Once they sat here being served by their skilled staff of the finest chefs imported from the best restaurants in New York. Just in the mood for a snack or a drink? Try The Pantry and The Bar

Golfers can play on one of four courses – including Great Dunes, designed for the Jekyll Island Club. In front of the clubhouse you can play croquet on a lawn as plush as a green carpet, splash in the sparkling pool, or just loll in one of the many wicker rockers adorning the hotel veranda.

Several other buildings are worthy of attention. The Gould casino, although not restored, is interesting just for its sheer size. The power plant, now the award-winning Georgia Sea Turtle Center, is a delight any time of year.

The Infirmary, once a bookstore, has its own resident ghost, a woman who will not come beyond the top of the staircase.

For something a little out the ordinary, explore off the beaten path, take a dirt road that is located across from the airport, and you will discover an old silo and the ruins of an old cabin.

The silo is all that remains of a dairy barn that existed during the club era. The cabin was used as part of the Skeet and Trap Shooting range in the 1920s. If the road is followed farther back into the island, it shows signs of being used as a horseback-riding trail.

The marina, located in the historical district, was where the famous yachts once anchored. Today it is the site of a restaurant, The Wharf, and is the boarding point of the water taxi, which operates several tours and trips to St. Simons.

The Jekyll Harbor provides hookups for long term docking. Dolphin tours are popular here. The playful sea mammals can often be seen for the shore and positively love to follow the tour boats.

If you're a camper, the Jekyll Island Campground is located on the north end of the island and can provide you with everything from primitive to full hookup. The campers' store is staffed by friendly personnel and even has bike rentals. Incidentally, bikes are a great way to navigate the island. The twenty miles of paved bike trails wander through places you can't reach by car.

Whether you hunt for pirate treasure, just plain fun or secrets from beyond the grave, Jekyll is a great place to look.

Chapter 4 St Marys, The Old and The New

St. Marys is one of the fastest growing small towns in Georgia thanks to the Kings Bay Trident Submarine Base located nearby. It's still the kind of quaint little town you love to visit and hate to leave. In fact, some of its residents have refused to leave for over a century. We're talking disembodied residents.

The most commanding building in the historic downtown area is Orange Hall. This magnificent Greek Revival mansion was a house museum demonstrating life in the Antebellum South. It is now closed down for renovation. It was the home of Reverend Horace Pratt--his portrait hangs over the mantle in the upstairs parlor--and his second wife, Isabel Drysdale. The house was a gift from his first wife's family. This first wife, Jane Wood, had died in 1829, after six years of marriage and the distraught pastor mourned for three years. Eventually he married one of Jane's friends. When their first child was born, there was no question of her name. She was called Jane.

Jane grew into a delightful and inquisitive child. It was only natural when a shipload of Acadians heading for Louisiana docked at St. Marys that Jane dashed off to view the unusual occurrence. Sadly, the Acadian ship carried an invisible passenger, Yellow Fever. The beautiful child sickened and died.

Today, visitors report spotting a pretty child playing in Jane's bright airy second floor bedroom overlooking the front lawn. There is only one entryway open, the stairway leading from the basement into the living quarters, an attendant is always on duty and would have noticed any child who entered the building. However, the child is seen when the attendant has not admitted any little girl fitting the description. There is reason to believe Jane may feel the house is too confining for her playful spirit. She is sometimes seen strolling up the walk out front.

Reportedly there are two other spirits there, an older gentleman, though and a woman dressed in purple.

The Riverview Hotel is another town landmark. It was built as a hotel in 1916 on the banks of the St. Marys River. In the 1920s, Miss Sally Brandon bought it. Miss Sally along with her sisters, Miss Semora and Miss Ethel, made the inn a popular stopping place for visitors from all over. One famous guest, Roy Crane stayed there and developed the comic strip "Wash Tubbs" based on the town and its railcar. A waterfront restaurant, Trolleys, commemorates the cartoon. For 95 years it was owned by the Brandon family..

The innkeepers for many years were Jerry and Gaila Brandon. They recently sold it. The new owner is Bert Guy. Jerry is a lifelong resident of St. Marys and served as mayor. He grew up in the hotel and tells of some hair-raising events that happened there. One strange episode concerns a guest in room nine, Red Myers. Mr. Myers stayed there during the time he was working at the bag factory. One day, a friend came looking for him. The desk clerk let him into room nine to wait and the visitor fell asleep. He awoke when he felt someone pulling on his leg. He jumped up and found no one there. He rushed downstairs believing Red was playing a trick on him and asked a group of people downstairs, "Did you see Red come out here?"

They assured him they had not. Further, they informed him, "Red has gone to Douglas for the weekend."

Upon discussing it with Red, his friend found that the same thing had happened to Red on several occasions.

Jerry informed me he had not seen anything personally but "My sister, who is not a believer in the supernatural, swears she saw an apparition. It happened in the fifties when the hotel was not operating. The family still lived here but didn't use the upstairs. She and her friend were in the second floor hallway and clearly saw what appeared to be the figure of a man. It scared her so bad she wouldn't go up there for a couple of weeks. No one ever saw the man again."

The Riverview has a restaurant, Seagle's, with great steaks and seafood and a quiet little bar. Seagle's Saloon.

Mardja Gray owns the Goodbread House, which was built in 1870 by Samuel Burns. Steamboat captain Walton Goodbread bought it in 1901. Legends claim it is haunted by the ghost of Dr. Eaton who was murdered on the front porch.

The Spencer House is another bed and breakfast. It was built in 1872. Both are worth a peek for their architecture alone even if you are staying elsewhere. Any of the three are a great place to stay if you want to catch the flavor of St. Marys.

The Presbyterian Church, built in 1808, was the one Horace Pratt came to as minister in 1821. One interesting story about this church concerns the belfry. As in any seaport, there is temptation for smugglers. One day the town was startled to hear the ball clanging wildly. The astounded townspeople looked up to see a horse in the belfry. The story goes that the horse was placed there as a distraction while the smugglers got their loot safely hidden. As to how anyone got the animal up into the belfry, no one knows.

Among the other attractions in St. Marys, is the Cumberland Island National Seashore Museum. Since St. Marys is the ferry port to visit Cumberland, the museum is a great place to get oriented before you visit the island or to get an overview if you cannot go to the island itself.

Another museum The St. Marys Submarine Museum is located on Osborne St, the main street in the historic section. You enter the converted movie theater, step past a sailor lounging in the corner and catch a fascinating glimpse of life aboard a submarine. Be sure to peek at the town through the periscope, which extends through the roof.

Another site you want to visit is the Riverview Park. It is located next to the ferry dock and boat launch. It boasts lots of white gazebos and attractive landscaping and is a great spot to enjoy the view.

For campers, Crooked River State Park is four miles away on the banks of the St. Marys River. The park accommodates anything from tents to the largest RV. The park offers great fishing and a boat launch. It has cabin rentals. In certain times of the year, you will want to be well provided with bug repellent as is occasionally has a gnat and mosquito problem.

Between the park and the city, visit the ruins of the old McIntosh Sugar Mill built in 1825. Some people believe the ruins are that of an old mission built long before the sugar mill. Whatever it is the moss draped trees and wooded surroundings allow your imagination to supply the site with spirits of long deceased inhabitants.

Chapter 5 Cumberland Island, Wild Horses & Castles

Cumberland Island nestles close to the mainland at the southernmost tip of Georgia. It's a place of rare natural beauty, although it has been inhabited for over 4,000 years; man has trod lightly here on this, the largest of Georgia's barrier islands. Camped among the moss-shrouded trees where there is no electricity, few cars and little technological development, it is easy to imagine spectral shapes among the mists.

The island can be divided into three separate ecosystems: saltwater marsh, maritime forest, and beach. The marshes are the first view of the island since it must be reached by boat. The National Park Service provides ferry service. Private and charter boats also visit the island.

During low tide, the marshes appear to be a vast plain of tall grass. In the low muddy places, fiddler crabs scurry about as they have done since primeval time. Many species of wading birds search for food in the shallows. At high tide, only the tips of the grasses show as the tides once again provide the nutrients needed to nourish the marsh and its inhabitants.

As the salt loving plant life gives way to the forest, tall pine and moss draped live oak seem to muffle the sounds and diffuse the light.

A feeling of peace and tranquility reign. Here you will sometimes spot the newest addition to the island's animal population as he rustles through the underbrush, poking his snoot in the soft sand as he searches for an easy meal. The armadillo has only been seen in Cumberland since 1974. In the evenings, the raccoons amble out of the woods to the shore to snack on crabs and shellfish.

In some areas, the grass has been grazed as neatly as if trimmed by a mower. The park like effect is the result of the feral horses and wild deer that feed under the stately oaks. Nestled into the crooks of branches, the Resurrection Fern spring to life after every rain. Bright flashes of red, blue and yellow dart among the branches as the island birds announce their presence with burst of song. Deep in the forest, small rain-fed ponds glisten in the sun. Occasionally, the eyeballs of a lone alligator break the surface. On the eastern side, the forests are thick with undergrowth. The Saw Palmetto intertwines with vines and grasses to form an almost impenetrable barrier to anyone striving to reach the dunes beyond.

At dune's edge, heat and light rise noticeably. Low shrubs and sand spurs cover the leading edge of rolling dunes. White sand, broken only by deer and horse hoof prints, forms the dune crests. Atlantic breakers tease small sea birds playing at water's edge, scurrying to and fro with the waves' rhythm.

Occasionally, humans and horses disturb the pristine shoreline, weaving their way through driftwood at the high-water mark.

At night, sea turtles lumber ashore to lay eggs in over 200 nests, according to former National Park Service Resource Specialist, Jennifer Bjork. The tiny reptiles hatch in 60 days and, guided by instinct, they rush home to sea.

Spend even one night primitive camping among the moss dripping oaks and you will sense a presence on the island. Perhaps it is its turbulent history. Perhaps, something else roams the pristine island at night.

Spanish explorers visited Cumberland Island in the mid-1500s. They met the Quale, a branch of the Timucuan tribe of Native American who had inhabited the island for thousands of years. When the Spanish departed, they left their Arabian and Barb horses to fend for themselves on the island. With no natural predators, the horses thrived. Today, National Park Service Rangers try to prevent overgrazing by the herd.

Shortly after the Revolutionary War, General Nathaniel Greene purchased land on the island to build a home for his family. Greene planned the home on the site of an old hunting camp belonging to General Oglethorpe. The General died before it could be built. His wife, Catherine, constructed the elegant four-story mansion and named it "Dungeness." Catherine lived in Dungeness with her second husband, Phineas Miller, and her children. The house was left unfinished because an old, family superstition predicted disaster should Dungeness ever be completed. But even that attempt to thwart disaster failed. The family remained at Dungeness until the Civil War drove them away. The elegant home survived the war, but was burned during reconstruction.

With the abolition of slavery, cotton, the island's chief crop, was no longer profitable. Human activity on the island diminished and the feral horses interbred with those abandoned by planters.

In 1882, Thomas Carnegie acquired most of the island. America had entered the "gilded age" and new money flowed freely. Jekyll Island, a few miles north, became the summer playground of the nation's wealthy, but Thomas and brother, Andrew, despite their sizable fortunes, were not invited because of their Scots ancestry.

In 1884, Thomas answered the snub with a Scottish castle on Cumberland Island. In defiance of the old superstition surrounding the original house, he built the magnificent, turreted mansion on the site of the old Dungeness ruins and called his new home by the same name. Thomas, with his wife Lucy and their nine children, made the new Dungeness the social center of the area. Thomas, like Nathaniel Greene, did not have long to enjoy his mansion. He died in 1886. Lucy continued using Dungeness as a seasonal home. Over time, Lucy divided the surrounding acres among her children as they married. Gradually, the magnificent showplace fell into disrepair. A fire ravaged the castle in 1959, leaving a skeleton standing. The horses, their gene pool increased by the Carnegies' fancy, saddle horses, now graze on the once-manicured lawns of Dungeness.

Some say it is home to the ghost of Thomas Hutchinson, the designer of a golf course that existed on the island in its heyday. He was killed while riding his horse beneath a low hanging branch after leaving a boisterous party at the mansion. Many partygoers reported that he had a disagreement and fled in anger after a dispute with his host, others claimed that he was merely going to fetch more spirits to liven the party. Whichever the case, he was riding recklessly across the island and thrown from his horse by a low hanging branch. His body lay for several days on the lonely beach before he was discovered. He is sighted frequently by staff and visitors.

The Carnegies later deeded the land to the National Park Service. Some homes in the area still have Life Estate arrangements and are marked as private property, but the bulk of the island is preserved in a natural state. When the Carnegies gave the land to the Park Service, one stipulation was that, to preserve the island's natural character, no bridge could be built from the mainland.

The first parcel granted to the park service was Plum Orchard. A wedding gift from Lucy Carnegie to her son George and his bride, Margaret Thaw, the Georgian Revival mansion is open to visitors.

The next occupants were Nancy Carnegie, the youngest child, and her second husband Marius Johnston. Nancy seemed to be a bit headstrong and didn't care how much scandal she stirred up. In 1904 she married the Carnegie's coachman, a heavy drinking Irishman named James Hever. The marriage was not peaceful and Nancy often retreated to her mother's home on Cumberland Island. There she met the island doctor, Marius Johnston, and fell in love. After Hever's death in 1911, she married Johnston. Her heir's remained in Plum Orchard until they deeded it to the Park service in the 1970s.

Plum Orchard is the only place that has drinkable water other than Dungeness Dock, Historic area, and Sea Camp.

Here too, you find the lawn well-grazed. "There are more than 200 horses on the island. Since there is only so much grassland, competition is fierce, and the strongest horses get the best grazing spots," Cox explains.

The mansion offers a glimpse of life among one of the wealthiest families in America. Everything was of the finest—Tiffany lamps, a pink marble kitchen sink, a library, plus their own indoor swimming pool and squash court.

The current resident, the spirit of a troubled Lady of the Evening, prefers solitude. Many staff members have heard the dumb waiter raising and returning in the empty house. Some have experienced the smell of fresh tobacco smoke and heard footsteps in the mansion. Many people have seen a woman in red in the servant's quarters. It is believed that a prostitute died on the island while "visiting" the quarters. She is reputedly buried in the Stafford Cemetery. Caretakers have seen her trying to leave the cemetery.

Since Plum Orchard is about an hour's walk from the dock, a better way to see it is on a Land and Legacy Tour. The tour is a five to six hour tour in a ten seat van over a 30 mile unpaved road that takes you to the north end of the island to view Plum Orchard, Stafford Cemetery, and the African American Settlement including the small church where JFK, Jr. was married.

The Settlement is located fifteen miles north of the Sea Camp Dock area at the northern end of Cumberland Island National Seashore. It was settled by former slaves in the early 1890s. Then the former enslaved people found work at a once flourishing hotel or in agriculture. Prior to the Civil War, the largest plantation owner on Cumberland Island was Robert Stafford. The newly freed people found work on his plantation. He had previously allowed his slaves to work during their free time and retain their earning so Cumberland Island freed people had more experience with paid work and managing money. Today, most of the former residents have left the island.

The most famous building remaining in the Settlement is the First African Baptist Church where JFK, Jr. got married. The originally church was just a log structure built when The Settlement was founded. It was replaced by a simple white clapboard building in 1937. It's open daily and the tour guide gives some history about it.

The only other intact house is that of Beulah Alberty, a descendant of one of the original settlers. The house is open but the rooms are unfurnished. It does have a restroom. There are several other ruins around the Settlement.

Of the other Carnegie mansions originally existing on the island, Greyfield is the only one open to visitors. Now operating as an inn, it was the location of John F. Kennedy Jr. and Caroline Bessette's wedding reception. It is the only lodging on the island. It was built by the Carnegies in 1890 for their daughter, Margaret Ricketson. Her daughter, Lucy R. Ferguson, converted to a 15 room inn with two additional cottages in 1962. Prices are not cheap, starting at over $600 a night for a couple, but it is a present day reflection of life during the Gilded Age.

Guests are furnished meals and have access to bicycles and kayaks plus private island tours. It's on the National Historic Registry.

Among the Carnegie homes not open to the public, the original Stafford is quite interesting. It was the home of William and Gertrude Ely Carnegie. It burned to the ground in the late 1890s. The couple then lived in the little tabby house that is still standing. Gertrude died in 1906 and William became severely depressed. He later married his nurse, Betty.

Betty, too, abandoned him by committing suicide shortly afterwards. Today, family members report that Gertrude's presence is felt in the Stafford House and even more so in the tabby house. Guests there reported jewelry moved and shades rolling up by themselves. A family member once saw Gertrude's apparition there. A woman in white is frequently seen around the old carriage house.

Today, Cumberland Island offers a nature lovers' paradise with miles of hiking trails, dirt roads and sandy beaches. Fortunately, water and restrooms are available.

Cumberland Island offers both salt-water and fresh water fishing. Anglers catch red fish, sea trout, blue fish, drum and croaker. The beaches are perfect for swimming, sunning, shelling or napping.

Former Park Ranger, Zack Kirkland, told of a letter written to the Park Service by a man who visited the island. He wrote about a deserted beach. He looked up, saw a crowd of people approaching, and got angry at seeing other people on his beach. As the crowd came closer, he realized they were not people, but horses. The man urged the park service "never to increase the limit of 300 people per day allowed on the island." Perhaps the island spirits also prefer the relative isolation as they drift between heaven and earth in this peaceful haven.

The Waving Girl

Carri Nation at Prohibition Museum

St. Simons Tree Spirits

Fort Frederica

St Simons Lighthouse

Horton House

Dungeness Castle on Cumberland Island

Section 2 Georgia's Antebellum Legacy

Deep in Georgia's heartland, lies a portion of the Old South that is well-preserved and waiting for you to explore. If the spirit of Scarlet and Rhett still linger anywhere, they would feel most at home here. Mammy would not be left out. Many spirits of African Americans still cry out for justice from the afterlife.

Geographically, it consists of the stretch of Highway 441 from Athens to Milledgeville with off shoots to Macon at the south end and Washington at the north.

But the Antebellum south is more a state of mind than an actual place. It comes alive here for its charm and warm Southern Hospitality. It also boasts the presence of many souls who remain behind from its turbulent past.

Chapter 6 Athens, The Classic City

College towns seem to attract haunts. So do historic districts, Athens, with its eclectic mix of brash young college students and descendants of the legendary antebellum gentry, is a natural habitat of ghostly legends.

The Hamilton-Phinizy-Segrest House on S. Milledge Ave is a perfect example of the marriage of two cultures. Built in 1859, it is now the home of Phi Mu Sorority. It is also the home of a long dead woman. Frequently, neighbors across the street called to say there was a woman on the roof. Residents would go out and look and she would be gone. Many people have seen her. One interesting incident occurred during summer classes several years ago. There were only four girls staying there. One stayed out a bit late one night and got locked out. She knocked and heard the lock click open. On entering, no one was there. She thought one of her sorority sisters had got up, opened the door and went back to bed. The next day, when she asked who had let her in, no one had. They had to assume it was their friendly ghostly resident. Sorority sisters believe it was Anna Powell, who died in the house grieving for her husband who committed suicide. At a certain time of day, a beam of sunlight cast a glowing cross upon the very spot where he died.

Sorority houses must be very hospitable to ghosts. The Alpha Gamma Delta House AKA Thomas Carithers House at 530 S. Milledge Ave has its own spiritual sister, Susie. Susie's father donated the house to the sorority in her honor. She was to be married in the house however, the groom failed to show up and the bereaved girl hung herself from a beam in the attic. The girls who live in the room directly under the spot all seem to become engaged or pinned during their tenure there. The house is worth seeing for its architectural value as well. It is shaped like a three-tiered wedding cake.

The university campus also has its resident ghost. Many students tell of seeing a man in Confederate uniform around Demosthenian Hall. He is believed to be Robert Toombs who had been dismissed from the college in his youth. Toombs led such a rambunctious life that he spawned many legends. He was a United States senator, cabinet member of the Confederate government and later a brigadier general. He fled to France after the war. He lived long and died peacefully in 1885, still refusing allegiance to the United States. There is also a story that after his expulsion in 1825, he returned during commencement ceremonies and spoke outside the chapel. His speech was so eloquent that everyone left the chapel to hear him speak under a large oak. The story, although so typical of his behavior, is untrue but the oak is still named Toombs Oak. He later served on the board of trustees.

Another campus building that hosts a ghost is Lustrat House, located on the old North Campus. Their resident spook here is a former English Department head, Major Charles Morris. The fact that he is usually spotted wearing a Confederate uniform makes him a bit more dashing. Lustrat Hall houses the university's Office of Legal Affairs.

The Taylor-Grady House, 640 Prince Ave., is worth a look for historical and architectural value as well as its ghostly gossip. The stately white house with its thirteen columns, representing the original thirteen colonies, was the home of Henry Grady. Grady was one of the chief supporters of the New South. He was managing editor of the Atlanta Constitution and used it as a forum to help heal the wounds of war. He fought for the rebuilding of the ruined southern economy. The university's School of Journalism is named in his honor.

It is his father, Henry who moved the Gradys into the house but was called to fight for the South. He was killed and is said to roam the house looking for his family.

Much of the development Grady sought has occurred in Athens. One fine example is the Classic Center. The Classic Center facilities house a 2000 seat theater, convention and meeting rooms and, what else, its own ghost. The center is a blend of old and new. The old represented in part by Fire Hall Number 1.

The story goes that this firehouse was the workplace of an older fireman named Hiram Peeler. On February 22, 1928 when he was killed fighting a fire, he was 67 years old and had 47 years of service. Apparently he liked his job and didn't want to leave. He probably still doesn't. Security guards at the hall report strange noises where there shouldn't be any and objects moved or overturned without any explanation.

Hiram is buried in the Oconee Hill Cemetery. Not surprisingly, there are stories of the residents frolicking on Halloween night. Supposedly, if you sit under the bridge then you will see a hunchback haunt drive a wagon and two horses through the cemetery. The cemetery sits just beside Sanford Stadium, where the UGA Bulldogs play so if you are watching a game you may get another surprise.

The Old Athens Cemetery also on UGA's Campus, just up the hill from Oconee Hills. It has its resident spirit, a girl of about 12 who prowls at night.

There is plenty for the living to enjoy here as well. Athens is a double-barreled city. Like its famous Double-Barreled Cannon, Athens, Georgia is a city with two faces. Both of them are lots of fun for visitors. If you're planning a vacation packed with wild nightlife, Athens is the place. If you're looking for culture and natural beauty, Athens is the place. If you're looking for a vibrant youthful city, Athens is the place. If you are looking for a rich historical legacy, Athens is the place. No matter what you want in a vacation, you will enjoy Athens.

If you want to eat, drink and be merry, Athens offers lots of choices. The bars almost outnumber the churches. The bars make up for their numerical deficiency by their wide variety of styles. They range from Trappeze Pub, that offers uniquely crafted beers from all over at their 30 rotating taps as well as a 20 page bottled beer selection. Not that is variety. They offer a good variety of soups, salads and sandwiches. Like the beer, their food is beautifully crafted.

Speaking of beer, The Terrapin Brewery, which creates many interesting brews, offers tours and tastings. It's fun even if you are not a beer aficionado as you get to see the brewing process first hand.

You'll find the conventional chains like Chile's and Applebee's. You'll also find the unusual. Graduate Athens, now a hotel was the site where the world's only double-barreled cannon was built for the Civil War now on display at the Athens-Clarke County Courthouse, the hotel is designed to replicate row houses built in the 1820's, it also preserves on-site historical buildings from that time period.

When dining, Athens's restaurants are hard to beat both in number and in excellent cuisine.

A restaurant that blends true southern food with the musical heritage of Athens is Weaver D's, When they won a Grammy for their 1992 release of *Automatic for the People*. Weaver D's became another shrine to the R.E.M. legend. This was a popular soul food restaurant frequented by R.E.M, the B-52's and many other bands in the late 1980's. It was, and is, a small unpretentious restaurant. The tables are communal and covered with checkered oilcloth tablecloths.. The food is Southern Soul Food at its best, fried chicken, greens, and homemade mashed potatoes and squash casserole, Weaver's signature dish. When the boys from R.E.M. came to Dexter Weaver with a request to use his "Automatic for the People" slogan on their album, Weaver D's suddenly became a part of the R.E.M. legend. Dexter was suddenly besieged with television crews and star-struck fans wanting a glimpse into the everyday life of these music phenomena.. He was offered a contract to write a book, "Automatic Y'all — Weaver D's Guide to the Soul." Weaver D's now serves over 300 people a day. No matter how long the line, his food is worth any wait.

If you wish to stroll into Athens past, there are sixteen neighborhoods listed on the National Registry of Historic Places. Many located near downtown lend themselves to walking tours. A great place to start is at the Athens Welcome Center. It is located in what is believed to be the oldest house in Athens, the Church-Waddel-Brumby House at 280 E. Dougherty St.

Classic City Tours, which is a great way to get a glimpse of many of the neighborhoods as well as other historic attractions. They offer daily tours. You can purchase their self-guided tour brochure at the Welcome Center. It can also be downloaded free at https://www.visitathensga.com/

The Morton Theater is another must see. It was built by Monroe Bowers "Pink" Morton, a wealthy black entrepreneur, in 1910. This makes it one of the first vaudeville theaters owned and operated by African Americans. In 2010, Athens celebrated the theater's centennial with a year long celebration. Along with the theater, the Morton Building housed doctor's offices, a drug store, a pool hall, and miscellaneous businesses. It is located on Washington and Hull Streets, once called "The Hot Corner" because it was the center of life for African Americans in Athens. The theater has been magnificently restored and once again presents dramatic and musical performances. Actors report spooky occurrences in the dressing rooms.

Strangely enough the Morton, even when it was closed to the public, still nurtured Athens immense musical heritage. In the 1970's two as yet unknown women, Cindy Wilson and Kate Pierson, worked in a restaurant called El Dorado located in the Morton building. In October, 1976, they along with three other unknown musicians, Ricky Wilson, Cindy's brother, Fred Schneider and Keith Strickland decided to form a band. They used one of the rooms in the closed theater to practice.

They played their first gig on Valentine's Day, 1977, calling themselves The B-52's. Little did they know at the time they were launching a new era in the history of rock music. They were the nucleus of what had come to be called "the Athens music scene."

The B-52's were followed by dozens of other new wave bands; Love Tractor, Widespread Panic, Python and then the most famous of them all, R.E.M.

R.E.M. began their career in a converted church where they lived at the time. The church has since been torn down and all that remains is the steeple but it is noted on a self-guided walking tour put together by the Athens/ Welcome Center and Flagpole Magazine.

Another old favorite theater in Athens, the Georgia Theater was ravaged by fire in 2009 but has since reopened.

The University of Georgia, charted in 1785, is the oldest state chartered university in the United States. Its main library houses the original Constitution of the Confederate States of America. The Founders Memorial garden on colorful North Campus commemorates honors the birthplace of the Athens Garden Club, the first garden club in America. Its Sanford Stadium is the most visited site in Athens.

The second most visited site related to the university is The State Botanical Garden. This oasis is a 313-acre expanse of soul refreshing greenery punctuated with eye dazzling blazes of color. Seven color designated trails wind through the varied gardens. Birders especially frequent one trail, The Orange Trail, for its varied bird population. It's not unusual to come upon a raccoon, rabbit or fox as you ramble on any of the trails.

The Garden's Visitor Center provides a feast for the eyes. The three-story glass conservatory flaunts exotic orchids, an Angel Trumpet plant with its delicate but deadly blooms, and myriads of other tropical plants. The center also houses a classroom, which may be rented, and a theater showing an orientation film.

The Day Chapel soars heavenward from among a majestic stand of hardwoods. Its cypress and glass exterior are a perfect marriage of nature and light. However stunning the exterior is, the interior is heart stopping in its beauty. The doors leading from the vestibule to the sanctuary are an art masterpiece worthy of Monet. The softly patined mahogany forms the trunk and branches of an intertwining dogwood tree. The dogwood flower and the Cherokee rose are vivid glass images set amongst the crystal. The vividly hued rug in the vestibule reflect the same motif as the doors and include the state bird, brown thrasher, and state butterfly, eastern yellow swallowtail. The chapel is a favorite spot for weddings and receptions.

For campers, there is a terrific little campground nearby. Pine Lakes Campground is about halfway between Athens and Watkinsville. It sits on a lake and can accommodate just about any RV or tent.

Chapter 7 Watkinsville, Wicked Watkinsville

Watkinsville, a delightful town that caters to artists and craftspeople, harbors a host of spirits at its oldest building, a ghostly milliner and a haunted cemetery.

Miss Ida Murray built her home in 1900. For much of her life she produced delightful hats for the local ladies. She died in 1952 at 92 but she didn't want to leave the home she had built mainly with her own hands. It is said her ghost still makes hats there. It's known as the Murray Home and is number 14 on the Watkinsville Walking Tour.

In the early 1800s, Watkinsville was considered so rowdy that it was declared "off limits" to students at Athens' newly founded university. The center of this riotous living was the Eagle Tavern. The Eagle was a stopping off point for almost anyone traveling between Milledgeville and Athens. The earliest use for the site was a fort built as early as 1789. Somewhere between 1794 and 1801, the present day tavern was built. Through the years, owners added to the original structure. Watkinsville, as well as being a stagecoach stop, was also the county seat of Clark County. In 1821 Richard Richardson purchased the inn and began the long string of additions with six rooms to take care of court and stagecoach business. His daughter, Martha, married a man named Edward Billups. When they were killed by Indians, their daughter, Belle, took over the business.

Popular legend claims Watkinsville was rejected as a site for the university because of the "Wicked Tavern" located there. Former tavern director, Bonnie Murphy, declared the town was never considered as a site of the university. It played a part in the life of the early students however as a forbidden place to steal away and indulge in some drinking and a little illegal fun.

For half a dollar, guests were fed a button-popping meal of chicken, ham, bacon, sausage, greens, bread and whatever wild game the owner had been lucky enough to bag. All this was washed down with ale, whiskey or brandy. He was then permitted to toss his bedroll on the floor with the other patrons who couldn't afford the price of one of the two upstairs rooms.

By the 1840s, the Eagle Tavern had achieved a measure of respectability. Harold W. Mann mentioned the tavern in his 1965 biography of 19th century Methodist preacher Rev. Atticus G. Haygood of Watkinsville. Mann wrote: "Most of the liquor was consumed in three established saloons, one of them at Watkinsville in the Eagle Hotel, where Athens lawyers stayed during the court sessions. Liquor drinking by respectable gentlemen in the 1840s is not to be confused with the riotous backwoods life of Georgia, especially two and three decades earlier."

Fortunately, the building escaped destruction when General Sherman marched through the area. In 1959, it was deeded to Georgia Historical Commission and later to Oconee County.

The tavern houses many artifacts relevant to life in the 19th century. Halford Lowder loaned one of the displays, a large loom and spinning wheel used by women of the era to spin the cotton into thread and weave cloth.

Today, the tavern houses the Oconee County Welcome Center and Watkinsville. It may be a gathering place for the other worldly. Ghosts of Georgia Paranormal Investigations did an investigation there and across the street in the Old Jail. Unfortunately, the Old Jail had been torn down to make way for "progress."

Many of the investigators saw or sensed things. One saw a lady in a red dress with dark hair who seemed to be a madam. She sensed that there were three "girls" who "worked" upstairs. She also sensed a salesman who drove a buggy with his goods on and stopped at the tavern often to eat.

Another worker sensed a young woman wearing a pink dress dancing downstairs and that the bedroom was used as a brothel.

The tavern room and the bedroom were the rooms with the most activity. One of the other investigators likewise got the impression that there might have been some brothel type activities that took place there.

Other visitors and workers have reported activity as well. A cleaning woman encountered the dancing girl in one of the downstairs rooms. People have sensed male spirits in the tavern, heard footsteps and smelled tobacco.

Melissa Piche, who used to do North Georgia Tours says, "When the psychic investigators came, one spirit they discovered was a Confederate soldier. We do know a soldier was hidden from Stoneman's Raiders here."

Melissa tells of a former docent, Anita 's, encounter at the Tavern, with a spirit called Henry. Melissa believes there are many other spirits in the old tavern, both benign and evil. The basement seems to be the focus for the evil spirits.

You will enjoy the down home atmosphere as you view the historic sites and browse the colorful downtown area. Art objects, crafts and antiques combine to provide a shopper's delight. Historic treasures, such as the Elder Mill Bridge, recall a more peaceful time. The bridge, built in 1880, is one of the few remaining covered bridges left in the state.

No visit to the bridge would be complete without a word about its self-appointed guardian, Al Cumings. When Al retired and built his home next to the bridge, it was in serious disrepair. Al successfully lobbied then Governor Carter for funds to stabilize the bridge. He continued with his efforts to improve the plight of the bridge until it was brought up to par. He guarded the bridge like its own personal troll until his death. His property has recently been purchased by someone else. Let's hope that he continues to cherish the old bridge as Al did, and I would bet, still does.

Not too far from there, on Salem Road, there is all that remains of what was once a major stagecoach stop, Salem. The town has long since disappeared into the mists of time but the old church and cemetery remain. Strange orbs are often seen here at night.

You will never find Happy Valley Pottery accidentally. Even if you wandered down its quaint gravel drive, you would think it was still another farm as it once was. Today, however, Happy Valley is a thriving artist community. It provides an artistic home base for other disciplines as well as pottery. Founder, Jerry Chappelle, and his wife, Kathy, opened the farm to over 175 various artists since its inception in 1970. Jerry recalls it wasn't all sunshine in the beginning. They moved to the farm and began turning chicken houses into studios. "From the day we moved in, everybody laughed at us because they didn't know what a potter was. Our first little summer festival we had thirty-five people. This year (2006) we expect 2,500 to 3,000."

Jerry and Kathy retired recently and closed their Chappelle Gallery, but they can still be found on a regular basis at Happy Valley Pottery. The studio is open seven days a week and has an honor code. If no one is at the register to check customers out, patrons are encouraged to write down the name of the artist, the price of the item, add the seven percent sales tax and drop it in the cash jar. How does that speak for the honesty of small towns?

You can watch artists throw a clay pop on their wheel, or create a mosaic in stained-glass. Learn the magic of glassblowing as an artist creates a Witch Bottles.

The Witch Bottle legend began in medieval European Glassblowing studios. Often the craftsmen would be called to war and have to leave their studio. The last object created would be a colorful ornament with a hole left in the center. The evil spirits would be attracted by the bright colors and find their way inside. When the artist returned, he would throw the bottle into his newly fired furnace thus destroying the malignant spirit.

Another magnificent haunted home is The Ashford on Main, now a wedding venue but formerly the Ashford Manor Bed and Breakfast. Ashford manor had remained in the Ashford family since A.W. Ashford built it in 1893.

Dave Sheron, Mario Castro, and Dave's brother, Jim Sheron, bought it and turned the historic home into an inn in 1997. The new owners arrived in town the day before the closing. They stayed in the manor that night. Around midnight, they heard a crash and, on investigating, found one of the dining room chandelier arms had turned downward, shattering its glass. They mentioned it to the Ashfords at the closing and found that it had recently been soldered. During the following weeks as the renovation progressed, all three partners had a feeling of being watched. When one of the carpenters saw the figure of a man cross the hall when no one else was in the house, everyone began to put all the events together. Upon investigation, they discovered that A. W. Ashford had died in that room after the stock market crash of 1929. His son had committed suicide in the family bank. Another murder victim died in the same room after being stabbed near the creek behind the house. I asked Dave about the spirit. "If the presence is A. W. Ashford," Dave stated, "he seems to be happy with what we're doing with his house and is leaving us alone now."

Dave and Mario closed down the inn in the 2020s.

Harris Shoals Park boast a great nature trail that winds along a secluded creek and crosses a small lake, a picnic area and lots of wooded spots is a great place to enjoy nature at its best.

History buff, art connoisseur or just plain tourist, you'll agree that whatever its past, it's now earned the title "Wonderful Watkinsville."

Chapter 8 Social Circle, Monroe, and Madison

Tiny Social Circle is a lovely little town that is most famous for one special eatery, The Blue Willow. The Blue Willow is a shrine to good old fashion Southern cooking. If Scarlett O'Hara were alive today, she wouldn't be thinking of Rhett at all. Instead, she would be contriving to hire the entire staff at Blue Willow.

If you haven't eaten any of their "To Die For Southern Fried Chicken" or fried green tomatoes, washed down with "Champagne of the South," their special iced tea, run don't walk to Social Circle, Georgia to remedy that unfortunate situation. After you have partaken of the vast array of plantation style food, you will not be able to run. A slow walk or a dignified waddle will be the best you can manage. Legendary columnist, Lewis Gizzard frequented it often. He gave The Blue Willow his highest accolade, "5 bowls of turnip greens."

It all began on Thanksgiving 1991. A hundred and fifty guests came to see what this new southern-style restaurant was all about. Operating on a shoestring, owners Louis and Billie Van Dyke had to make do with old broken-down equipment so they faced quite a challenge. But you can't keep good southern cooking down no matter what so the guest left well fed and happy and told all their friends. They and the friends and eventually friends of the friends and then strangers from all over the country and even the world began to visit The Blue Willow.

The Van Dykes were justly proud of the inn's achievements. The days of beat up equipment are long gone. From the moment you step through the door of this historic Greek Revival home, you experience the best of the "Old South." Built in 1917 by John Upshaw, the house frequently played host to Margaret Mitchell who married Red Upshaw. Red is said to be the inspiration for Rhett Butler in *Gone with the Wind*. Tara looks a lot like The Blue Willow. Louis passed away in November 2010 and later Miss Billie sold the restaurant. I have heard the new owners are keeping to the old traditions and using the traditional recipes.

I wasn't surprised to learn, there is a resident ghost. Former owner, Louis Van Dyke, told me they believe she is Miss Bertha Upshaw.

Miss Bertha was the last Upshaw owner. She had donated the house and grounds to the clubs of Social Circle in 1961.

A paranormal group investigated and found evidence of not only Miss Bertha but other spirits. A physic who visited was able to "speak" with Miss Bertha who told her she was happy with the restaurant and all the renovations but was not happy about the Pecan Grove. The physic had no idea what had happened to "the pecan grove" to upset Miss Bertha."

The cook explained that there had been a pecan grove of about 80 trees behind the restaurant that had been taken down to build "The Village," a cluster of boutiques and shops including an ice cream parlor (as if anyone needs more food.)

Louis, who didn't believe in ghosts, had to admit that something is happening. He told me, "Miss Bertha is a gentle spirit but one day the hall chandelier began swinging. Luckily we got a worker up there to secure it before it fell."

The present owners have closed it temporarily while they are remodeling. I doubt the renovations will scare off the spirits.

Another Walton County place where the past is alive in more ways the one is the William Harris Homestead. It was featured on ABC's *Georgia's Hidden Treasures*. It was built around 1825 by William and Harriet Harris and lived in until 1935.

The farm was part of the original land lottery when the land came into the possession of the United States after purchase from the Creeks. The homestead showcases life in pioneer Georgia and is a complete farm. It features a log house built high off the ground to allow for a large cellar underneath, and several outbuildings One thing that makes this place unique is that it has always remained in the same family. The current director is Dotty Zazworsky, a great-granddaughter of William and Harriet.

The house is one and a half stories with two rooms upstairs. Judy Hardegree, whose great-grandmother was born in the house, told us the children slept upstairs and the parents slept downstairs in what is now used as a kitchen.

Dotty explained that an earlier member of the Harris family is still in residence. Todd Bishop, one of the contractors, was working in the upstairs bedroom and saw a little girl with pigtails and wearing a pinafore walking across the pasture. She was carrying a basket and then disappeared in front of his eyes.

Another time two women were riding horses across the pasture and saw the same little girl who also disappeared. It is believed the spirit is that of Viola Harris, one of the granddaughters who never married and died at the age of 42. Perhaps the spirit was reliving happy memories of her childhood in this Georgia treasure.

Madison, in neighboring Morgan County, is one of the prettiest little towns in Georgia. Madison is billed as "the town Sherman refused to burn." Actually Sherman didn't come to Madison. He sent Major-General Slocum instead. History records that in November 1864 the Union troops occupied Madison, Senator Joshua Hill led a delegation to plead with Slocum to spare the town. When Union Troops moved on towards Milledgeville, the town was not torched. Thanks to this fortunate circumstance, you can still view the wonderful old collection of plantations and town homes planters built when cotton was king. Much remains the same. You will stroll down tree lined brick sidewalks and catch a fleeting glance of the South that is now mostly Gone With The Wind.

There is still an old-fashioned square where the courthouse sits in all its splendor. It was built prior to 1910 and is the only courthouse built from that plan. Hollywood director Rob Letterman while filming *Goosebumps* said, "I loved Madison for the nerdiest reason," said. "The clock tower in *Back to Future* reminded me of the courthouse there." This would be appropriate; as the city is a perfect blend of old-fashioned charm and modern convenience. While *Back to the Future* wasn't filmed here, Madison has been the setting for many other films and TV series including, *In the Heat of the Night, Hidden Figures, Vampire Diaries, The Originals*, and many more.

What was once the city hall and fire station is now the Madison Welcome Center. Go down the hall to the restrooms and you will see the original fireman's pole still there. Madison offers a self-guided walking tour app people can download on their phones and walk around Madison learning about the historical sites and homes.

Madison has one of Georgia's largest designated historic districts boasting classic displays of Antebellum and Victorian architecture. A great place to start your tour is The Madison-Morgan Cultural

Center. Built in 1895 as one of the first graded schools in the South, it provides a glimpse into early life in the community.

Rose Cottage and Rogers House give a glimpse into the life of middle class family of the nineteenth century. The Rogers House was built and occupied by the Ruben Rogers family in 1809. It is a classic example of the Piedmont Plain style common to the rural South.

Adeline Rose built the Rose Cottage in 1891. The cottage still reflects the personality of this industrious African American who was able to construct such cozy home on her earnings as a wash woman. She did much of the washing and ironing for residents at the Hardy Boarding House, owned by the mother of Oliver Hardy. Her charge was fifty cents per load.

After her death in 1959, her daughter lived in the house for a time. Then her beloved home fell into disrepair and was finally sold for back taxes. The city of Madison then bought and restored the little house built as a labor of love by a former slave.

One of the best places to find the true antebellum flavor is Heritage Hall. It was constructed between 1833 and 1835. The hall is famous for some of its window etchings made by the original owner's children. It was built for Dr. Elijah Evans Jones for his wife and five children. The building is furnished with authentic period furnishings and many of the doctor's implements. But there is something that draws visitors to the hall besides its historic importance.

When you visit the Heritage House, you may feel a presence in the "Ghost Bedroom." In separate instances, two people claimed they could detect the presence of a young woman in the bed, holding a baby, and a servant kneeling at the foot of the bed. Both claimed that a tragedy had occurred in the room. There is an outline of the three figures on the hearth that cannot be removed by cleaning. The docent when I visited, Betty Jo Booth, relayed a personal experience she had. "I was closing for the night when a lady rushed up. 'Please don't close the door. I was here fourteen years ago and I need to go into a certain room and see if I have the same experience.' I stepped back and watched to see what room she would enter. She went right to the ghost bedroom, right in front of the fireplace and began shouting, 'I knew it! I feel it! There is a presence in this room!'"

The restless spirit is believed to be one of the Jones' daughters, Virginia, who died in that room. There is a stain in the hearth that will not be eradicated despite all the cleaning efforts. Ask the docent, most, like Betty Jo, will tell you the tale of Virginia's unhappy marriage, lost infant and subsequent death.

Of course, Betty Jo reminded us that no one knows for sure if there really is a ghost in the house but, she added, "If I have to come here at night when the alarm goes off, I let someone else check the upstairs."

Another interesting house in Madison is the Wade-Porter-Fitzpatrick-Kelly House. The ghost of a murdered servant girl named Mathuda roams the rooms at night. When the former owners, the Kelly's, bought the place, the previous owners warned them to always leave refreshments out for Mathuda if they had a party. At the housewarming, they forgot. That night they were awakened by a loud crash. A huge antique bed in the guestroom collapsed.

Lula Hearst was your average small town Georgia girl, with one little difference. She could levitate. As a young girl, her father decided Lula's talent should be used. She began to travel with Paul Atkinson who owned and displayed the famous cyclorama painting of the Battle of Atlanta. She was able to raise a chair containing two men while she stood on a scale. The scale registered only her weight.

A romance developed and Paul and Lula were married. When she abandoned her career to raise her family, they settled in Madison. Lula didn't want to be considered a freak so she stopped levitating. However, there may have been one other time she preformed. Shortly before her death in 1949, there was fire in her home. By the time the fire department arrived, all of her massive furniture was sitting on the lawn. Lula never discussed how it got there. Her home, Jessup-Atkinson House, also known as Luhurst in her honor, is one of the Victorian beauties that make a walk through Madison's historic district memorable.

One downtown lodging is a home-town treat. It incorporates the heritage of downtown with the most up to date conveniences. The James Madison Inn has a great view of Madison's newest park, Town Park. The inn features local creativity. The cozy beds are built by a local craftsman. The art on the walls is created by local artists. Even the nightly chocolate is made by a local chocolatier. Each room or suite is named for one of Madison's historic homes. This inn makes new look historic. Even the Greek columns on the front porch mirror the park's Parthenon-like bandstand. Both were rescued from a St. Simon's Island house that was demolished.

For art lovers, the Steffen Thomas Museum offers an opportunity to view an extensive collection of this famous German-American Artist. The museum, with over 5,000 feet of exhibition space is the brainchild of his widow, Sara Douglass Thomas.

Don't skip nearby Lake Oconee. With its 374 miles of shoreline, it offers a haven for fishermen, boaters and nature lovers.

Campers looking for a haunted hideaway? Try Hard Labor State Park. Two ghosts reportedly haunt it. A little boy named Ethan, and a man who is very noisy. There is also a figure spotted near the small graveyard, wandering back and forth along the trail.

Monica Cosper, a former park volunteer, tells her experiences,

> Ethan is pretty young, maybe 5 (as far as how he manifests himself). I have not had the opportunity to study him and his features/clothing because like most 5-year-olds he likes to play games. He loves to giggle and dart so you only see him out of the corner of your eye. He has a red ball that he likes to bounce across paths. I heard a story once about a couple who had driven up the road leading to the graveyard to make out. The windows were fogged up so they couldn't see anything but the car started rocking by itself. They drove off and when they got into the main encampment they got out to look at the car. On the side were the letters "ETH" and then a line, presumably made when they drove off. Most of the time Ethan doesn't try to do things to scare people. Like I said, he likes to play. In fact the only times I have known him to try to scare people is when The Man is coming.

Monica has had a totally different experience with The Man who she perceives as malevolent specter. She explained about the one night he terrified her.

> I was staying in the counselor cabin closest to the graveyard on Halloween that year (lack of planning on my part). Usually, no matter what time of year, we try to either be in bed or out of that area by 10:30pm every night. Well this night I had changed clothes in a friend's cabin and wanted to put my clothes in my cabin so I didn't lose track of them. I didn't realize that it was nearly mid-

night. And this time Ethan didn't give me a warning. He probably wanted to be clear of the area himself. I walked into the cabin, which really only has room for a bed. It's more like a closet in the counselor's cabin. I closed the door behind me and put my stuff on the bed. I was checking my pockets to make sure I had everything I needed so I wouldn't have to come back until much later. The shutters were closed too. I couldn't see outside at all. (They open toward the inside, not the outside) Two sides of the cabin have a window with screens, one side has nothing, and the door is in the other side. I heard a tap on one of my screens then the back wall then the other screen then my door. At first I thought it was my friends playing with me but it kept getting faster and faster around and around my cabin until it was like a roar and the cabin was vibrating. It went on for a good three minutes (which is a long time when you're having a heart attack.) I was terrified, and then I got mad. I clenched my hands into fists and screamed "STOP!" and it stopped suddenly like someone flipped a switch. I threw the door open and jumped out of the cabin. There was nothing outside.

She explained that her nearest neighbors were in a cabin fifty yards away and could not have gotten away from her cabin that quickly if they had been playing a trick on her. Oddly enough, her friend in the other cabin didn't hear her screams or the pounding.

Although this is the only physical manifestation she has experienced, she said you are often aware of the presence of the two spirits. "You can feel them, watching you...following you. They feel different too. Ethan makes you feel like you are being toyed with, the man makes you terrified. The kind of fear that used to make you cry at night in your bed and pull the covers over your head"

Two of her friends have talked to Ethan. She believes the old graveyard on the grounds that may account for the presences. Her experiences go to show that haunting is not limited to buildings but occurs out of doors as well. I bet spooky tales told over a camp fire at Hard Labor State Park would give a whole new meaning to the expression "Somebody just walked on my grave!"

Chapter 9 Eatonton, Home of Brer Rabbit

The little town of Eatonton, located on Georgia's Antebellum Trail between Athens and Macon, has a rather snooty spook. Sylvia is reputed to reside at Panola Hall. Many people have seen Sylvia, but only those she considers "her social equals." One visitor not only saw her; he smelled the fragrance of the Damask Rose in her hair.

Panola Hall is not Eatonton's only phantom. Another private home on the Walking Tour is The Riley-Williams House. Gayle Riley, a wealthy cotton factor, built this classic revival house for his family. Today it's the home of Carol and Zeke Williams. The family has all heard footsteps that sounded like a woman walking down the stairs at night. Duncan, the William's son, actually witnessed the figure of the woman who vanished before his eyes. A psychic brought in to investigate sensed a female presence, possibly Mrs. Riley.

Eatonton is one of the most literary towns along the trail. It nourished three famous writers, Joel Chandler Harris, creator of *Uncle Remus Tales*, Flannery O'Conner, best known for *A Good Man is Hard to Find* and other classic tales, and Alice Walker, world-renowned author of *The Color Purple*. The Uncle Remus Museum contains memorabilia immortalizing Brer Rabbit.

A tour of the places that are part of Alice Walker's life allows you to envision the birth of her creative spirit. The Alice Walker Driving Tour brochure is available at the Visitors Center and gives a timeline of important events in Walker's life. There is a Georgia Writers Museum to honor them and other Georgia writers. It is the home of the Georgia Writers Hall of Fame exhibit.

Little is known about the origin of two other intriguing creations in the area. The giant Rock Eagle Effigy is a stone mound or tumulus in the shape of a bird with outstretched wings. The wing span is 120 feet. The body stands about ten feet high. Native Americans in the area when the settlers arrived stated they didn't know who built the mound. It was there when their ancestors arrived. Scientists believe it to be built by a mound-building culture about 3000 BC, which would make it older than the Great Pyramid of Egypt.

Not too far away is a similar mound called the Rock Hawk. The area around this mound has recently been upgraded into a huge outdoor classroom and park. It comprises about 1,000 acres with trails, camping, canoeing or kayaking, wildlife watching, playground and a swimming beach. Two towers are built for viewing the mysterious effigy. One theory is that these mounds were religious sites perhaps associated with burials. It was a common practice among Native Americans to place a rock on a grave when they passed by. There is a legend in the area that some early settlers used some of the effigy's stones to construct a path to the Oconee River. Those who did this became sick and died immediately after.

For a light lunch or snack, visit Hannah's in the downtown district, it is close to antique shops and boutiques. Hannah's offers lunch and dinner with a Caribbean and southern influence. Menu items include fish tacos, an avocado burger, shrimp po' boy, Cuban sandwich, crab cakes, salads and many different specials.

Eatonton's Blackwell Furniture Store occupied the site of some of the oldest structures in town. Fortunately, the owners have maintained the feel of the historic structures. The Adel Theater has been restored including a box office with an authentic ticket taker. The stage area transports you back to 1914 when the theater was a silent movie house and a vaudeville show. Unfortunately, the furniture store closed down in 2023 so the theater viewing is in limbo.

The complex includes the town's oldest building there is a peep-hole door used to screen members of a secret male society in 1818. Downstairs was originally a stagecoach depot. Surely there must be some lingering spirits in these ancient buildings, but they choose not to manifest themselves.

The original Eatonton School built in 1916, now houses the Plaza Arts Center and the Old School History Museum. Four of the classrooms are devoted to the history of the area.

Nearby Lake Oconee offers camping and recreational opportunities at three sites provided by Georgia Power and Light, located on the lake, Laurence Shoals, Parks Ferry and Old Salem. There are lodges: Cuscowilla on Lake Oconee and The Lodge on Lake Oconee. Legend has it that an old cemetery located near the Old Salem area is haunted. If you camp there, you may get to find out firsthand.

Eatonton combines the opportunity for water and nature fun with the ambience of a small town of the Old South.

Chapter 10 Milledgeville, Confederate Capital

Shades of Tara! Scarlett would feel right at home in Milledgeville, Georgia. And with good reason. This charming city was the capital of Georgia during the Civil War. It witnessed some of history's most turbulent moments. It played host, willingly or unwillingly, to many fascinating people. Flannery O'Connor, Susan Myrick, who made sure the dialect in *Gone With the Wind* was correct, Oliver Hardy, Governor Joe Brown and many others. General Sherman paused on his march to the sea long enough to eat Thanksgiving dinner in its hastily abandoned governor's mansion.

Fortunately for the modern traveler, Milledgeville managed to preserve much of its antebellum architecture and flavor. You can still tour The Old Governor's Mansion, one of the South's best examples of Greek Revival architecture. St Stephen's Episcopal Church, where Sherman's soldiers stabled their horses, is still in use as a house of worship. The tale of a child who got the pipe organ replaced after Federal troops poured molasses into the original organ is a case of fact being more interesting than fiction.

The Old Governor's Mansion seems to have multiple spirits. There is Molly, who spent her life as the cook. Delicious smells emanate from the basement kitchen although the huge red brick fireplace is no longer used for cooking. When you tour the mansion you may witness unusual phenomena. Others have. At a tour in 1992, all the lights flickered as if keeping time to unheard music. Workers have heard footsteps and even seen apparitions. Servants tell of beds being unmade by spirits after the room is cleaned.

In an interview with James C. Turner, past curator of the Mansion, he stated "This was a house of life and death. Governor Brown's younger brother, John Brown, returned here in 1864 severely wounded in battle. He died here and was laid out in the rotunda. From time to time people have heard him groaning in his pain. Like-wise, Governor Cobb's three-year-old daughter, Aurora died on the upper floor. People sometimes hear a little girl crying, 'Mama, Mama.'"

Are these spirits still earthbound in this place and era of so much tragedy? You can judge for yourself. Tours are held Tuesday through Sunday.

Another multi-ghosted house is The Homestead. Of course, many old Southern homes have their ghosts but The Homestead, built in 1818, is reputed to have several. The most interesting one being "Miss Sue," who is occasionally seen working in her garden and loves to flush toilets. Miss Sue was the fiery, redhead daughter of the original owner. Her husband, Honest Jack, has also been reported hanging around the mansion. There are conflicting stories about his death, He either committed suicide to escape Sue's nagging or died of malaria.

There is also a lady in gray. The Gray Lady is believed to be a banshee who followed the original occupants from Wales. If so, she has been there since 1818 when Peter Williams built the home for his bride, Lucinda. If you do see her, you can be sure you will soon hear of the death of someone you know.

Footsteps and noises occur in the upstairs hall. One possible source is revealed in a story from 1864. A Confederate general was a guest in the home. He had contracted pneumonia and was unable to leave when Sherman captured the city. Hidden upstairs, he finally died in an upstairs bedroom. Ever since, strange occurrences – door slamming, falling pictures, imprints in the unoccupied bed - have emanated from the room now called "The General's Room," happen. Perhaps, he is still there waiting until he feels the coast is clear so he can rejoin his troops. The Homestead is a private residence but the trolley tour does include the exterior. Please respect the owner's privacy.

When Daniel Reese Tucker sought a home for the third time, he vowed he would have one "Neither fire or wind could destroy." He purchased a lovely Greek Revival home in 1851 to replace two earlier ones. The first had been destroyed by a tornado; the second by fire. He was right but has he and his family paid for his pride by being trapped forever in his magnificent showplace? Had pride cast a spell on this lofty mansion from its very beginning?

A "Yankee entrepreneur," R. J. Nichols, built Rose Hill, as it was original named, in 1838. He wanted it to be the grandest home in the city. It even overshadowed the new governor's mansion. However, he was not able to enjoy his triumph long. He died, leaving no will, about ten years later.

Daniel Tucker bought it at auction from the estate. He and his wife, Martha, raised nine children there. It was so grand it was chosen as the site of the gubernatorial inaugural ball in 1853. But have any of the prideful residents known peace in the house?

Daniel was only able to enjoy the full use of the mansion for about ten years. He was stricken with a crippling disease and was confined to a wheelchair on the first floor for the remaining eighteen years of his life. Emma, his daughter, supposedly had a rather unhappy marriage. Daniel remained in the house, an invalid unable to vacate when Sherman marched past. The soldiers took food and burned the outbuildings but left the house intact. Daniel's boast held true and has to this day. Daniel, Martha, Emma and her husband, George Sibley died in the house.

After the Civil War, much of the land was stripped away and given to the former slaves. After all they were the ones who had built the home and the wealth for the owner. A British family changed the name to Lockerly Hall in 1928. The estate eventually disintegrated until it was almost a candidate for the bulldozers. Then another Northerner purchased it. Edward Grassmann needed a guesthouse. He restored the manor to showcase the fine china made by his Georgia Kaolin company. He set up fifty acres as Lockerly Arboretum. In 1998, the manor was rejoined to the arboretum. Both are now open to the public and part of the Historic Trolley Tour.

Throughout the years, Lockerly Hall gained the reputation of being a "haunted house." Visitors have claimed encounters with the restless spirit of Emma Tucker Sibley. Others have reported seeing an elderly man in an antebellum costume in the downstairs hall. Does Daniel still roam the halls of his magnificent mansion?

As might be expected in a town as rich in Antebellum and Victorian architecture, Milledgeville has many homes equipped with their own resident spook. Sam Walker was considered the "meanest man in Georgia." He is reputed to walk the floors of the Tate House, which is now converted to apartments. Debbie Thompson braved the eerie events to create apartments for college students. She later sold the house. In 2001, the estate was purchased by Holbrook Properties

Debbie was kind enough to let me roam among the workmen to get the feel of the place. I experienced one strange occurrence in the house. I use a tape recorder so I will remember information accurately. It was in its holster strapped to my belt. Suddenly it jumped out and crashed to the floor. It was thrown open and the batteries fell out. I picked it up and put it back together. It worked fine but I had forgotten what we were discussing just before. Perhaps Sam was showing his displeasure at my intrusion. Perhaps it was just an accident however, it never fell from that holster before or since.

Memory Hill Cemetery has more ghosts per square foot than any other place in Georgia. One story commonly told relates to a man named Thomas Fish. His wife and child died shortly after he returned home from the Civil War. It was his final defeat. He walled himself up alive inside the tomb of his dead wife. Unfortunately it is an old urban myth. Yes, they had those way back when.

Dixie Haygood who could lift a table with five men seated on it is reputed to be a witch. She is buried there in an marked grave. Dixie performed before the royalty of Europe and even the President of the United States. Her super human powers came about after a strange spell in her middle age. In spite of her "gift," she spent much of her later years in the state mental hospital and died at fifty-four. Her nickname was "The Little Georgia Magnet."

John Yates was believed to be a warlock. His grave is frequently disturbed by a large sinkhole. Attempts to fill the hole with cement have not been successful. Perhaps he and Dixie are feuding even in death.

Frank Gobert was the first of many tragic deaths that occurred in the house at 520 W. Hancock. He shot himself over his cotton failure around 1904. Elenore Wade, a later owner was murdered in the 1980s. The house's latest victim was Walter Park. He went to investigate noises in the yard and was killed when he stepped in a hole and the gun he was carrying discharged. The house used to serve as a bed and breakfast, but the ghost did not seem intent on harming the visitors.

The Old State Capitol Building was restored in 2000. Today, it houses Georgia Military College and perhaps a few Confederate Soldiers who have been hanging around since 1861. This building was the midwife of the Confederate State of Georgia, when the Secession Convention severed the state's bonds with the Union in January 1861. In 1864, it witnessed the death throes of that same Confederacy as Sherman burned the state records and the books from its vast library. On dark and moonless nights, the tramp of marching soldiers echoes across its parade grounds. Many have watched a lone Confederate sentry march between the capital gates and the governor's mansion.

Milledgeville is the Antebellum Grande Dame of Georgia.

Chapter 11 Macon, Music and Mansions

Macon can truly be called the city of "White Columns and Cherry Blossoms." It was founded in 1823, and one of its most beautiful white columns, the 1842 Inn, was built less than two decades later. Its history and the city's are intertwined. Judge John Gresham built the gracious Greek Revival home as his family residence. A successful cotton broker, he served two non-consecutive terms as mayor of Macon. Gresham was very proud of his stately mansion, with its stately columns, shady veranda and lush magnolia trees. It was and still is the perfect Southern image of hospitality. So proud was he that he refused to part with it after death. Many claim he still inhabits the Gresham Suite and he is not alone.

Guests have seen a small girl, perhaps his daughter. The suite has a unique floral smell that is different from the rest of the house. But it is not the only place to experience paranormal activities. One lady who was in the Dogwood Room "met" John Gresham in her room when she came out of the shower. At first she was frightened but the man's expression made her feel protected instead of threatened.

Mayor Gresham will not harm you. He is a very gracious host. There is a tall blond female spirit who visits the inn. The staff has no idea who she might be but she is also benign.

He and his home have played host to many famous people over the years. Jefferson Davis, president of the Confederacy, stayed there in 1865 as he fled south to avoid capture.

The Gresham family was not the only one to leave its mark on the Inn. They owned it until the early 1900s, when B.F. Adams purchased it for his family's residence. The Adamses added two side porches and additional columns, and replaced the flooring with parquet flooring. It was around the same time that the Victorian cottage located across the courtyard from the main house was built in the neighboring Vineville area. The cottage was moved to its current location in the early 1980s and is now part of the inn. It features 12-foot ceilings, original heart-of-pine flooring, and a wide front porch. Including the cottage, the inn offers a total of 19 rooms.

Each room is named for some prominent person or place that has a connection to Macon. Georgia Belle, Dogwood and Magnolia rooms pay homage to the South's favorite flowers, both literally and figuratively. Of course, Jefferson Davis has a namesake room. The Cotton Merchant's room is named for B.F. Adams; it's no surprise to find rooms named in honor of Sidney Lanier, Georgia's most famous poet, and William Bartram, the naturalist who traveled though Georgia. What is unusual in this bastion of Southern heritage is to find a room (it's actually not a sleeping room but a public parlor) named in honor of William Howard Taft. The reason? Taft stayed here in 1909 shortly after his election.

The home was used as an apartment building from about 1930 to the early 1980s, when it became an inn.

As a city, Macon's history began when President Thomas Jefferson commissioned the building of Fort Hawkins near the Ocmulgee Old Fields just across the river from present day Macon. At that time, due to the latest treaty with the Creek Indians, the Ocmulgee River was the southwestern border of the United States. As usually happens, a settlement called New Town grew up around the fort and in 1823, the citizens laid out a new city across the river, named Macon. The fort saw action during the Civil War. Although by then the old fort was in ruins, it succeeded twice in repelling Federal raids. Perhaps even then, Macon's guardian angel protected the city. Does some mysterious presence still patrol the watchtowers of the old fort? At least one resident of the area has seen the spectral sentry by the light of a full moon as he patrols high on the top watchtower of the reconstructed fort.

Hugh earthen mounds a guarded by the spirit dogs are all that is left at the nearby Ocmulgee National Monument of an ancient Mississippian settlement dating back to around 900AD. Actually these people displaced earlier groups of nomads and started a farming culture on the banks of the river. Several mounds and a reconstructed earth lodge offer a glimpse into a way of life that stretches back into prehistory. The earliest mention of ghosts in the area dates to 1775. A trader, James Adair, recorded in his diary tales of ghostly Indians at dawn.

Marty Willett, who portrayed the poet Sidney Lanier, on a ghost tour for the Historic Macon Foundation, reported that staff and visitors to the Indian Mounds often see and hear ghost dogs. The wolf like animals howl pitifully at night but towards dawn, the cries become joyful.

Indian legends claim the dogs are souls of the people buried there. Another legend says the black dog is a spirit left to guard the sacred place. There is also a legend that the last of the Creek-Muskogee were driven from their homes, they cursed the land and said then no one who came here would be able to leave. Sounds of drumming are still heard in the area where their sacred lodge stood.

Animal spirits are not the only ones found there. Sylvia Flowers, retired Master Ranger, tells of employees hearing a child laugh in the building but when they searched no child was ever found. One visitor at a Cherry Blossom Lantern Light Tour reported seeing a Confederate Soldier in the mists. Many people over the years have reported a small white dog that disappears when you approach.

Perhaps these souls are holdovers from a later time. During the War Between the States, Samuel Dunlap's plantation stood there. It's not known if he had any children but he did have a small white dog.

One of Macon's grand old antebellum dowagers is the Cannonball House. Whenever there is a party planned there, hosts are careful to invite Miss Elizabeth. Once they forgot to invite her to a mint-julep party. The next day, they realized their oversight. The leftover bourbon and simple syrup was dumped all over the room. If she feels slighted, she is sure to make her presence felt. One docent saw a woman dressed in a green antebellum style dress. Many have heard voices. One was told by a young girl's voice, "It's late. Go home."

It was during the Battle of Dunlap Hill that the now famous cannonball came to be lodged in Judge Asa Holt's residence, now known as the Cannonball House. The shot was aimed for the home of William Butler Johnson (The Hay House), who was the Treasurer of the Confederacy. Instead it glanced off a portico column and passed through the parlor wall and settled unexploded at the bottom of the stairs. It is still there.

Judge Holt's problems with the Yankees did not end with the cannon ball in his home. Sadie Crumbley, co-author of *Macon's Trea-*

sures Remembered, told about the Judge's near brush with death. When he learned the Union troops were approaching Macon, he and his wife fled the house for the supposedly safer environment of their plantation in Jefferson County but his wife did not want to lose all her good china and silverware. So she had it bagged up and loaded on a carriage to take with them. One of the men loading the bags commented, "Lord Miz Holt, you mus' have a lot of gold in these here bags. They sur' are heavy."

Instead of avoiding Sherman, the Holts plantation was right in the army's path. Some of Sherman's men had heard the story about the "heavy bags of gold" and dragged the 75 year-old judge out into the woods to make him tell where the gold was buried. Judge Holt took his captors to the place the bags had been buried. When the bummers found that it was china and crystal not gold they believed the judge was holding out on them. They hung him until he was almost dead and then cut him down. The judge still tried to tell them there was no gold. Unconvinced, they gave him until the next day to lead them to the gold. On the next day, the soldiers again hanged the judge and cut him down at the last minute. Finally on the third day, they left him hanging. His wife begged for mercy and some soldiers cut down the limp body and tossed it on the porch. Miraculously, the tough old judge was not dead and revived to live a few more years.

In spite of the judge's luck at surviving hanging, the Cannonball House has had more than its share of unlucky happenings. After Judge Holt's death, His widow remarried. Her daughter and son-in-law both died from a wasting form of dysentery. Two of their children, John William Martin and Canning Martin, came to unhappy ends in the home. John, a veteran of the Spanish-American War, became depressed and shot himself on sleeping porch in 1903 Charles hung himself in the tool shed in 1909.

While there, be sure to visit the original brick servants' quarters and kitchen in the rear.

Macon's Hay House is now owned by the National Historic Trust and is open to the public as a museum. Although the former owners' and the director's official statements are "There are no ghost in Hay House," the numerous sightings tell another story. The wave of sightings began in 1980 when the 18,000 square foot palace was undergoing extensive renovation.

Built in 1860, the Hay House had such amenities as hot and cold running water, walk-in closets, and its own heating and cooling system. The White House didn't have all the luxuries taken for granted at William Johnston's home. Johnston made his fortune in insurance, real estate and banking. His young wife, Anne, called Hay House "her fairy palace." Perhaps she liked it so well she would not leave even after her death. During the renovations, the family butler, Chester Davis, saw Anne. She was elegantly dressed in period clothing and seemed to be inspecting the work. Other members of the staff saw her as well. A psychic who came to the house detected the presence of Anne and believed she was concerned about the renovations. She has not been seen since the renovation.

Davis also glimpsed other former residents of the house. He sighted Judge William H. Felton, the homes second owner, and his daughter-in-law, Luisa. He hesitated to mention any of the apparitions for fear people would doubt his sanity. However, when other staff members mentioned similar sightings, he came forward with his story

Whatever the truth is, when you ask the tour guides at the mansion, the answer will be "We're instructed not to discuss that."

One of Macon's most unusual Southern beauties is the Bennett House. It is built over the spring used for the water source of the Hay House. It was the first house built when inheritance dictated the division of the original Johnston Estate. One daughter inheriting the house, the other the land sprawling up the hill. The spring is housed in a domed room on the lowest level of the house. The house also boasts a matched pair of ghosts; Uncle Pliny and his wife, Mamie.

In life they were known as Mamie and Mansfield Pliny Hall. They were the second owners, moving there in the first decade of the 1900s. Maim loved to move around a lot. Pliny was an attorney and tired of having to build a new clientele every time they moved. Before they bought the house from Eugene and Mary Harris, Pliny announced he was going to stop practicing law if they moved. Keeping his word, he retired and the couple became popular host in

Macon. Perhaps this was what Mamie wanted all along since they never moved again even after death.

The later corporeal owners of the house, Susan and Gilbert Bennett have come to consider their ghostly guests part of the family. They consider footsteps, voices and event apparitions a normal part of life in the Bennett House.

Woodruff House is a Greek Revival mansion currently owned by Mercer University. Because of its Doric columns and triglyph frieze it resembles the Parthenon. Originally named Overlook because of its location atop Coleman Hill. The house has sheltered many of the rich and famous in its time. It was the residence of Reconstruction Military Governor General James Wilson. Wilson incidentally "captured" Macon several weeks after the war ended

The otherworldly occurrences seem to date to the occupancy of the second owner, Colonel Joseph Bond. His former overseer, Lucius Brown, killed Col. Bond in 1859 during an argument over the mistreatment of one of Bond's servants. After his death, his widow, Henrietta remained in the house until her death in 1879. For some reason, she is not buried in Rose Hill Cemetery next to her husband but on her family's homestead in Twiggs County.

When George Woodruff donated one million dollars to Mercer University in 1993 to renovate the mansion, the college renamed it Woodruff House in his honor. It was then that the phenomenon began occurring. Pat Wood of the Mercer Police force was assigned to protect the house from vandals. She encountered strong feelings of hostility when she entered the house and became convinced Col. Bond was upset at strangers in "his "house. She began the practice of speaking to him and explaining her presence and the plans for the house. Gradually she sensed a lessening of the hostility. When the alarm system was installed her presence was no longer necessary. However, the alarm began to go off several times a night. There was no mechanical or electrical reason so once again. Wood explained to the colonel, what was happening. After that the alarm functioned properly.

The lights would flicker, though no electrical problem could be found. The portrait of Henrietta would repeatedly turn itself to face the wall. A rug would be pulled from under a table. In the upper floors, a baby could be heard crying from the attic. A psychic visiting the building claimed to sense a presence there

On other occasions, a visitor in the house saw a man dressed in clothing of the 1860s and a security guard reported seeing the Colonel several times. The guard also saw a female presence wearing a long black dress. He has seen the same woman in Willingham Chapel, another Mercer property nearby.

Willingham Chapel, located on the main Mercer campus, houses the College's Back Door Theater. Drama students blame mysterious happenings on an unseen entity they call "Oscar." But even before the theater was installed in the chapel basement, there were rumors of unexplained occurrences. Students in the early nineteen hundreds claim to have sighted the spirit of a Confederate soldier who was killed there in the 1860s.

Some places seem to attract ethereal spirits. Theaters are one of those places. Perhaps old actors continue to believe "The play's the thing." The Grand Lady of Mulberry, Macon's Grand Opera House certainly lives up to a theater's expected level of haunting. Built in 1884, it once claimed the largest stage south of the Mason-Dixon Line. You can still catch a performance however now it is mainly used for concerts but many local performances are held there as well. The theater suffered a decline with the era of movies and then television. It was destined to become another high-rise parking lot when it was rescued through the efforts of Supporters of the Grand Old Opera House in 1967. It was Macon's first building to appear on the National Register of Historic Places.

The theater experiences regular poltergeist activity. Some of this is blamed on "Randy." Randall Widner, the former managing director, committed suicide in a room called the Thunder Room above the stage in 1971. The place on the floor where Randall's body lay for four days before being discovered will never collect dust. Since then whoever opens the Grand Opera House always greets Randall as if he were there--and perhaps he is.

Whenever a group performs that is somewhat disrespectful of the theater's history they seem to have technical problems but groups that are mindful of the theater and respect its history have no problems. One doubting-Thomas technical director was in the theater when it was closed and no one was there except himself and a few friends. As they stood near the stage, he shouted "Randall, if you are here, show yourself."

Immediately there was the sound of loud stomping back and forth across the room directly above them. They shined their flashlights on the ceiling above and saw dust falling as the clattering continued. They were directly under the Thunder Room where Randall had died. I'll bet that technician never called Randall's name in vain again.

Another unexplained phenomena related to the theater's spring-loaded seats. When he was alive, Randall frequently sat in one of the seats and ate his lunch there. Frequently, people have observed the seats popping from the down position to the up as if someone had just gotten up from the seat.

Bob Mavity, the senior technical director, was doing "fire-watch" duty to make sure no embers caught the theater on fire after a day of welding sets. He experienced lights flashing, mysterious music and footsteps.

But the strange events predate Randy. Another employee hung himself in the elevator shaft. In 1937, the Macon Telegraph reported a night watchman, J. D. Jones, claimed to see a woman in a long white gown floating across the stage. Many others have reported footsteps and cold spots in the theater. So catch a performance when you visit Macon. You may get more than you bargain for.

The newest--it was built in 1921--in Macon's trio of supernaturally inhabited theaters is Douglass Theater. The Douglass is one of the few historical theaters built, designed, owned and operated by an African-American. Charles Douglass was a man ahead of his time. His theater offered patrons the opportunity to see three or four short films on its golden screen and traveling vaudeville performers. During its heyday, it hosted the like of Duke Ellington, Ma Rainey, Little Richard, Otis Redding and James Brown.

Then in 1972 the theatre closed its doors. But the dream didn't die there. It reopened in 1997 after a more than three million dollar facelift. Shortly after reopening many strange events occurred. Lights would mysteriously dim and brighter repeatedly, projectors and curtains began unusual malfunctions. The staff has come to believe the dynamic personality of Charles Douglass is proud of his newly reopened theater and trying to communicate. The theater now runs films, special screenings, the Macon Opera Guild and stage performances and boasts one of the finest sound system in Georgia.

What was once one of Macon's finest and most haunted restaurant has undergone several reincarnations. Beall's was acquired by the G. H. Bell Family Partnership, an engineering firm that specializing in restoring historically significant buildings. They transformed it into elegant offices but the businesslike atmosphere may not have driven away the resident haunts? In 2008, the Bell family donated the historic structure to Mercer University to be used by the Engineering Department. Wonder if the spirits are still in residence.

The magnificent structure has had its ups and downs. Built in 1860, the home became a casualty of the war that ravaged so much of Dixie. When it was used as the backdrop for the first Allman Brothers Band album cover, it looked like a derelict who had known better times. In the 1970s and 80s, it was renovated and became the home of several restaurants. Always the stories of the eerie events drew people as well as the hope of good food. Many were not disappointed. A group of Confederate reenactors held a banquet in the upstairs dining hall. Picture the surprise of the diners, all clad in their Confederate uniforms when the huge brass chandelier overhead began to blink an unplanned and electrically impossible cadence.

Another event this time, a ladies' luncheon, was held in the library. Suddenly, books started flying from the bookcases. That lunch ended suddenly. The staff frequently reported electrical abnormalities like self-starting blenders, lights turning off and on and ice that flew out of glasses when bartenders tried to mix drinks.

Guests frequently spotted a lady, dressed in a long white gown, sitting at the end of the bar when no one was really there–or was she. Some guests even claimed to be pinched by a playful spirit. Another mystery that refuses to be cleared up is the stain that remains outside the building in spite of numerous attempts to remove it. Reportedly it marks the spot where a distraught young woman committed suicide when she threw herself out of a second story window.

Hardeman-Mayer building, now the home of Lawrence Mayer Florist, has a history that explains its strange happenings. Items have been known to fly off the shelf and doors opening and closing. Employees have seen a strange dark image downstairs.

In the 1840's the building housed Paine Apothecary on the ground floor and a concert hall upstairs. Dr. Ambrose Baber, Macon's first practicing physician, prescribed a dose of cyanide of potassium according to the instructions in Ellis' Formulary for a patient. When the pharmacist seeing that there was something wrong with the prescription refused to fill it, Dr. Baber became indignant and went behind the counter and filled it himself. He took a dose to prove it was exactly according to the formula in his book. It was. However, the book had a typographical error that was corrected in the next edition. It was too late to help Dr. Baber as he died instantly upon taking a dose of the prescription he had insisted was correct.

The Macon Convention & Visitors Bureau's Haunted History podcast tour provides a haunting look at the city's past, and may be downloaded free from the CVB's website at www.visitmacon.org

Tours are a must in Macon. They have some of the most beautiful historic homes and buildings as well as unrivaled museums. Your feet may ache from walking the areas included in the Self-guided Tour Map of Macon but it's worth the effort.

The Tubman African American Museum's exhibits make it a unique attraction. From military hero such as Crispus Attucks, the first Black to die in the American Revolution, and Rodney Davis, Macon's only Medal of Honor recipient, to entertainment greats such as Otis Redding and blind singer-guitar player Rev. Pearly Brown, the museum makes a positive statement about Black history. Rev. Brown performed at Carnegie Hall and became the first Black entertainer to perform at the Grand Ole Opry.

The Museum of Arts and Sciences and Planetarium allows you to view a 40-million- year-old whale skeleton found near Macon, view art exhibits and interact with exhibits.

Macon is also very much a city of the present. The state of the art Georgia Sports Hall of Fame, opened, April 24, 1999, this Macon museum allow participation not just appreciation. Your tour begins with a fast paced video introducing you to the world of Georgia sports in a 205 seat theater modeled after a ball park stadium. When the cheers die away, you emerge into a colorful display of jerseys and banners. The museum merges interactive activities such as an interactive wheelchair race or your chance to sit in the sportscaster's chair and make the call for one of sports history's great moments.

A riveting display is Bill Elliott's NASCAR car, featured prominently on the second floor. No way could it have been driven to that spot. Robbie Burns, the museum's former publicity director told me the secret. "It was hoisted and maneuvered through an opening on the second floor where a huge, curved window had been removed to allow the car's access."

Although Macon was already a star in the music constellation with Otis Redding's Soul Music and Little Richard's Rock and Roll, it was Capricorn Studio that flamed like a blazing meteor through the musical sky with the Allman Brothers Band and the birth of Southern Rock. Like a meteor, its life was short. Loss of two of the Allman Brothers Band in motorcycle accidents within a year, an economic recession, and new genres like punk ended Capricorn's success. By the 1980s it was gone as a musical force. Last time I visited Macon a few years ago, it was just a group of huddled decaying buildings destined for the wrecker.

Today, Mercer College has revived Capricorn. Downstairs, you can tour their brand-new working studio completed in 2019. It's an active recording studio. Across the lobby is the original studio where musicians like the Allman Brothers Band, James Brown, Lynyrd Skynyrd, Marshal Tucker Band, Wet Willie, and Charlie Daniels recorded in the 1970s. I could feel the old vibes there. I refrained from singing "Sweet Home Alabama" here in Georgia. There is a small museum on the second floor. It has a digital collection of all the old albums that made the original Capricorn Studio unforgettable.

The Allman Brothers Band created a new genre, Southern Rock. It was a mix of Rock and Roll, Country, Jazz, and Blues. The Big House was where they and some of their friends lived while they were creating this music. It was their home from 1970 to 1973. The three-story house is filled with their personal possessions, albums, instruments, scraps of paper where they wrote songs. There is a painting of the band next to their many gold records.

The Allman Brothers Band were a big influence in electing one of their fans president. One of my favorite exhibits is one showing Jimmy Carter wearing the band's tee shirt with "Win, Lose, or Draw" on it. Under he is quoted, "I don't intend to lose."

Some spirits still inhabit the house. There are many accounts by former residents and workers of an apparition at the Big House. Kristin and Kirk West owned the house before it became a museum, . Kristin once saw a face of " a young female ghost hovering over her bed. When she asked who it was, the apparation replied, "this was my daddy's house." Linda Oakley who lived in the Big House wiht her husband and baby also told Kristine about seeing a apparition. Kirsten said. "She was very aware of it and so were anyone associated with the Allman Brothers."

Richard Brent, Director of Collections is another who has experienced strange occurrences. He said, "On a handful of occasions it's been really noisy; I've heard footsteps a lot." he said.

The Rock Candy Tour is a great way to see places related to music in Macon. Rex Dooley, my guide on the Rock Candy Tour, took me to all the places related to music in Macon. Many were little out-of-the-way spots with a big significance like the Downtown Grill, hidden away in an alley. It used to be Le Bistro when Capricorn Records Vice President Frank Fente opened it in 1973. Rex said, "Mick Jagger sent his personal chef to cook for the opening night."

It played host to many famous people like Andy Warhol, President Jimmy Carter and the Allman Brothers Band. It is famed in music history as the place Gregg Allman proposed to Cher.

My tour touched on the Otis Redding Foundation and Douglass Theater. Rock Candy Tours offers a variety of different tours, even a ghost tour. I'm not sure if those folks get to see the ghost of dead rock stars but it might be a fun tour.

You will find so much to see and do in Macon that this just scratches the surface. There are magnificent churches, such as St Joseph's Catholic Church, cultural offerings, such as the restored Douglass Theater and the Grand Opera House. Parks and gardens abound.

Lake Tobesofkee Recreation Area provides three parks and 1800 acres of fresh water fun. They offer fishing, boating, picnicking, tennis and swimming. Two of the parks, Arrowhead and Claystone, offer camping along the lake's 35 miles of shore.

Macon's biggest festival revolves around the Yoshino Cherry Tree. This tree produces no fruit. Its sole purpose in life is to create beauty. Each year, in early spring, the trees drape the city of Macon in a blanket of pearly pink blossoms. The residents are so intoxicated with nature's blushing masterpiece they want to share it with the world.

In 1983 they decided to wrap the city with pink bows, put together a plethora of varied and fun activities, invite artists and craftspersons and throw a terrific city-wide block party. The first International Cherry Blossom Festival was born.

The festival traces its roots to William Fickling who began propagating the trees and sharing them with the community. As a result of his generosity, over 330,000 Yoshino Cherry Trees burst into bloom all over Macon's parks and neighborhoods in mid March. The city is transformed into a fragrant pink bower earning it the title "Cherry Blossom Capital of the World. The azaleas, dogwood and tulips must be jealous since they all decide to erupt in a floral display at the same time.

The whirlwind of activities begins with the ribbon cutting in Central City Park. For the next ten days, the city pulls out all stops to entertain you like royalty. Complementary refreshment and free carriage rides are offered. Carnival rides, animal shows and shopping will compete for your attention. Golfers of all ages can whack little white balls in one of the four golf tournaments. Softball, volleyball, archery, running and bicycling are also on the agenda. If you're not the energetic type, the ongoing arts and crafts in the park and various displays offer something for everyone.

On stage activities run the gamete from concerts to plays and everything in between. Magicians mystify, dancers strut and thespians entertain with world class plays.

For those who wouldn't leave home without Fido, you'll enjoy the Canine Frisbee Disk Championship and the Humane Services Fins, Furs and Feathers Festival. Their contests include smallest pet, largest pet, pet trick contest and even a most unique pet contest with prizes in all categories.

And then there are those of you who like to eat. You won't feel slighted here. The Pink Pancake Breakfast, International Food Fair and the pizza eating contest should fulfill your every food fantasy.

Only in Georgia will you find a "Peanut Boil," provided by the fire department.

Even the skies are filled with entertainment. Multicolored hot air balloons and fireworks provide drama and spectacle. To avoid heavy weekend traffic during the festival, take advantage of the free shuttle bus that runs from the Coliseum to Central City Park. The Red Cross provides a first aid station on site. They also offer free blood pressure readings.

Although most of the activities are free, some of the big name concerts do cost additional. Tickets for these events can be purchased at any Ticketmaster location or at the Coliseum. The Cherry Blossom Festival was named in the Top 20 Events in the Southeast, a Top 75 Event in the United States and a Top Hundred Event in North America. It has something for every taste. It can be as sweet as a chocolate covered cherry or as intoxication as a Cherry Jubilee.

Chapter 12 Washington, A Confederate Treasure

There is some debate as to the birthplace of the Confederate States of America; however, there is little doubt Washington, Georgia was the deathbed of the Confederacy. In May 1885, President Jefferson Davis convened his last cabinet meeting there and signed the papers officially dissolving the Confederate States of America. He had fled to Washington carrying with him the Southern treasury and other bank money for safekeeping, estimated at over half a million dollars in gold.

There are many stories about what happened to the gold, but they all agree that the Union soldiers only recovered about a third of the treasure. About a million dollars worth of gold in today's market is still missing. To this day, legends claim it lies buried in or around Washington.

As you stare at the ancient iron and leather chest that once held a portion of that gold, you are transported back to that turbulent time. The chest is located in the Mary Willis Library in Washington. It reclines beneath a priceless Tiffany stained glass window in the foyer of the first, free-library in Georgia.

A tattered news clipping tells the story of the chest's recent history. Whether or not you believe the stories of the hidden Confederate gold, the tiny city is a treasure in itself. The Visitors Guide, which can be picked up free at the Chamber of Commerce in Washington boasts over 70 historic sites in the area and more antebellum homes than any other Georgia city its size.

Start at the Washington Historical Museum. At the time of the War Between the States, it was owned by Samuel Barnett, Georgia's first Railroad Commissioner. It is furnished in the antebellum style. The sight of Jefferson Davis' camp chest and an astonishing collection of Confederate relics and memorabilia of the Reconstruction period will draw you back to the fateful days of the Civil War. While Stephanie Macchia, the curator of the museum does not know who it is, there seems to be a spirit in the building.

Some visitors have said there is a presence around a display of letters posted on the wall. Stephanie also told me the motion detector lights often go on when no one is in the museum.

Washington's most controversial citizen was Robert Toombs. His stately, white columned mansion is preserved as a State Historical Site. As the guide conducting the tour explained, "He was a man who fit his times." Toombs' home reflects his personality, a forceful lawyer, a successful planter a consummate statesman. As a United States Senator, he originally argued for Unionism. However, as events escalated, he became convinced North and South no longer shared common goals.

On January 24, 1860, he exhorted his fellow senators, "Defend yourself; the enemy is at your door!" When succession became inevitable, he was an ardent Rebel. He served as Confederate Secretary of State for a short time then resigned to become a brigadier general. At the end of the war, he escaped from Federal soldiers by taking refuge with a neighbor. He spent several years in exile in France but scorned the idea of a pardon. However, in 1867 he did return home. In 1880 he boasted, "I am not loyal to the existing government of the United States and do not wish to be suspected of loyalty." Toombs ghost is reputed to frequent his alma mater, the University of Georgia campus in Athens, but he returns home occasionally.

Guests who are touring the lower floor have heard footsteps overhead in Toombs' bedroom. One gentleman of a decidedly Northern persuasion with little admiration for the Confederacy heard a heavy stomping above his head. Perhaps Toombs was upset by the gentleman's "Yankee" ways and was trying to kick him out of his home. Guests are not the only ones hearing General Toombs. One worker became so upset over the presence he left and refused to return after hearing footsteps when he knew he was alone in the house.

Toombs' spirit has some permanent company. That's not surprising as in life he entertained lavishly. When there was talk of building a hotel in town, he is reported to have said, "What do we need with a hotel. If a man is a gentleman, he can stay at my house, if he's not a gentleman, we do not need him here."

The other spirit who still inhabits the home is known as "The Lady in White." She is believed to be Toombs great-niece, Kathleen Colley. She and her sister, Marion were the last private owners of the home. A lady gliding across an upstairs room was first seen in the late 1970s by then site manager, Nita Edwards Riley. Ms. Riley was so upset she refused to go upstairs alone again.

Curator, Marcia Campbell, told of a conversation between two gentlemen visitors several years ago. They were on the porch and one of the men remarked, "I had so much fun on this porch. Miss Kathleen (Colley) would serve cookies when we came to visit and I would sit out here and eat them while the ladies visited. I remember Miss Kathleen would never wear anything but white."

A statement from a man who used to deliver milk to the sisters as an 18 year-old confirms the idea of Kathleen Colley as the resident spirit. At the time he was the milk man, the house was in poor repair due the sisters' age and finances. He considered the house scary. He would pick up the empty bottles and leave milk at the bottom step of a rundown back porch. One day, the bottles were not there and he had to climb the steps. Just when he reached the porch, the door creaked open, a long white arm holding a bottle extended towards him. In the doorway, he spied an old lady with flowing white hair hanging around her shoulders. Even though he knew it was a real person, he grabbed the bottle and ran.

Robert Toombs is buried in Resthaven Cemetery in Wilkes County. It has its own share of unearthly activity. According to Elaine Filipiak, who does Miss Fanny's Tours, she knew of two ladies, one a local and one a visitor, who went to Resthaven. After the visit, the visitor asked her hostess, "Who were the reenactors at the cemetery?"

Her hostess had not seen anything but her guest had seen several Confederate soldiers. Elaine said many people have gotten pictures of orbs at that cemetery.

For those of you seeking history and ghostly lore, make sure you take one of "Miss Fanny's Tours." Miss Fanny, AKA Elaine Filipiak, knows where all the bodies are buried and which closets are filled with skeletons.

She told me about the old Saint Joseph's Boys' Orphanage. Founded in 1876 under the leadership of Father James O'Brian, the orphanage was staffed by the order of the Sisters of Saint Joseph. The next year, the nuns opened Saint Joseph Academy for girls where Joel Chandler Harris' daughter attended school. During the late 1800s, many of the sisters died of plague. When a sister died, she would be laid out in her habit and the young orphan boys would file by to pay respect.

In later years, the place became Wilkes Academy. They added a gymnasium. After the school was closed it eventually came into possession of the city which uses the gym for their recreational department but the rest of the buildings remain vacant; vacant of human habitation that is. Stories are rampant of the long dead nuns who still roam the halls and grounds.

Another spot where the old South is close at hand is Callaway Plantation. It is easy to see why people have claimed to spot Confederate soldiers riding across the plantation at in the early morning fog. Perhaps these phantoms are guarding the Confederate treasury until the South has need of it again. Michael Horgan, a local attorney, had an eerie experience. He was then living at Callaway Plantation as a caretaker. He had a friend over one night and the two men were awakened by Michael's dog's frantic barking. Michael grabbed his gun and they went to check on the disturbance. A short distance from his trailer, they discovered several cavalrymen. They were wearing Confederate uniforms and they were utterly soundless. Not a squeak from a saddle. Not a whinny from a horse. Just dead silence while the two groups confronted one another. He quickly realized his gun would be of no use against these visitors. They were already dead. As quickly as they had arrived, the horsemen turned and galloped silently into the darkness.

The original plantation, begun around 1784, was 3000 acres. Self-contained, like all plantations of the time, it resembled a small village with a schoolhouse, country store, cemetery and other buildings. One significant building is the boyhood home of former governor George R. Gilmer.

The oldest structure rough-hewn log cabin was probably built around 1785 and is similar in style to the cabin Job Calloway, his wife and their seven children lived in for six years. The existing cabin is of the same era and is preserved along with the furnishings and tools used then. Later as the owners prospered, they built a four room, Federal Plainstyle home, which is maintained and furnished in a typical 1790's style.

Although the War Between the States devastated many local planters, Job's great-grandson, Aristedes Callaway, was wise enough to keep his cotton profits in an English bank.

In 1869, he built the crowning jewel of Callaway Plantation. The red brick mansion recalls a bygone era when cotton was king. In fact, you will enjoy seeing the tiny plot of cotton grown there as a memento of that vanished South. One step into the softly patined wood floor of the Greek Revival style manor house, and you are immersed in a lifestyle that is no more. In the drawing room, the piano, its sheet music lying open, awaits the delicate fingers of a southern bell. The round oak table in the dining room is set with everyday china, a blue willow pattern. Perhaps the reason the house invokes such a lived-in feeling is that it remained in the same family since it was built.

There is something besides memories of the Callaways remaining in the stately mansion. Olivia Jackson, former curator for the plantation, told me many of the docents have seen Aristedes' young bride, Martha, walking between the master bedroom and the nursery, just across the hall. Since Martha died when she was only 45, she probably is still trying to care for her nine children. However she doesn't just confine herself to her motherly duties. She takes time out to greet guests.

The plantation is open Tuesday through Saturday. One family came to visit the plantation on a Monday and found it closed. They decided to look around the grounds and return the following day to visit the home. The wife took some pictures of the front of the mansion and noticed a woman waving to them from the front window. The next day when they arrived to take the house tour, they asked, "Who is the lady that lives in the house?"

Their docent, Buddy Patterson, replied that no one would have been in the house on that day. "It is empty and locked on days when it is closed."

Olivia has had her own experience while walking around the grounds. A paranormal group was investigating at the plantation one day and photographed a ball of light following her from building to building. Another time, she had observed a similar ball of light following a city worker as he entered one of the houses. She feels the spirits are benevolent. "I have never felt afraid or threatened by them," she commented.

As might be expected Washington is home to a historic haunted hotel, The Fitzpatrick. As an architectural treasure it holds its own in a town filled with architectural eye candy. As a historical landmark, it can match histories with the best in a town with a colorful history. For comfort and amenities, it holds court with the finest hotels of today while reminiscent of the luxury of an earlier era.

Its story began on June 11, 1895 when the worst fire in Washington-Wilkes history broke out. It devastated much of the town square. Two Irish brothers, John and Thomas Fitzpatrick, were successful merchants who operated in Washington and South Carolina. They decided to build a hotel on the square to replace an older one that was destroyed by the fire.

When it opened in 1898, it was the epitome of luxury. It was built in the Queen Anne style that was popular in that era. Stained-glass windows and beautiful gas lights illuminated the building. There were three storefronts on the ground floor and a gracious lobby. There was a special entrance where ladies could enter more discreetly while the gentlemen entered the main lobby. The hotel boasted the first telephone system in Washington. Of course, it helped that the Fitzpatrick brothers owned the first telephone company in Wilkes County.

The brothers were in competition with the owners of the Johnson Hotel around the corner. In order to compete, the Fitzpatrick Hotel offered their version of limo service, a mule-drawn trolley ride from the depot to bring customers to the hotel.

After the brother's death, the hotel continued to operate under different owners until it closed in 1951. Like many old building, it had degenerated until it was in sad shape.

Today, it has been completely renovated maintaining the elegant Victorian furnishing, even several claw-foot tubs. You feel you have stepped back in time to an era of gracious living. To meet the needs of today's traveler, you are provided with internet service and satellite TV in each room. Of course, the cordial southern hospitality is always included.

Naturally, there are a few invisible residents to keep you company. When I asked about ghost stories, Ashley Herring, the front desk clerk when I visited, took me into the conference room and showed me an old painting. It was of an old couple standing in a field being harvested. It portrays an horse pulling a wagon loaded with baskets of produce. It was by an obscure Dutch artist named Josef Veltman. But the painting's history is what leads to the rest of the story.

The painting belonged to a daughter of the Pope family. She loved it but her mother disliked the painting. When the daughter grew up and moved away, the mother gave the painting to the Fitzpatrick Hotel. The staff has always felt something odd in the conference room where the painting hangs but never associated it with the artwork. Recently a paranormal group investigated the haunting in the old hotel. They saw an old woman walking in a "U" pattern around the painting. They believed this is the Pope daughter protecting "her" favorite work of art after her death.

The protective woman is not the only spirit that remains from an earlier era. I spent a peaceful night in room 205. This room and its neighboring one 206, are known as the tower rooms. These rooms are frequently the haunt of a phantom dancing girl. If the young lady waltzed around my room, I slept right through her visit. Blame it on the peaceful ambience and comfortable bed. Who this girl is, is not known.

There is another female sprit that can be identified through an odd coincidence. When the ghost hunters visited the hotel, they noticed a lavender smell in room 208.

This was one of the rooms used as their living area by the Fitzpatrick family in the early days of the hotel. During the renovation, a bottle of lavender perfume was found behind the fireplace where it had fallen all those years ago. Research revealed that lavender was Mrs. John Fitzpatrick's favorite scent. She "told" physics that she is happy about the renovations and reopening of the hotel.

Wilkes County was not always noted for its southern chivalry to women. It was the first county in Georgia to hang a free, white woman. The trial of Mary "Polly" Jenkins Barclay had all the ingredients of a thriller. A thirty-two-year-old widow standing trial for conspiring with a younger man, Robert Rafferty, to murder her husband, John, riveted the attention of the entire county and beyond.

She was found guilty. Prime evidence was statements of guests at her home when the killing occurred. They all heard her husband ride into the barn and shots ring out. Then Polly exclaimed, "Oh, they have killed John!" Not a smart statement.

On Friday the 13th of May 1806, the beautiful widow was hanged from a tree west of downtown Washington. The tree is no longer there. Does Polly's restless spirit still visit the lovely town where she lived so tumultuously?

In days gone by travelers didn't have the luxury of an airport. They depended on horse and wagon. One nefarious citizen of Wilkes County took advantage of their limitations to defraud travelers.

Abram Simons was a Revolutionary War veteran turned cotton farmer but he had another more sinister means of support. In the early 1800s, he lived along what was then Augusta Road, now South Smyrna Church Road. He had a two-story house with lots of rooms. He had built a racehorse track on part of his property, converted some of his house into a tavern and gambling hall, and used many of the rooms in his house for an inn. The road in front of his house was the route used by the wagoneers hauling supplies from Augusta.

Simons would have his slaves douse the dirt road with water causing the wagons to get mired in the mud. He would then rent them rooms, ply them with liquor and induce them to gamble away their money.

According to old county records, some of his victims reported his activities but to no avail. Old Simons died a wealthy man in 1825. In order to ward off his just reward, he insisted on being buried standing up with a musket in one hand and a bottle of whisky in the other. He believed if he couldn't bribe the devil with the whisky, he would shoot him with the musket.

The house and tavern have long been torn down but the gravestone remains, well hidden off the old road behind a stone fence, which he believed would keep the devil out. Passersby on the lonely road claim to have heard him riding his horse around a ghostly track as if pursued by the devil himself.

Since horse and wagons have long become obsolete, Wilkes County has recently built a multi-million dollar motoplex, Aonia Passis a popular spot for auto race fans..

A great way to see many of the historic homes in Washington is to visit during their Tour of Homes. The tour is held in April and features private homes open for this event.

Another event that provides access to homes not open at other times is the Christmas Dinner and Holiday Tour in early December. Other Christmas events are the Christmas Parade and Tree Lighting and the Candlelight Christmas Open House held the Tuesday before Thanksgiving. At the same time of year, Callaway Plantation provides a glimpse of how Christmas was celebrated on a plantation with Christmas at Callaway Plantation.

The biggest event is Mule Day Southern Heritage Festival in early October at Callaway Plantation. This is a fabulous celebration of plantation life in the Old South. You will enjoy watching humans lock wills with mules in the contests, crafters provide a colorful array of unique objects, and demonstrations of primitive skills remind you of how different life was a hundred years ago. The airport sponsors their Fly-in at with activities for the entire family.

For campers, there are two state parks nearby, Alex H. Stephens or Elijah Clark. Callaway Plantation has a small campground as well.

Dining in Wilkes County is a real pleasure. Your choices range from upscale places like the Jockey Club, with a history stretching back to Washington's early horse racing days to small diners and local restaurants.

A visit to Washington/Wilkes County is a trip into the past. Even though the gold may be lost, the treasure remains in the relics of the Old South still found here.

Dicy Ann Roberts Grave in Athens

Balcony of Morton Theater in Athens

Eagle Tavern in Watkinsville

Brer Rabbit Museum

Rock Eagle Eatonton

Heritage Hall Milledgeville

Old Governors Mansion

Ocmulgee Mounds

Seat that ghost uses at Macon Opera House

Treasure Chest in Washington

Allman Brother's Band exhibit inside The Big House

Section 3 The Presidential Way

This stretch of Western Georgia bears the stamp of two of modern history's most influential men; Franklin Delano Roosevelt and Jimmy Carter. It follows a crescent in the central part of West Georgia. You will find many strange and unexplained occurrences as you trace the legacy of two presidents.

Chapter 13 Andersonville, Hell on Earth

If any place deserves to be haunted, the site of the infamous Confederate prison at Andersonville is the spot. Andersonville, its very name conjured up horror during the Civil War. Today, it spreads a message of hope. During the fourteen months the prison functioned as Camp Sumter, 45,000 Union soldiers were imprisoned there. Of that number, 13,000 died from starvation, disease, unsanitary conditions, or exposure to a bitter winter cold. Conditions were so bad there that one prisoner, Sgt. David Kennedy, described it as "this hell on earth where it takes seven of its occupants to make a shadow."

The officer in charge of the prisoners was Captain Henry Wirz. He was the only Confederate officer hanged for war crimes. His malevolent presence is rumored to still haunt the site. Wirz was not a natural-born Southerner. He was a Bavarian who had joined the fourth Louisiana Infantry. Assigned as commander of Camp Sumter in March of 1864, he was placed in an untenable position. The war was taking its toll on the South's resources. Sherman's march to the sea had left behind a blazing trail of destruction.

There was no food to feed the citizens. Soldiers lived on what they could forage off the land which was little. The Union blockade had cut off most supplies to the South including medicine and anesthetics. The situation would have eased if the prisoners could have been swapped for confederate prisoners languishing in Northern prison camps but General Grant believed an exchange would benefit the Confederacy. He felt the exchanged prisoners would return to fight for the South thereby prolonging the war.

The prison had been built early in 1864. It consisted of little more than a 15-foot high stockade enclosing about 16 ½ acres. In June, that was enlarged to enclose 26 ½ acres. Sentry boxes, called pigeon roost, by the prisoners were built every thirty feet along the wall. About nineteen feet within the wall was the "deadline." Any prisoner who entered this space was subject to be shot. The only water in the camp was a tiny stream that meandered through the stockade. The stream was used for all of the prisoner's sanitation needs as well as cooking and drinking. Naturally disease was rampant. Shelter consisted of what the prisoners themselves could fashion from their limited resources. During the fourteen months of its existence, the prison housed approximately 45,000 prisoners in all with up to 32,000 prisoners held at one time.

As is usually the case in situations like this, bullies arose within the prison. A group of the dregs of the Union prisoners preyed on their weaker compatriots. Led by Willie Collins and others, these renegades called themselves "The Raiders." They stole what little other prisoners had and often killed other prisoners. Finally the prisoners informed Wirz. He allowed the prisoners themselves to try The Raiders. They convict several of outlaws. Six of them were hung from a makeshift gallows inside the stockade to the cheers of the prisoners. Willie went to his death defiant and cursing his accusers. The graves of the raiders are located near the front of the cemetery. This is not a spot where I would choose to be late at night. There are those who say he and some of his raiders still remain within the walls of Andersonville Prison.

Wirz was charged with the responsibility for their care. Had he been a saint, he would have been able to accomplish little under these conditions. At the end of the war, horrified Federal officers brought Wirz to trial as a war criminal. He was accused of conspiracy to "murder in violation of the laws of war." There was no conspiracy but the conditions horrified the Northerners so that Wirz was convicted and hanged. The United Daughters of the Confederacy have since tried to clear his name, claiming he was a scapegoat. They have erected a monument to Capt. Wirz in the town of Andersonville. Wirz's spirit is still bound to the prison in the hope of making people understand that there was nothing he could have done to change the conditions that created the horror of Andersonville Prison.

In spite of the impossibility of the situation, there was one man who tried to ease the pain of the wretched prisoners trapped in this hellhole. If you are strolling on the prison grounds and come upon a little man dressed in ragged black carrying an umbrella you may be face to face with the prison chaplain, Father Whelan. Whelan was the only chaplain who chose to consistently endure the conditions at the prison. Although he was a Southerner, he ministered to Protestant as well as Catholic prisoners. He begged the archdiocese to send help, food and medicine.

Other priests came but could not stand the conditions and left. There was no money to send. Father Whelan used what little money he had to buy flour and make bread, which he took to the starving men in the compound. By the time the war ended, 45,000 men had passed through Andersonville's gates almost 13,000 died there. That's 29% of the population, the largest number of any Civil War prison camp.

Those who died were transported to the "Dead House"; a small building made of tree branches outside the South Gate, until interment in the prison cemetery.

Perhaps the suffering of so many helpless souls caused physic energy to emanate from the site as early as August 9, 1864. A strange-some say miraculous-event occurred then. As the prisoners huddled in a fierce summer rainstorm, a spring burst forth from the ground. Because of the unsanitary conditions of the stream in the camp, fresh water was one of the most pressing needs of the prisoners. Many had tried to dig wells to no avail.

Today, it is a national historic site and houses the National Prisoner of War Museum as well as the Andersonville National Cemetery. The National Prisoner of War Museum honors all Americans who suffered imprisonment for their country. The exhibits are graphic. A moving film depicting interviews with former POWs gives a deeper understanding of what it is like to be a prisoner.

The little town of Andersonville offers eateries, antique shops, collectible shops and museums. A yearly historic festival is held in October. As you stroll the streets of the tiny Civil War Village during the festival, you are apt to meet Abraham Lincoln, Robert E. Lee and other personages of the time. Music, dancing and a reenactment are among the entertainments.

The heart of the village is the Depot Museum housing memorabilia of the time and the Drummer Boy Civil War Museum housing a fantastic collection of original uniforms, weaponry, diaries and many one-of-a-kind items.

The Andersonville Guild, the historic preservation society in partner with the South Georgia Paranormal Association now offers ghost tours of the village once a month.

Be sure to visit the old log church west of town and the Pioneer Farm at the north end of the village. The 7-acre Pioneer Farm depicts life on a one-man farm in the mid-1800s. There is an authentic log cabin, log barns, an operating grist mill and a Blacksmith shop.

If you plan to visit during the festival accommodations are filled to overflowing so plan ahead.

Andersonville RV Campground is convenient and reasonably priced. It is comfortable but not fancy. It does offer both RV and tent camping. There are some chain motels outside of town or you can stay in Americus, a few miles away.

Andersonville is a part of our American heritage and should be seen by every man, woman and child to understand the terrible cost of war.

Chapter 14 Americus and Plains, The Making of a President

The excitement of the movement that transformed "Jimmy who?" to President Jimmy Carter still lurks in the streets of the small rural town of Plains. Feel the spirit of The Jimmy Carter National Historic Site, his residence, boyhood home, high school, the railroad depot that served as campaign headquarters and the National Preservation District that protects the heritage of a town that is the home of America's longest lived president.

One fun attraction is the SAM Shortline Excursion Train. These scenic 1949 vintage railcars carry visitors from Cordele to Plains, Americus and Archer, a tiny hamlet outside Plains where Carter's boyhood home is located. The farm that Jimmy Carter grew up on is an unpretentious rural slice of Americana, with its rural farmhouse, country store, blacksmith shop and an outhouse.

On the way to visit the Boyhood Farm Site, you will pass a very different residence of the former first family. This Federal Style home, known as the Rylander House, sheltered the Carter family from 1956 to 1961. The house was built by Matthew Rylander 1n the mid 1800s. Stories of a ghostly woman who kept a lamp lit in the attic to guide Confederate soldiers to a safe haven during the Civil War.

According to Fred Boyles, former supervisor of the Jimmy Carter National Historic Site, this house "is believed to be the oldest house in Sumter County. It predates the Civil War." He said there is no secret to the fact that it is supposed to be haunted. "It is labeled on the NPS map as 'Haunted House.' Jimmy Carter refers to the house in his book, *Why Not the Best?* In spite of this, the Carters loved the house and tried to buy it but the owner would not sell."

Although the Carters knew of its reputation before they moved in, the spooky stories were reinforced almost at once. In an article in the *Examiner,* "Mrs. Carter said that one night they were startled by the sound of a loud crash coming from the front room. 'We waited a bit, then the whole family trooped in together, thinking a window had fallen shut. But the window was still wide open,' she shuddered."

Union soldiers occupied the house during the Civil War and it is their spirits that are supposed to haunt the dwelling. Along with the soldiers, there are other spirits present. There is a small white dog that vanishes mysteriously when anyone tries to pet him.

There is a woman in a long white gown. She appears to be weeping. The ghostly activities seem to center on the living room. Adding to the mystery, there are two small rooms hidden in the space between the attic and the ceiling. Jack, the oldest of the Carter children found several loose bricks in the hearth of the attic fireplace and discovered one room. It was furnished with only a ladder.

A former cook who worked in the house shortly before the Carters moved in had this to say, "Things would happen in that room. I could hear knocking on the door. Then it would open and shut and I'd hear walking. I'd see a woman with a long white dress coming from the cemetery. Dr. Wise, the man I worked for, could see her too. He'd say it was our imagination, but when he spoke to the woman, she and the light she carried both vanished. Sometimes I'd hear her walking on the attic stairs."

Even the area nearby seems charged with a mysterious energy. People have seen a woman in a white dress walking from Lebanon Cemetery toward the house. Others have seen ghostly dogs and a light near a spring across the road.

Countless tragedies in the home add to the reasons for spirits to remain in the antebellum mansion.

Matthew and Sarah Rylander moved here from Bibb County, Georgia in 1853. Matthew's estate surrounding the home included more than 1,000 acres. He was a harsh slave master and at the beginning of the Civil War, he owned at least forty enslaved people. Both his sons fought for the Confederacy and were killed in battle.

Finally there is hope that this historic treasure will be preserved. I have heard that the Better Home Town Committee of Plains acquired the house and is planning on restoring it.

A great time to visit the area is for the annual September Peanut Festival. Along with visiting all the other attractions, you might meet President and Mrs. Carter who usually autograph their books at the festival.

As children, Jimmy, Billy and Ruth would have considered a trip to nearby Americus as a visit to a big city. Although it really is a small town, it does have a lot of big attractions. Perhaps the biggest of them all is the Windsor Hotel.

The Windsor opened to fanfare and a great ball on June 16, 1892. Thousands attended the opening and over 100 guests registered the first day. However, the hotel's popularity declined and the building went on the auction block. On September 5, 1899, Charles A. Fricker, the jeweler, bought the Windsor for $40,000 at public sale. Even though the hotel was completely renovated with electric lights, new elevators, telephones, and steam heat, it never regained its former Victorian-era glory until recently. In August 1974, having operated for some time as apartments, the hotel closed her doors after 82 years.

The bankrupt hotel came into the possession of the City of Americus and the hotel reopened on September 20, 1991 after considerable restoration to return the elderly dowager to her youthful beauty. The original golden oak woodwork in the lobby was refinished, as was the original marble floor.

The mirror on the back wall of the lobby dates back to before the Civil War. The mahogany phone booth, one of the highlights of the lobby, is authentic although not original to the hotel. The clock on the second-floor lobby is the only original furnishing. It came from the Windsor jewelry shop. It has been restored, and is on permanent loan from the Sumter Historic Trust.

The Roosevelt Boardroom has been nicknamed the "Lucky Room" because so many successful political campaigns began there.

In her time, the Windsor played host to the famous and the infamous. John L. Sullivan, former heavy-weight boxing champion, Congressman William Jennings Bryan, three-time Democratic presidential nominee, The Governor of New York and soon-to-be President Franklin D. Roosevelt and, Al Capone, who posted an armed guard at the foot of the stairs. Lindbergh played pool there. President and Roselyn Carter are frequent visitors even though they have never stayed at the hotel. Jessica Tandy did stay there and has a room named for her.

There is someone else still at the hotel. She has been there through all the renovations and isn't likely to ever leave. In life, she worked there in the early 1900s as head housekeeper. She and her small daughter lived in the hotel. The woman was murdered and her ghost is said to haunt the Windsor. She is a restless but not a dangerous ghost.

Just down the street stands the Rylander Theatre. For decades after it closed in 1951, it sat, hidden behind a row of offices. Just a few old timers remembered its existence. In its glory days it featured the Ziegfeld Follies or World War I sharpshooter Sgt. Alvin York. But until fall of 1999, only the termites graced the stage. The moths and perhaps the restless spirits of former actors were the only ones occupying the costume vaults.

The owner of the local Ford dealership a descendant of Matthew Rylander, who saw silent movies in 1919 when he visited New York City, built the Rylander. He decided Americus should have this luxury. Two years later, in 1921, the Rylander opened. It boasted a stage and dressing rooms for live shows as well. . It closed when the company running it opened a new movie theater elsewhere in town.

Today the Rylander has been completely restored to its former glory. It features live performances. Much of the new has been added but whenever possible the original craftsmanship was restored. Of course, the spirit is still there and lets its presence be felt occasionally with a flicker of lights or a cold spot in an otherwise warm theater.

On the Northeast side of Americus, drive past a restored antebellum home. Built around 1852 for Colonel George Fish and his wife, Martha Hansell Fish, Today it is a private home. It was moved from Oglethorpe to its present location in 1969 by Mr. and Mrs. Donald Nelson, who did major restoration on the old home. However the move and the restoration did not dislodge the presence of Col. Fish.

An associate, John Holsenback, murdered him in the Macon Court House. Although the murderer was brought to justice and hanged, Col. Fish still remains in his former home. His presence is felt most often in the front parlor specifically in an antique chair that was his favorite when he was alive.

Donald Nelson claims to have spoken with the ghost of Fish while he was relaxing in his renovated home. He stated, "I was not really asleep, but I was not afraid. We had a pleasant conversation. He told me that he had been very upset about the house being moved; however, since we were restoring it to his liking, he was happy and peaceful. I went to the other room and told Marsha I had talked with Colonel Fish."

Another spot in Americus where it is rumored you might have an otherworldly encounter is at the bridge on Lee Bell Road. The apparition of a little girl has been seen and heard walking across the bridge.

Americus Garden Inn Bed & Breakfast was built in 1847 by James Kelso Daniel, a former Georgia State Senator. During the 1860s it was the home of William A. Wilson, president of the Furlow Masonic Female College.

It was converted to a bed and breakfast in the 1990s. Visitors have felt a welcoming presence and experienced strange happenings at at the inn. Footsteps are heard in unoccupied rooms Doors open on their own which could be handy if carrying in heavy luggage. The clock radios have turned themselves on and off and guests have experienced the smell of strange perfume during the night. Guests have captured a host of "orbs" in their pictures. Voices ranging from children to Civil War soldiers are sometimes heard.

Kim and Susan Egelseer, the owners have captured ghostly occurrences in photos and on tape. They were thrilled when they were awarded 2020 TripAdvisor Travelers' Choice Awards for the Best of the Best. Americus Garden Inn Bed and Breakfast was named as the Number One Best Bed and Breakfast in the United States and Number 3 Best Bed and Breakfast in the World.

Americus is filled with Victorian homes. Many of them may have their own restless spirit. Viewing these lovely buildings reminds us of a time when homes were built for beauty rather than convenience and economy. The spirit of a more elegant era lives on in Americus.

Chapter 15 Columbus, The River City

Columbus is a city often overlooked by travelers. What a pity! They don't know what they are missing. It is home to some of the state's most interesting spirits.

Georgia's State Theater, The Springer Opera House, is located here. Visualize yourself seated in the Springer in 1876. The five-year-old theater is renowned for its curved double balconies, delicate tulip lights and high proscenium arch. Wealthy merchants, planters, and steamboat passengers declared it the finest theater between Washington and New Orleans. You lean back in your seat and watch the plush velvet curtain rise. The incomparable Edwin Booth, brother of man who shot President Lincoln, strides unto the stage to portray Hamlet as only he can do. The audience is captivated by the charisma of this legendary actor.

Throughout its career, the Springer hosted the cream of the crop. Ethel Barrymore, Oscar Wilde, Buffalo Bill, Lilly Langtry and hosts of other famous thespians have trod the boards of the Springer's stage. It provided a hotel on the upper floors where many of the actors stayed. Then, with the coming of the great depression, touring companies no longer travel to the great stagers of America and Europe. The Springer begins a slow decline. It served as a movie house for a time and was on a collision course with the wrecker's ball. In 1964, a group of civic-minded citizens realized that an irreplaceable treasure was being lost forever. They partially restored the aging dowager and once again it fulfilled the purpose for which it was born, live theater.

No one expected anything spectacular when a traveling company preformed one show in 1981. They preformed *Hamlet* for the first time in almost a century. When they assembled for a curtain call, cast and audience alike were in for a big surprise. As the audience offered thunderous applause, the tulip lights began to blink in an almost musical rhythm. The tulip lights were connected so they could dim or brighten. Their electrical connection was not configured for blinking. Yet they blinked! Was Edwin Booth expressing his approval that Shakespeare was once again being performed here?

The Springer envelops you in Edwardian splendor as you watch some of Broadway's biggest hits. The hand stenciled designs, the gold leaf topped columns, the lavish antiques and paintings filling its lobby and halls; all conspire to transport you to the early 1900a. You feel the magic that only a live performance can produce.

Perhaps, you may feel the touch of something else; something as mysterious as the *Phantom of the Opera*. Actors and those connected with the theater have always had an aura of the melodramatic about them.

In an interview with Amy Bishop, the theater's former educational coordinator and frequent performer in the productions, I learned that the Springer is inhabited by a whole a wide cast of ghosts.

Along with Booth, who has been sighted by many people, she tells of her own experiences with the supernatural. "I was walking in the hallway on the third floor. Keep in mind that this was the old hotel. It is the office suite now for everyone else but me. There are framed posters on the wall of productions we have done. I glanced at a poster of *The Sound of Music* and there behind me was the reflection of a man. When I turned there was no one there. It happened so fast. I began looking in the offices trying to explain it. Was someone in an office where the poster could catch a reflection? Nobody was on the floor but Laura and she was in her office at the other end of the hall. This is the same man who frequently passes my office. Usually he's wearing a top hat."

Amy tells of a strange occurrence about ten years ago. The gentleman who was to have had the lead in *The Oldest Living Graduate* died just before Christmas. The play went on as scheduled in January and February. "Lots of crazy thing happened in that production," she recalled, "like gloves being misplaced, the cast would come in and find everything lined up when it hadn't been the night before, jewelry pooping off of people on stage. Tim Chitwood who is a reporter for the Ledger wanted to search for the ghosts so he stayed in the theater overnight. While there he began playing with a Ouija board."

"Some of the information it gave was the name Levi and some numbers. Tim Chitwood wrote about it in the paper. Shortly after, Paul Pierce, the artistic director, got a phone call from a lady named Daye Lane, her husband; Art Lane was the man who was to have performed in the Oldest Graduate production. She said 'Paul, my children and I have been very upset by Tim Chitwood's article but we decided we needed to call and tell you some information. Art Lane was a vaudeville performer who came over to this country by way of Ellis Island. He performed in New York under the stage name of Art Levi. He had changed his name to Art Lane. No one in Columbus knew that except his wife and family. The only two places Art and I lived in our married life started with those two numbers.'"

Amy said she feel most of the spirits at the Springer are people who have preformed there in the past and are happy about the theater's progress. However, one spirit is believed to be that of a young girl who was killed outside the theater by runaway horses at the turn of the century. She seems to frequent the costume loft. Costumes, shoes and jewelry are often found on the floor as if a child had been playing dress up. People have glimpsed the child at play here.

The ghosts are not disruptive though. Actually they help. Ralph Wimberly who was costume designer before Donna Pierce, the current designer, always felt that if he needed a certain belt that he couldn't find, he would think about it. When he came back into the belt section it would be sitting on top of the others waiting for him.

Amy is not the only member of the Springer to have a ghostly tale to tell. Paul Pierce had an experience with an otherworldly mimic. He was working late and walked across the stage. He heard footsteps and looked back to spot a bent old man in period costume. The "man" seemed to be imitating him. He continued to walk and so did his imitator until he crossed an area where a curtain separated the two. The footfalls continued but when he reached the end of the curtain the "man" was no longer there.

Laura Kratt, the former managing director, pointed out a certain box on the top level third from the stage. "During a closed rehearsal of a traveling company, the director stopped the play and shouted, 'who's up in that box. No one is supposed to be in the theater!' Everyone looked up at the box and no one was there. The director began the rehearsal again only to stop in a minute and shout, 'Someone's in that box! Go look!' The assistant director approached the box entering through one door. The stage manager went in through the only other entrance. No one was there."

Another incident occurred involving the same box. "It was a Friday opening night show and the cast planned a party afterwards. One actress brought a red sequined dress in a dry cleaner bag and left it in the dressing room. After the show the dress was nowhere to be found. It didn't show up again until about three months later. Still in its bag. It was draped over one of the seats in that box."

The Springer offers Broadway hits and tours of the theater can be arranged. You may not encounter any ghostly presence but you will certainly be touched by the performances. They are top notch. If you want to see more of the famed opera house, there are tours on Monday and Wednesday at 3:30. Who knows you might have your own ethereal encounter.

The phantoms of the Springer Opera House are not the only spirits afloat in this river city. Walk along the charming red-brick river walk with its statue of the four ages of Christopher Columbus. That tumbling river is the Chattahoochee; one day a tiny trickle you can almost ford, the next a raging flood threatening the nearest buildings. It flows through Georgia from high in the mountainous north and here marks the border with Alabama. Columbus sits on the fall line beyond which large oceangoing boats cannot pass. But in the 1800, this was a thriving steamboat stop. In fact it was the main naval base for the Confederate Navy.

Today Port Columbus hosts the Civil War Navel Museum. Opened April 10, 2001, this is the only museum of its kind in the world. It houses the 225-foot hull of the *CSS Jackson*. This massive ironclad was built at the Confederate shipyards just a few miles from the present site. The museum also has a scale replica of the *USS Waterwitch*. The Waterwitch was serving as a Union blockader in the waters just off Savannah. Confederate forces succeeded in capturing her on June 3, 1864. Interestingly enough the confederates were piloted by an Black man, Moses Dallas. Dallas held the rank, if not the authority of an officer in the Confederate Navy. Both Dallas and his commander, Lieutenant Pelot, were among the first killed in the ensuing fight. Ironically, after fighting so hard to take the ship, the Confederate navy could not get it safely back to Savannah and on December 19, 1864, it was burned to keep it from falling into the hands of General Sherman's advancing troops.

The most interesting exhibit is the reconstruction of the ironclad *CSS Albermarle*. The *Albemarle* was terrorizing the Union fleet until a young Union Lieutenant in a small steam powered launch sank it in a daring raid on the Roanoke River. Inside you will experience life aboard a Confederate ship under attach up to the moment of its sinking. It's so realistic, I swear you can feel the flow of the river and the impact of the missiles.

And that may not be all you feel. According to Bruce Smith, Executive Director at the museum, "This began October 2009 but we have been having unexplained things happening almost since we opened in 2001."

Books fly off the shelves in the museum gift shop. One hit a customer in the back. Others land across the room, rearranged as if they were neatly stacked there by an unseen hand. Trinkets on display in the gift shop move around of their own volition.

Susan Ingram, director of visitor services, sees this sort of thing frequently. The unexplained events were accepted as the norm by the staff at the museum. Then one day at a party, some workers were discussing various incidents they had experienced and a newspaper reporter heard them and ran an article about the paranormal happenings in the local newspaper.

When the Alabama Paranormal Research Team saw the article they were intrigued and asked to perform an investigation, Bruce said he was a bit skeptical but, after checking references, allowed them to come and conduct the investigation.

The group led by Faith Serafin came they did a study. Bruce said "I didn't think they would find much since it is a new building, but they got a lot of recordings and said 'This place is hopping.' The activity relates to the big ships and artifacts in the museum."

One exhibit, the *CSS Chattahoochee*, the only surviving Confederate gunboat, had a lot of activity. The ship suffered a terrible boiler explosion in May 1863. There were 19 men killed in that blast. It's only natural that this boat generated a lot of paranormal recordings.

It's not only in the real artifacts that strange events occur. Several staff members were sitting with the Alabama ghost hunters in the ward room the replica of Admiral David Farragut's flagship, the *USS Hartford* when Susan Ingram felt something touch her. The invisible presence moved around the table touching many of the others at the table. Then a flashlight turned itself on.

The ghost hunters also heard footsteps that sounded like hard shoes striding across a boat deck. They were able to rule out any actual person as the walker. The group leader asked the presence to respond to questions by tapping and got responses.

The staff has learned not only to co-exist with their otherworldly companions but to offer these spirits a chance to be heard. The museum now holds ghost tours on the last Thursday every month.

Effigy Paranormal located in Columbus heard of the happenings and now conducts a quarterly investigation where people can participate in an actual ghost hunt. The first one resulted in some impressive phenomena. If you have a yen to do an actual investigation here is your chance.

The Chattahoochee River holds the secrets of a love lost to its turbulent waters. In the 1800s, Rebecca Effringham was steaming to Columbus aboard the Chattahoochee Princess. The ship was sunk in a storm, and she was lost beneath the swirling waters. Rebecca was never reunited with her betrothed in life. She is patient, though, on dark nights you might see her swirling white gown and the lantern she hold aloft as she drifts along the banks seeking her lover.

Another legend about the riverbank claims you can hear the Confederate officers and their laughing partners dancing at a phantom party many nights.

If you are looking for more worldly pursuits, try their white water rafting. It is an experience you will never forget.

Another branch of the armed forces offers a tribute to the infantry's heroes, past and present. Although the museum boasts no ghosts to speak of, it is well worth a visit. This huge museum pays tribute to the two centuries of service by the American infantryman. Its exhibits range widely. From armor of the medieval knights to Hitler's henchmen's artwork you will enjoy this museum even if you are not militarily inclined.

The National Infantry Museum and Soldier Center has re-located and is now just off post and is housed in a new, $100 million facility.

Just in front of the building formerly housing the museum is a memorial stone to a four-legged comrade who did much to boost the morale of lonely soldiers. Calculator was so named because he would limp on three legs to gain attention. Soldiers said he knew how to "put down three and carry one."

In the 1920s he was every Fort Benning soldier's favorite mascot. He was no one-man dog but was willing to hitch a ride with anyone going into Columbus. Many an officer made a stop at the Ralston Hotel on his way back to the base just to pick up Calc. He offered comfort and companionship to the lonely soldiers.

When some miscreant poisoned Calculator in 1923, the soldiers took up a collection to bury him and place a monument to his memory. The inscription on the monument reads "Calculator-Born? Died August 29, 1923. He made a better dog of us all." Although the old building is no longer open to the public, the monument to the faithful dog is still there to offer inspiration to all.

Columbus has much to see and do it's impossible to include it all. The Riverwalk, Columbus Museum, The Coca-Cola Space Science Center, and the home of Dr. Pemberton, creator of Coca-Cola.

Nearby Oxbow Meadows, while not having any ghostly creatures, has many of the wild kind and lots of nature.

If you have an urge to share your bedroom with a ghost, try the Rothchild-Pound House. This place is so good it is included in Fodor's Guide, a publication with no advertising. You can't buy your way into this guide. They choose the top inns that offer "special warmth, unusual decor, superlative charm."

The inn certainly meets all of the criteria plus one other. It boasts its own resident ghost. The owners, Mamie and Gary Pound made his acquaintance not long after they moved into the house. Mamie tells of that first occurrence. "Gary and I were sleeping in the front upstairs bedroom. We had installed locks anticipating guests so all the doors were locked. We heard footsteps in the upstairs hall. We both sat up in bed. Gary didn't even ask 'Did you hear that?' He just got up and looked around. No one was there but the footsteps were a very pronounced man's footstep."

Not too long after, Mamie was preparing to take a bath. She had run the water and left the bathroom for a short time. While she was out the extremely heavy stained-glass window fell into the tub. A short time later, the marble mantelpiece crashed with a "sound like a bomb." Again this was around 3AM. Also the air conditioning vent in this room fell. After that the crashing and falling seemed to stop. Perhaps the ghost decided to coexist peacefully with the house's living inhabitants.

All of the activity seems to occur in or around this certain bedroom, The Redd Room. Mamie is not sure why except that Mr. Rothchild did die in the house. Perhaps he is still around. Several instances involving guests have occurred. One guest was asleep in one of the room's twin beds. She heard someone walk past her bed and go into the bathroom and start rattling around in the dark. She turned over and saw her friend still in the other bed. Several other guests have reported similar experiences.

The inn has several cottages adjourning the main house and a strange visitation occurred to an insurance representative in one of these as well. He was sleeping and felt the hair on the back of his neck rise. He opened his eyes and saw an elderly black man standing over him. He blinked and the man was gone.

Even if you don't experience any unearthly visitations on your stay there, the quality of the food, usually fresh fruit and quiches or French toast for breakfast and the hors d'oeuvers with wine or one of their special Mint Juleps or Peach Daiquiris in the evening, will be one of your favorite earthly memories.

If you pass near the First African Baptist Church, don't be surprised if you hear the sounds of the great concertos echoing through its empty sanctuary. Tom Wiggins, born into slavery attended that church. Tom was not only blind but considered an "idiot savant" by the doctors of his time. After having heard them once, "Blind Tom" could reproduce the masterpieces of the great composers. His master sent him on tour through the great music halls of America and Europe to play for the great and famous. On moonlit nights in October, many people have claimed to hear the strains of Tom's music coming from the church.

Columbus's newest attraction, Historic Westville, is a living history recreation of a typical Georgia town in the 1800s. It's like stepping back in time. So do some time travel and meet some fascinating folks who lived and died long ago. They will tell you about their way of life in Westville. I would not be surprised if there were some paranormal activities in these old buildings. Maybe you could be the first to meet one of its resident spirits.

Westville was never a real town. It was created by Colonel John West, a history professor who saw progress destroying history. He began trying to preserve it by buying up old buildings destined to be destroyed. Originally, it was situated in Lumpkin, Georgia. On June 22, 2019 the recreated Westville reopened in Columbus. The buildings are restored to reflect the mid-19th century and range from modest homes like the Singer House, home of Belgian immigrants to the McDonald House, a gorgeous Antebellum home.

Each of the buildings has a period costumed docent who tells you about life in 19th century Georgia. The shoemaker, Timothy at Johann Singer's Boots and Shoes Shop, was busy making boots when we entered the Singer family shoemaker's shop.

He told us about the Singers. "Johann Singer was the first boot maker in the area. When the Singers first moved here, the shop was in the house. That's why it has two front doors. One was the boot shop and the other was the family entrance. He became very popular. In just over a year he built the house in 1837 and he built the shop in 1838."

Entering the Singer home, we met Sarah who was quilting but took time away from her work to show us how to do carding of the wool. The McDonald House has fireplaces in each of the rooms and is furnished with beautiful antiques applicable to the period. The housekeeper at McDonald House, Jacque, was sewing an authentic looking blue and white checked apron by hand in the parlor. She led us through the home which was built in 1843. Mr. McDonald became rich from a cotton warehouse he started and then when the trains came through in 1859 he invested in that.

Native American people who lived in the area often mingled with the white settlers before the Indian Removal Act of 1826 forced them to move to Oklahoma. The Creek people had been there for thousands of years before the white settlers arrived. Jeremy, the docent in the Yuchi House/ Wells House is an authentic Creek. This house is the oldest in the village. The Wells family, owned it for over 100 years and left oral and written records that the original structure, a simple log pen cabin and a shed with a dirt floor, had been built and lived in by Yuchi Indians, a tribe related to the Creek Nation.

The blacksmith shop is equipped with a restored bellows that might have been used in 1850. A blacksmith was an essential worker for any town of the time. Cameron, Westville's blacksmith, was hammering on a red-hot piece of iron to pound out a sharp point when we stepped into the smitty. He crafted a tool right in front of our eyes and explained the working of the bellows and fire.

A doctor was another very important person in any small town. We met medical assistant, Lena, at Dr. William Paullin's office. The office was built in 1845 and he used it until his death in 1880 however he frequently made house calls. Lena showed us how the doctor would make prescription pills from herbs he grew in the backyard. The doctor's office displays the "latest" surgical equipment he used. One was a valuable surgical kit dated back to the 1800s. Just one look at the saws convinced me I was feeling much better without any medical assistance.

These and many others, like dressmaker, Chelsea, at Adams Clothier and Fine Fashions Shop bring to life what it was like to live in a small Georgia town in the 1900s.

You'll find the last wooden courthouse left in Georgia from Chattahoochee County. There are two churches here. The Methodist Church, dating to 1836, has original art on its walls and ceiling painted by an itinerant German painter who traveled around trading his skill at painting public buildings for room and board.

Another new attraction in Columbus is Ma Rainey's House. Ma Rainey is known as "Mother of the Blues." She released over 100 records with Paramount. Her home, a two-story clapboard house in what was the traditionally "Black" section of Columbus, is open to the public for free. She built the house for her mother in her hometown of Columbus, Georgia. It was where Ma Rainey retired after her stage career slacked during the Depression. Each room is filled with memorabilia about her, the Blues, and contemporary musicians who were influenced by Rainey. It's a good mix between Ma Rainey as a person and her musical image with many of her original records and posters from her career.

The most notable feature in the home is her bedroom set. It's a hand-carved tiger wood set. Ma Rainey's niece, who was her heir, sold the set to a local antique dealer for $200. When the dealer learned the city was restoring the house he charged them $15k for the set. Free enterprise or highway robbery, you decide? The house was in such a terrible state the city was able to buy it for $5,000 but the restoration cost over $90,000. The purchased was approved by a narrow vote. The mayor had to cast the tie breaking vote. Ma Rainey was not well known in her hometown. Had she been better known, shocked citizens might have objected to restoring her home. Outrageous behavior by musicians is nothing new. Ma Rainey stirred a bit of controversy wherever she went.

Perhaps she is still stirring things up. Folks have reported hearing a woman singing in the house and the piano playing but the docents only play music on CDs. Some people have even reported seeing a Black woman in 1900s dress dancing on the balcony.

Other strange activities have occurred in the house like the curator finding the water running and shade drawn when no one was in those rooms. Ma Rainey just can't stop misbehaving.

She may still be acting out at another of her Columbus haunts, Liberty Theater. Workers at the theater had seen a silhouette of a large woman with jangling jewelry on the stage.

After her move back to Columbus, Ma Rainey managed and often performed at the Liberty. The theater was built because of Jim Crow Laws; Black people were only allowed to sit in the upper balcony of the Springer so in 1925, Roy E. Martin, owner of the Martin Theater chain built this Black theater. It showed live performances, silent movies and then talkies and was the local hotspot for black entertainers. Copying Hollywood, the Liberty Theater's has its own Walk of Fame. Naturally, Ma Rainey has a star along with many others who performed at the Liberty.

The theater is a simple two-story, red brick building with small windows, twin sets of double doors set in a recessed entry way into the lobby. After integration, the theater attendance declined and it remained vacant until it was opened as The Liberty Theatre and Cultural Center. It's open for events and tours and offer about four live performances each year. Liberty Theater is on the National Register of Historic Places.

The centerpiece of the lobby is a large oil painting of some of Liberty Theater's legendary performers Louis Armstrong, Nat King Cole, Cab Calloway, Marian Anderson, and Ma Rainey called After Hours by Najee Dorsey. Other greats that performed there included Fletcher Henderson, Bessie Smith, and Jackie Robinson. It's not surprising that the spirits of some of this group may also be singing and dancing here as well.

As for dining, it's varied and great. Some of my personal favorites are The Loft Downstairs for fine dining, The Cannon Brew Pub for fun and a great pizza, Country's Barbecue at either location if you have a really big appetite for barbecue and after you tour the Columbus Museum, Meritage Cafe is just around the corner for deli style sandwiches and homemade soup. Of course there are countless other fine restaurants here as well.

A fun annual event is the Aflac Outdoor Games held in May, a big 3-day, outdoor event taking place in Uptown Columbus and along the Chattahoochee RiverWalk. It consists of competitions in archery, cycling, agility and air dog, lumberjack, barbecue and lots of live entertainment.

Chapter 16 Warm Springs and Pine Mountain, A Presidents Hope

Before the white man settled in this part of Georgia, Native Americans visited the warm mineral springs. They thought of them as a sacred place, a place of healing. Later these healing waters drew settlers. In 1832 David Rose began the first "resort area" in Warm Springs. It became a popular summer resort. Later, in 1893, Charles Davis built a 300 room Victorian called Meriwether Inn. The inn had all the latest amenities and of course, the main draw, the 90-degree springs flowing from the hillside of Pine Mountain. At the turn of the century, the resort and the town fell into a decline and were almost forgotten except by the few lucky residents.

In 1907, Hotel Warm Springs was built on the site of the oldest building in the town. The hotel changed hands and at one time was named Tuscawilla Hotel after a Creek princess. The owner at that time, Mr. Butts, was so enthralled with the name that he named his oldest daughter, Tuscawilla. The name is still part of the hotel history and lore and lives on in the ice cream parlor, known as the Tuscawilla Soda Shop, once frequented by President Roosevelt.

The hotel has been the scene of a gruesome double murder and is known to have its own resident specters. The murders occurred when the hotel was owned by the Thompson family. Mr. and Mrs. Thompson and their five children lived in the hotel. To bolster the family income during these lean times, Mr. Thompson did deliveries from one train to another and sometimes delivered parcels arriving by train to families living outside town. For this reason, he always carried a gun.

At the same time, he leased a pharmacy in the hotel to a pharmacist, Mr. Bulloch. Bulloch was a rowdy character. He liked to indulge in loud late night poker games in a room he kept at the hotel. He had a "fancy" lady he kept there. He often got violent with the woman; slapped her and locked her in the room.

Thompson had repeatedly warned Bulloch that this kind of behavior would not be tolerated in his inn. Things came to a head one day in 1915. Thompson had returned from delivering some packages. He was tired, hot and wanted to eat lunch and relax. His wife, pregnant with their sixth child, met him as he came in and told him that Bulloch was up to his old ways. Bulloch had slapped his woman and locked her in the room. When Mrs. Thompson told him that he could not do that, Bulloch turned on her with threatening words. This was more than Thompson was going to tolerate. He approached Bulloch and told him that he could keep his pharmacy in the hotel but the woman had to go, and he would no longer be allowed to maintain a room in the hotel. That settled, Thompson went into the lunchroom to eat.

Bulloch went to his drawer in the pharmacy and took out his gun. He followed Thompson into the dining room and shot him. Thompson's niece tried to prop her wounded uncle up. Thompson then drew his gun and shot and killed Bulloch. Thomson died a few days later.

You would think after such a dramatic double murder either Bulloch or Thompson would still be haunting the hotel. Strangely enough, the ghosts at Hotel Warm Springs seem to have nothing to do with either victim.

Gerri Thompson, the current owner and no relation to the ill-fated former owner, told me though she had never seen anything, there seems to be several presences in the hotel. Once she was leading a woman up the stairs to her room when the woman began to shake her shoulders rapidly. Fearing that the woman was having an attack or something, she asked, "What's wrong?"

The woman grabbed her and said, "Don't you feel it?"

Gerri replied that the only thing she felt was the woman's hand grabbing her. The woman proceeded to tell her, "I'm psychic. There are ghosts in the hotel."

The next day, the woman was telling other guests about the ghost. "I felt him in the hall."

When they asked how she knew it was a man, the woman replied, "I could smell his cologne."

When two different guests at different times told her of seeing children's ghosts, she began to think there must be something here. One family saw the children standing at the end of the bathtub in their room. The other saw them playing in the hall.

One night when Gerri had gone to a wedding and returned to the hotel to meet another wedding party who was going to be staying at the hotel. She saw a guest sitting on the porch waiting for her return.

The wedding group pulled up right about the same time so the man just waited until she finished checking them in. Then he approached her and told her he wanted to ask her something but didn't want to ask in front of the guests she was checking in. She assumed he was going to complain, but that was not what he had on his mind.

He told her while he was sitting on the porch; he saw an apparition moving across the yard wearing a long white gown. He wanted to know if she could think of any event that might have triggered such a spirit.

At first she could not but then she remembered. The family who she bought the hotel from had brought the wife's mother to stay with them after her father had died. The mother was grief-stricken and would not be comforted. She refused to eat and stayed in her room in her nightgown. Finally one night, the distraught woman decided she did not want to live now that her husband was gone. She had taken her own life by jumping from a third story window.

Gerri says people are always saying they hear things. She has heard lots of thing too. She tried to dismiss them as the natural noises an old building makes. Funny thing is when she hears odd noises and goes to investigate, she never finds the source of the noise but often finds things that need to be done. "It's almost like they are looking after the hotel and me," she said. "Like one time I kept hearing a 'thump thump' and I started to look for something rubbing against something else that had worked loose. I never found anything like that but I did find a lit candle burning in a small holder in one of the rooms that was supposed to be cleaned and closed up. After I put out that candle, I never heard that noise again."

Yes, the wonderful old building has its resident spirits who protect its guests and want their home to be cared for so they will always have a home.

It took Gerri a while to realize that however. She has owned the hotel for nineteen years. Naturally in a historic building you are always fixing things. The first time anyone approached her about "ghosts" she was doing some stenciling on the front door. Three couples came in and one of the men asked, "Ya got any haints here?"

Not in the best of moods she replied, "If I saw a "haint" here, I'd slap a paint brush in his hand and put him to work."

It was the former President Franklin Delano Roosevelt who is credited with the town's twentieth century revival when, in 1924, he visited the town's naturally heated mineral springs as treatment for his polio related paralysis. He advocated the name change to Warm Springs to promote the healing mineral springs

Once FDR discovered Warm Springs, he wanted his own cottage there away from the hustle and bustle of politics. He built the modest home that came to be known as The Little White House while still governor of New York a year before being inaugurated as president.

This is the modest cottage where he developed his "New Deal." Here, he was able to escape into the charm of this small southern town where he took refuge from the pressures of leading a nation during the worst war the world has ever known. It was here that he died on April 12, 1945. He left behind a legacy in which any world leader could take pride.

The home is now a Georgia Historic Site and Museum. It was here, while posing for a portrait on April 12, 1945, that FDR suffered a stroke and died a short while later. Today, the "Unfinished Portrait" and many other pieces of Roosevelt memorabilia are housed at the museum dedicated to his memory. Standing in the dim room staring at the portrait I could feel why he always came back here in times of stress. Perhaps his soul still abides here in this home he loved. Many people have claimed to see a misty figure that resembles FDR in the house. There is a picture of the spirit circulating on the internet.

When you visit the village in Warm Springs you are looking at small-town Georgia life much as it was in Roosevelt's era. But one ghost is of a much earlier time. As you drive to the airport, you may notice a private residence, a big two-story house built before the Civil War. A prosperous family owned it. The man of the house had gone off to fight for the South. His loving wife tried to hold things together on the home front. Things went from bad to worse for the lady. She learned of the destruction of nearby Atlanta then was forced to harbor the hated Union forces. While these unwelcome guests were making themselves at home, she received the ultimate bad news. Her husband had been killed in battle. In despair, she either jumped or hung herself from the balcony.

To this day, when the light reflects just right on the house, you can still see the shadow of the woman as she flung herself off the balcony. One local resident, Johnny Craven, had this to say about the occurrence, "I did not believe this but I have seen a shadow of a person on the wall of this house many times when traveling from Greenville to Warm Springs. It is kind of spooky."

Johnny tells of an old slave cemetery nearby "in White Sulfur Springs about 15 min from Warm Springs on Mullins Cemetery Road. The graves have caved into the ground making it spooky enough but at night you can hear people talking in the woods around it when no living person is there."

Franklyn Delano Roosevelt State Park separates Warm Springs from Pine Mountain with a peaceful drive that combines history with outdoors activities. Spectacular waterfalls and unusual rock outcropping await you at this 10,000-acre park.

For spirited fun of a different kind, tour the Wild Animal Safari. It is filled with more-earthly adventures. Here, animals from every continent roam freely. You are the one encased in your car or the zebra striped bus that transverses the domain of these wild creatures. Perhaps an ostrich or a llama will stick its nose into your window hoping for a handout. Or a tiny fawn will stop besides your car and gaze in curiosity at you.

Cason and Virginia Callaway dreamed of building the prettiest garden since the Garden of Eden. In May of 1952, their dream became reality when the gates of Callaway Gardens swung open for the first time. For over a half-century, they provided visitors with a glimpse of heaven right here on earth. From the blooming Azalea Bowl, the world's largest, to Sibley Horticultural Center, a five acre conservatory featuring some of the most colorful plants in existence; from the Day Butterfly Center, aflutter with jewel toned "flying flowers" and darting hummingbirds, to the native wildlife, deer, raccoons, birds and others, all protected by the lush growth, the Garden is a photographer's paradise. The newest creature to inhabit the gardens is the American eagle. When you glimpse this majestic bird in flight you will understand why they are a national treasure as well as our national bird. Whether it's natural beauty, historic sites or outdoor activities, this area will please everybody.

Fallen soldier at Andersonville Reenactment

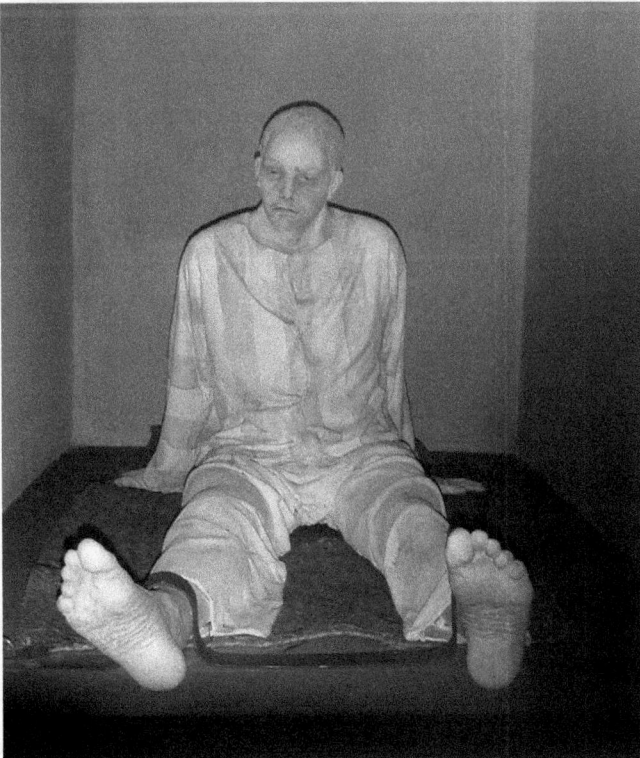

"Prisoner" at Andersonville POW Museum

Windsor Hotel

Exhibit in Andersonville Museum

Blacksmith at Westville

Creek Native American at Westville

"Sailor" at Civil War Naval Museum

Phantom of the Opera at Springer Opera House

Warm Springs Hotel

Little White House

Section 4 The Bloody Fields of War

In all of Civil War history the event that stands head and shoulders above the rest is Sherman's infamous march to the sea. There is no more dramatic scent in motion picture history than *Gone With the Wind*'s burning of Atlanta. However, the bloodiest fighting of the war took place in northwest Georgia where the towering mountains sought to protect Atlanta from the Federal's southward push. From Chickamauga to Kennesaw, brother stood against brother, American against American. Is it any wonder that there are more reported ghost sightings on the fields of battle than anywhere else?

Chapter 17 Chickamauga, Beginning of the End

On September 19, 1863, the wooded hills of Chickamauga rang with the clash of steel and the roar of gunfire as Confederate and Union troops locked in mortal combat in what was to become the bloodiest battle fought on Georgia soil. This battle calls attention to the "brother against brother" aspect of this war. When Lincoln was informed of the casualties at Chickamauga he was devastated. He had a reason for personal grief. His brother- in law, Benjamin Helms was one of the casualties. Helms was a Confederate officer who died at Chickamauga!

When the smoke cleared and the battle was done, the Confederates held the field with the Federals pushed back to Chattanooga. But at what price? They had lost over 18,000 men out of their 66,000 soldiers. The Union Army left 16,000 bloody corpses at Chickamauga. Twenty five years after the war, Chickamauga and Chattanooga National Military Park was officially dedicated on the anniversary of that bloody battle. Is it any wonder that countless visitors and staff alike have come face to face with the restless spirits whose life ended abruptly on these rolling hills?

The Federal government is the last to ever acknowledge the possibility of anything supernatural but as you tour the battlefield watch for something the government does not admit exists here, ghosts.

The most commonly seen specter is "Old Green Eyes." Actually, he has been seen at Chickamauga before the Civil War. According to

John Fogerty, a Confederate re-enactor, who has visited the site many time, "Union soldiers atop Snodgrass hill claimed they saw this creature lurking among the many thousands of maimed and mangled bodies on the evening of September 20th, after the heaviest fighting there. Park Rangers report seeing him/it on several occasions and Old Green Eyes never fails to terrify anyone so unfortunate to cross his path."

John knows one woman who visits the grave of "Johnny, the only Confederate with a known marked grave." This woman "talks" with Johnny and claims he hovers about and enjoys the attention. Many others have reported seeing his around the woods near Alexander Bridge Road.

John's girlfriend had a strange experience near where the Poe Cabin had been. "She heard someone moving through the grass behind her, whirled around to see who it was and actually saw the grass being stepped on as if some unseen human was walking towards her. She said, 'Are you friend or foe?' and the thing turned away from her and paced into the woods."

Nicky Reynolds, who worked as a ranger at the battlefield, tells a little about "Green Eyes." Visitors who come to the park look for the green eyes of a soldier killed in battle but that isn't the basis of the legend. The 125th Ohio Infantry, nicknamed "Opdycke's Tigers" or "The Tiger Regiment," fought heroically on Snodgrass Hill. Later a monument to the regiment was placed there, a statue of the regiment's leader, Emerson Opdycke, with a scene from the battle on a bas-relief slab. Atop the slab is a carved tiger. According to one legend the green eyes belong to the tiger.

Perhaps there is some truth to the earlier story since the Indians who camped on the banks of the creek were the ones who named it "Chickamauga," "The River of Death" since they lost so many of the tribe to Yellow Fever there. That might account for the creature seen by the Union soldiers and described as having long black hair, sharp fangs, talon-like claws and a pumpkin-like head with blazing greenish-orange eyes.

Other apparitions are more humanistic. There is the "Woman in White" reported frequently by visitors. She walks in the fields and disappears when approached. Specters appear frequently around the

Hunt Cemetery and Lost Corners areas. Naturally many of the specters are soldiers. Nicky tells of a Yankee re-enactor in uniform who was walking at sunset on one of the maintenance roads. He spotted what he thought was a Confederate re-enactor and hailed him. The Rebel panicked and pointed the gun at him then disappeared. To this day the re-enactor refuses to walk alone on that road.

Harper Harris, former historian at Kennesaw Civil War Museum and a Confederate re-enactor, tells of his first re-enactment at Chickamauga. "I shot on a cannon crew. I hadn't been with these guys long then. One day they said, 'we're shooting up at Chickamauga this weekend.' I thought that'd be great. They said 'Man, it's a real spooky place. We see some strange things every time we go up there.' I thought they were just pulling my leg. We camped out in front of Snodgrass Cabin. In the evening, we sat around the fireplace in the cabin. It got later and later and everybody else had drifted off. I was sitting alone by the fireplace. I began hearing all kinds of noises and figured all the guys were playing tricks so I just sat and ignored the noises. When I decided to turn in and headed out for my sleeping bag. I realized all the other guys were already asleep so something else was making the noises. I stayed up all night long. I still don't like to be up there by myself."

Perhaps all the deaths that occurred there attract death. For whatever reason, the battlefield is a favorite place for suicides.

Mountain Cove Farm in McLemore's Cove was doomed to be subdivided until Walker County Sole Commissioner, Bebe Heiskell convinced then Governor Perdue that the state should partner with Walker County and acquire this land to protect it.

It was the site of some earlier skirmishes before the actual battle. McLemore Cove is listed on the National Register of Historic Places. Walker County has restored the historic structures in the cove.

Chattooga Academy is believed to be one of Georgia's oldest remaining brick school buildings. The building, completed in 1836 is known as John B. Gordon Hall. It was Confederate General Braxton Bragg's home base from September 10 to 17th, 1863 and it's reported that he planned the campaign sitting under a big oak in the front yard. The oak, known ever since as Bragg's Oak, was destroyed by a storm in the 1920s.

The Academy saw action during the Battle of Lafayette on June 24, 1864. Confederate Capt. William V. Harrell using the building to store supplies while attacked Union troops. It is Georgia's oldest remaining brick schoolhouse.

Across Joe Stock Memorial Park from the Academy, Marsh House is another interesting stop. It was built by Spenser Marsh in 1836. During the war, the Marsh family relocated to Cassville, Georgia. When they returned after the war, they found that the house had been occupied by Union soldiers who rode the horses through the rooms and left bullet holes in the walls and blood stains on the pine floors. When the Marshes repaired the home, they left several of the bullet holes. Perhaps as a reminder of how swiftly life could be turned around.

Since the home was in the Marsh family for 150 years, much of the furniture is original to the home. Mary Smitherman, with the Marsh House Task Force that maintains and operates the house, believes the horses were probable stabled there as they were so valuable. She is proud to show off the "Certified Haunted" plaque from GHOST (Ghosts and History of Southeast Tennessee) investigators.

"I was concerned about compromising the integrity of the house, but we agreed. I was here with them. We never let anyone in without one of us being here. They put cameras everywhere. They found a lot of activity in the children's rooms and in the attic and servants quarters. The group was very professional." She commented the 'haunted' appellation had increased interest in the old home."

At this time, GHOST had completed about 50 investigations, and the Marsh House is just the fifth one to receive the haunted certification.

Lee and Gordon's Mills allow you to glimpse life in a gristmill of the old South. The mill was occupied by both Union and Confederate forces. Built by James Gordon in the late 1890s, the mill served as the first general store in Walker County. It stayed in the Gordon/ Lee family until 1929 when Tom Lee sold it to the Wallace brothers, Bill and Charley who operated it until 1967. When Bill retired in 1967, he retired the mill as well, refusing to sell or even lease it. It stood empty until 1993, when the Wallace heirs sold the mill property to Mr. Frank Pierce. He restored the mill to the condition it was in 167 years ago, although he passed away in 2003, the mill still lives on, a tribute to those who nurtured it over the years. The city of Chickamauga has recently entered into a lease agreement to operate the Mill.

The Gordon-Lee Mansion allows you to experience for yourself the lifestyle of the upper class Southerner. The home was built for James Gordon, the owner of Gordon Lee Mill. Construction was begun in 1840 but not completed in 1847. The bricks used in construction were made on the residence grounds.

During the War Between the States, the home was used by the Union Army for General Rosecrans' headquarters just before the Battle of Chickamauga. During the battle the house was converted into a temporary hospital. Many soldiers on both sides died in the house. From the many amputations and wounds, the floors were drenched with so much blood that the stains could not be removed and the floors had to be covered with mats. Some of soldiers scribbled a last message to loved ones on the walls as was a common practice in hospitals during the war. James Lee's female relatives tried to made copies of them and contact families of these dead soldiers after the battle.

Unlike any other Civil War hospital where there was so much loss of life, the manager of the site informed me there are no ghosts present in the mansion. Visitors have said otherwise. Many saw the spirit of a man in Confederate uniform inside the building. Other people have seen and one passerby even photographed a ghostly German shepard in a window of the mansion. The Gordons did have a German shepard when they lived in the home.

It would be hard to believe that so much death could not leave any psychic trace. Of course, there are always those who do not want to admit that humans are made of both a body and a soul.

The first railroad came to Chickamauga sometime around 1888-89.The Central of Georgia Railroad put up a stone depot and trains made round trips twice a day between Chattanooga and Cedartown, stopping in Chickamauga. Then railroads began to become outdated. Passenger service stopped in the early 50's and in the late 60's the depot was finally shut down.

But things weren't over for the little depot. It was used for many purposes until the City of Chickamauga was deeded the property in the late 1990's. They have restored it to its original state and it now houses the Walker County Regional Heritage and Model Train Museum. It also has a fine exhibit of Civil War collectables, Indian artifacts and Cherokee arrowheads, WWI artifacts, antique guns and furniture and a complete working display of Lionel Old Gauge model trains that date back to 1947. And the big Iron Horses are rolling once more. A vintage steam locomotive carries passengers on excursions and day trips from Chattanooga during the summer months, stopping just like old times at the Chickamauga Depot.

For Campers, Cloudland Canyon State Park is one of Georgia's most scenic parks. It also has cottages.

Of course, Walker County has many other attractions. In spite of common belief, Rock City is in Georgia and should not be missed. Its natural beauty is a delight to kids and grownups alike.

Chapter 18 Kennesaw and Marietta, Sherman's Last Mountain

In spite of the Rebel victory at Chickamauga, Sherman continued to advance towards Atlanta, Georgia's main stronghold. To take Atlanta Sherman had to confront not only the Confederates emboldened by their win, but one last natural obstacle, Kennesaw Mountain.

This time, Sherman and Johnson squared off. Johnson dug in to hold his position. Sherman outflanked him forcing a retreat. But a small chain of mountains just northwest of Atlanta stopped Sherman.

He could not leave the Confederates entrenched above his railway supply line. When he tried his outflanking maneuver once more, John Bell Hood boldly confronted him, making a battle inevitable.

Repeatedly the Union forces tried to break the Rebel lines but could not break through. The attack took its toll in lives and the weakened Johnson retreated to a position closer to Atlanta. Even though this had been a Rebel victory, Sherman had overcome his last mountain. Atlanta lies virtually unprotected before him.

Some of the greatest loss of lives occurred during an attack near Picketts' Mill at a place called New Hope. The Union forces unexpectedly confronted a makeshift Confederate battery of 16 cannons and 5,000 men on May 25, 1864. As the Union soldiers cleared the thick underbrush they emerged into deadly artillery fire. The churchyard was drenched with blood. As the slaughter continued, the sky darkened and a deadly storm broke over the area. The boom of cannons and the roll of thunder created a fearsome symphony. The wounded and dying Federal soldiers tried to escape the withering gunfire and the torrential downpour by crawling into nearby ravines. It is said that even over the cacophony their screams and moans were heard. The place became known as "The Hellhole"

Craig Dominey had an eerie encounter here one night. He was engaged in "relic hunting" and had pinpointed New Hope Church as a likely location. He left his car parked behind the church and proceeded into the Hellhole in the middle of the night. Suddenly he was in the midst of a torrential downpour. Thunder crashed. The sky, perfectly clear just a few minutes ago, darkened. He took shelter inside an abandoned car. It was then he heard the moans and smelled the sickening odor. He tried to rationalize the occurrence but the odor grew stronger and the moans louder. In the flashes of lightning, he was horrified to observe soldiers all around. He experienced devastating pain and total exhaustion. Unable to stand it any longer, he burst from the car and clawed his way through the forest back to his car. Strangely, the storm ceased as suddenly as it had begun.

He emerged to find the minister standing next to his car with a flashlight. Trying to avoid comment on what he was doing there, Craig tried to distract the man with a talk about the storm. The minister replied that they were common around the area on this date, May 25, the anniversary of the battle. His may be the most frightening story about this area but it is not the only one.

Tammy Bagley had a startling experience.

It was a gorgeous fall afternoon here in Georgia when I decided to play sick at my job so I could leave early. I went home to where my sister Teresa was babysitting my 4-year-old son Wesley, and suggested we go somewhere nice to enjoy the beautiful weather. We decided to go to a local Civil War National Battlefield Park. It is a gorgeous place with the typical numerous trails and various sites where soldiers were buried before they were relocated after the war, monuments, and the famous places where the battles were held. We went to a site where one of the most gruesome battles of the war took place. We were walking along one of the trails when we came upon a stream. Wesley had some toys that he brought with him, so he wanted to play in the water for a bit. We stayed there for about 15 minutes when I heard some voices. I asked my sister if she heard them too, and she did. My son heard them as well and asked me who it was. I picked up Wesley and told Teresa that we should follow the sounds of the voices to see who it was. It sounded like about 20 people that were marching and chanting like they do in the old war movies. I can't describe how eerie it sounded. The closer we got to these voices, the further they seemed away. We started running so we could find out what it was, when the sounds just stopped completely. I dismissed it at first, thinking that is was maybe some re-enactors, or maybe that it was some kids from a school field trip but then that seemed odd. It was around 2 o'clock in the afternoon on a Wednesday, and the re-enactors were usually there on weekends...not in the middle of the day. Before we left the park, we went to the information desk and asked if there were any re-enactments going on or any field trips there on that day and the lady said no. We told her what we had heard, and she told us that other people had heard the same thing in about the same place that we did, and that she couldn't explain it. I truly believe that Teresa, Wesley, and myself experienced a supernatural occurrence from the souls of those killed there. It is a memory I will always cherish.

The outcome of war is often decided by events other than battles. The Kennesaw/Marietta area was the scene of one of the Civil War's most daring spy stories. It began with a secret meeting in Fletcher House, also known as the Kennesaw House, now Marietta History Museum on the night of April 11, 1862. James Andrews and 21 other men plotted a daring train theft. The idea was to cut the Confederate supply lines. The target was The General, a Western and Atlantic engine on a routine run between Atlanta and Chattanooga. The Fletcher House was used because the owner, Fletcher was a Union sympathizer. The next morning Andrews and his Raiders boarded the train as passengers. When William Fuller, the conductor, and crew went to breakfast at the Lacey Hotel in Kennesaw, then known as Big Shanty, the raiders absconded with "The General" the plan was to move north towards Chattanooga destroying rails and burning bridges to facilitate an easy win for federal troops at Chattanooga.

The indignant crew of The General took the insult personally. Conductor William Fuller and two of his crew raced on foot the two miles to Moons Station where they commandeered a handcar and two maintenance men to help in the pursuit. The race was on in earnest now. When Fuller and his men encountered torn up track they continued on foot then on whichever different engines that were handy. Finally at Adairsville, the Confederates boarded a southbound engine, the Texas. They continued in hot pursuit in reverse.

Meantime, the Rebels had sent a rider to nearby Dalton where the telegraph lines had not been cut and sent a message to General Ledbetter in Chattanooga. Southern troops were swing north on the railway to meet the Raiders. Just at the top of Ringgold Gap, the gallant

General gave out. All twenty-two of the Raiders were caught. Andrews and seven others were tried and hanged in Atlanta. The other fourteen were sent to prison. In 1862, congress created the Medal of Honor and awarded it to some of the Raiders. Ironically, James Andrews was not eligible since he was not in the military.

The General continued in service for another thirty years. But that wasn't its last brush with death. In 1882 a man got drunk and stole the switch key. He maliciously opened the side rail in Kingston. The morning was foggy and the engineer did not see the switch sign and plowed into three boxcars. The fireman jumped in time but the engineer, Andrew West, was crushed. When they backed The General up, West's crumbled body fell to the ground. The perpetrator might have gotten away but he tried the same trick again and was caught and prosecuted, hanged in all probability.

The General remained a working engine until 1891 when it was retied. It was renovated and made appearances at festivals and reunions until it came to Kennesaw Civil War Museum. The museum was renovated and renamed The Southern Museum of Civil War & Locomotive History in 2003. It showcases *Railroads: Lifelines of the Civil War* and *Glover Machine Works: Casting a New South*. It has a great multi-media show telling the story of the daring train chase.

One of the exhibits is a rare regimental flag of the 65th Georgia Infantry. The flag, still proudly displays its 41 bullet holes and a bloodstain. This flag saw much action during the Civil War, including the entire Atlanta campaign. It survived many battles, including the Battles of Resaca, New Hope Church/Dallas/Pickett's Mill, Kennesaw Mountain, Peachtree Creek and Atlanta and is the only known surviving example of an Army of Tennessee flag with both unit and state designations. Perhaps it brings with it a few spirits of the brave men who died defending it.

Mike Bearrow, former museum's curator, and Harper Harris, the museum's former historian, have experienced some unnerving experiences while the General was housed in the old museum. Harris tells of hearing things at night. "At night, the place gets mighty creepy. This was an old cotton gin. It was originally built in the 1890s then it burned and was rebuilt in the 1930s. I hear stuff at night all the time. I usually keep the radio on and try not to stay that late but in the winter it starts getting dark early. Also when the alarm goes off I have to come in here. And sometimes I find stuff lying on the floor with no logical reason. You wonder 'How did that get there.' I know I didn't put it there. And then there's the noise. It's not like voices. It's more like thumping and scratching. One night it was real loud back in that room (where The General was displayed) I thought someone was in here. I've never seen anything but it's scary here sometimes." With all the deaths connected with The General, who knows what's lurking in the gleaming relic?

The former Fletcher House where the Raiders plotted now houses one of the most haunted spots in Georgia, The Marietta Museum of History. Dan Cox, the founder of the museum, has one of the most authentic "ghost photos" I have ever seen. He tells how he took it. "I saw this figure on the TV monitor in the back office. I thought someone was in the museum so I walked up front and no one was there. I went back and took a picture of the TV monitor."

Although Mr. Cox considers himself an unbeliever when it comes to ghosts, he has no explanation for some of the things he has seen and heard. Newspapers claim that there are 700 ghosts. He also admits that strange thing happen. There are places where he can hear his name being called at some places in the building. A tapping noise on the stairways one evening sounded like a man's wedding ring on the stair rail mysteriously kept starting and stopping. He would go to the stairwell when the noise occurred and it would stop. He would return to the office and it would resume. Finally, he walked all the way downstairs and out the building and then returned. The noise never occurred again. Doors there have a mind of their own. They close unless he props them open. The men's rest room door will close even if it is propped open. The elevator sometimes comes up when there is no one in it or no one pressing the button on any floor.

He described the most unexplainable manifestation. "My wife and I were waiting for the elevator in the lobby of the museum. I started to chuckle and my wife asked, 'what are you laughing at?' I replied 'I just saw someone standing beside me.' She asked, 'What did you see?' I said 'I'll tell you what I think I saw. There was a man standing there. He had on a little flat hat. I call it a riverboat gambler hat. He had on a cream colored coat that struck him about here (indicating thigh length). His pants were tucked into his boots. He looked like a Civil War surgeon to me.'"

He told me that the museum files do indicate there was a Dr. Wilder, a union officer and a surgeon who did come to the building to treat the people while it was used as a hospital. The local television stations have been there with "Ghost Hunters" and found "Cold Spots" and electromagnetic fields. There has never been any of the scary "Hollywood" type stuff. He has never felt threatened or intimidated. I did ask where I had the best chance of getting a "Ghost Photo." He suggested the mannequin dressed in an Antebellum wedding dress.

Never once dreaming that I would actually get anything out of the ordinary, I took two consecutive shots of the mannequin with the same camera. It was set on automatic. All I did was take a step and refocus. The result almost left me speechless (a feat that is almost as impossible as the photo I took.) The first picture was exactly what I saw when I looked through the lens. The second shows a halo type light around the mannequin's head. No light is actually there. If there were the light should have appeared in both shots. The photo on the front cover shows the orb. I put the other photo on the back.

Mr. Cox agrees that sort of thing is interesting and fun but he hopes people will not lose sight of the fact that this is a magnificent old building with some tremendous history attached. Dix Fletcher who was a Mason and a Unionist owned it. The room where The Raiders met is recreated here. It was common knowledge that Fletcher was a union sympathizer but no one has ever tied him to the raiders. Mr. Cox feels very close to proving that Fletcher did help James Andrews and his raiders. The museum is located on the second floor. The fourth floor accidentally burned when Sherman's troops occupied the building. It was removed. 1867.

Cobb County has several interesting graveyards. The Confederate Cemetery and the Marietta National Cemetery both house graves of soldiers killed in the Civil War. There is also a small 1800s cemetery near Marbleton off Concord Rd. known as "The Witch's Cemetery. Supposedly, a witch was killed and buried here and remains to vent her displeasure. Late at night, you night hear voices, footsteps and drums from underground. Often there is fog here when it is nowhere else. The Cemetery is on private property and heavily patrolled.

When dining in Marietta, you can combine your ghost hunting with lunch. Hemingway's on the square offers both. This building was once the city's morgue and visitors often smell formaldehyde in the basement. Servers report being called by name but when they look around, no one is there.

John Heyward Glover, Marietta's first mayor, built his first home, Bushy Park, a large Greek revival plantation, due south of Marietta just off South Cobb Drive. Bushy Park was converted into a restaurant first known as The Planters and subsequently The 1848 House. The restaurant closed in 2002.

Back when it was a restaurant, chairs would rock by themselves and the chandeliers swung and blinked. The clock would run back ways. It was believed these were caused by two resident spirits, George and Lillian. George is believed to be a soldier killed at the Battle of Bushy Park, fought here. There is still a bullet hole in the side of the house from that skirmish. The home was also used as a hospital by Union troops. What was the restaurant's Scarlet Room was the operating theater.

Marietta is graced with four National Historic Districts containing over 150 antebellum and Victorian homes. A free self-guided historic walking/driving tour is available at the Welcome Center in the old depot. You may find a ghost here that no one has discovered yet.

Another place to look for an interesting ghost would be the William Root House. Located Two blocks from the square, the Root House is one of the oldest surviving frame houses in Marietta. It was the home of William Root and his family. Root was the town's first druggist and a merchant. He was also a founder of St. James Episcopal Church and served as its Sunday School Superintendent for many years. He was the county coroner for two terms. It offers visitors an opportunity to experience how a middle class merchant and his family lived in the 1850's. One of his sons died at a young age but as yet I have not heard of any episodes which might be the boy. It has paranormal activity usually in the main bedroom of the house. People have seen the spirit of a woman, believed to be Mrs. Root. The bedroom is furnished with an antique rope bed that is sometimes appears to have been slept in at night. When docents open the house in the morning the ropes appeared loosened. The ropes are always tightened at night before closing.

The turn of the century town square offers delightful shops and restaurants and the Theater on the Square.

Kennesaw's quaintness and Marietta's grace and charm offer a delicious contrast to nearby Atlanta's hustle and bustle.

Chapter 19 Metro Atlanta, Gone with the Wind Territory

Atlanta is a well-preserved southern belle who loves to show off her treasures. Like a connoisseur of fine things, Atlanta has an entire jewelry box filled with both genuine diamonds and that fun costume stuff no southern lady would be without. Atlanta is more than a city: she is an entire metropolitan area composed of many small cities and towns. Put it all together, and Atlanta represents "the new South." Like the Roman god, Janus, it has two faces: one looking back on a rich past and the other gazing into a bright future.

A Segway Tours is a good way to save your feet and get a great overview of Atlanta. My segway tour guide, Jamaine, was patient in explaining how to handle the machine. He comments, "Even if you've never ridden one you will soon be zipping along." The three-hour-tour takes you most of the main attractions. You also visit places that have become a local tradition such as Varsity Restaurant, the World's Largest Drive-in. Jamaine describes it, "Varsity serves all those foods that give you a heart attack; hot dogs, fries, burgers but they're so good you want to eat them anyway."

If you are searching out Hotlanta's hottest haunts, Segway Tours provides a chilling ghost tour.

Downtown Atlanta is filled with many chain hotels but if you are looking for something special, one small boutique hotel stands out above the rest. The Ellis Hotel on Peachtree is that special little jewel every traveler loves to discover. It has style. It has history. It has ghostly legends. Most of all it has all the comforts and luxuries to coddle a weary traveler.

The hotel on this site originally was the Winecoff Hotel built in 1913 by renowned architect, William Lee Stoddard. In its time, the 15-story Winecoff Hotel was Atlanta's tallest and most luxurious hotel. Then on December 7, 1946, it was destroyed by the most deadly hotel fire in U. S. history. That night, 119 people lost their lives including some of Georgia's best and brightest high school students in town for a mock-legislative session at the Capital. From that fire came the fire codes now used in all hotels. A plaque outside the side entrance of the Ellis Hotel commemorates that tragic event.

A new hotel, the Peachtree Hotel on Peachtree, reopened; this time with fire escapes and alarms but it did not succeed. By 1967 the building was donated to the Georgia Baptist Convention for elderly housing. Then it went through over two decades as an abandoned blighted building. Has it not been for its historic location, its fate might well have been the wrecking ball.

A new angel stepped in to rescue this grand dame in distress. This owner poured $28 million into restoring the faded beauty and turning it into a fabulous European style boutique hotel.

In October 2007, this sleek 127 room beauty opened as the Ellis Hotel. Its history has earned it a spot on the National Historic Register. Its style and charm are fast earning it a place in the knowing traveler's heart as *the* place to stay in Atlanta. Enter the lobby and breathe in the distinctive scent of "Sea Island Cotton" while soothing music plays softly in the back ground, and you know this is your home away from home while in Atlanta.

Former Director of Sales and Marketing, Tracey Lyon-Mercado, told me, "We take pride in our service. In today's world of automation, people prefer the personal touch. We brand ourselves on unique and different and the personal touch is important to us.

For some great eats, try the hotel restaurant, The Terrace. The emphases is on natural organic local foods

I found this hotel to excel in those little thing that are important but often overlooked by chain hotels. You have free internet in every room sign in and you are online. For watching your favorite show or the news, each room is equipped with a large flat-screen television. Then there is the afternoon wine tasting at 5:30. You get to mix and mingle with other guests and sample some of the great wines that are served at the Ellis with $1 wines and free light appetizers.

Don't you hate to get a computer wake up call? At the Ellis, you will get a cheerful call from a real live person who will ask if you need another call. It starts your day on the right note.

You not only feel welcome at the Ellis, you feel secure. Should an intruder attempt to follow you, he will get no farther than the elevator. To use the elevators at the Ellis requires a room card be inserted.

Only then can you ascend to the floor of your choice. Even the location is geared for safety. The Peachtree Center MARTA Station is just steps out of the key-secured side door.

For women traveling alone there is one more incentive to choose the Ellis; its Women's Only floor. The tenth floor is complete with all the things a woman needs and some she only wants; curling irons as well as blow dryers, A cozy terry robe, an honor bar full of choices such as panty hose and other little necessities as well as chocolate and other nibbles and a full supply of drink choices. Although the Woman's Only floor is geared to women, all of the hotel's rooms offer a great honor bar. Then there is the great fitness room where guests can work out.

For the icing on the cake there is a ghostly legend. People have claimed to have seen spirits at the windows while the building stood empty. Considering the lives lost in the fire, it is easily understood that many of these people died with much of their lives unlived. Perhaps they enjoy seeing the new hotel, made safe for guests.

Some of the honors the Ellis Hotel has been awarded are: Recognized National Green Seal Property, Silver level , Atlanta Downtown Design Excellence Award for Best Hotel Design, 2008, Atlanta's Urban Design Commission Award for historic preservation, 2008 , *Convention South* readers named The Ellis "Best New Hotel for Small Meetings."

Don't take my word for it. Try the Ellis on your next trip to Atlanta and you, too, will be singing its praises. Maybe you will even glimpse one of the spirits that call the hotel home.

For any Southerner, *Gone With the Wind* is *the* top Southern classic. A visit to the Margaret Mitchell House ranks more as a pilgrimage than a tourist attraction. The author had a tiny apartment in this beautifully restored Victorian home then called the Crescent Apartments. According to tour guide Melissa, "Margaret referred to her apartment as 'the dump.' But she loved the apartment because it was small and easy to clean. Best of all, it was one-bedroom, giving her an excuse to avoid overnight guests. Margaret detested overnight guests."

It was here that she wrote her famous novel. Mitchell was a voracious reader, so when she was housebound with an injury, her husband, John, would bring her four or five books from the library each day. Finally in despair, he brought her home an old Remington typewriter and told her, "If you want something to read, write your own."

The rest is history. Today, the tiny apartment is only part of the shrine to a great Georgia author. Besides the apartment, there is a gallery with photographs and artifacts from her life. Across the courtyard is a wonderful tribute to the movie based on Mitchell's book. Visitors can get the inside scoop on why Clark Gable did not want to play Rhett, how Leslie Howard got talked into the role of Ashley, how Butterfly McQueen was transformed into Prissy and all you ever wanted to know about the making of GWTW.

According to the staff, Mitchell's ghost is not now in residence. However, I did find references to the possibility that her ghost had been active once: a blog site reported, "Some thought the fires that almost destroyed the Crescent Apartments on two occasions were set by Margaret's irate ghost."

If you are looking to meet Margaret Mitchell face to face, your best bet is a visit to the Grant Mansion. The mansion is now the home of the Atlanta Preservation Society but it travelled a bumpy road to reach this point. Naturally, Grant Park was not named for Ulysses S. Grant. It was a "converted" Yankee, Lemuel P. Grant, an engineer from Maine, who arrived in 1840 to help designing railroads, Atlanta's chief asset then.

He fell in love with the southern city, and in 1857, built an 8,250-square-foot Italianate mansion with nine fireplaces, etched cranberry glass over the entry and a widow's walk.

When war came, Grant enlisted in the Confederate army and became a colonel. He helped design trenches and ramparts around Atlanta to foil Sherman. His efforts were in vain but his home was spared, reputedly because Sherman's troops found Masonic regalia inside. Sherman did respect Masonry if not much else.

The house remained in the Grant family until the turn of the century. One of Grant's sons befriended a young couple and allowed them to share the home. These were the parents of golf legend Robert Tyre Jones who was born in the mansion.

The mansion was on a downward spiral and changed hands seven times between then and 1941. That is where Margaret Mitchell entered the picture. A fellow newspaperman named Boyd Taylor wanted to buy and restore the Grant Mansion and approached Mitchell for a loan. Naturally, realizing the historic value of the home–it was only one of six remaining homes of that type that survived Sherman's burning of Atlanta–she made the loan on stipulation that the home was to be properly restored.

"It was about to be cut up into apartments," Mitchell explained. "I've seen that happen to many old houses, and I couldn't stand to see this one go the same way. We haven't a thing like that in Atlanta to show tourists."

When Mitchell drove by and found Taylor had torn off the porches, she sued him and accused him of voiding the contract by not restoring as it should have been. She got a temporary injunction but later lost the case.

Taylor continued to live in the mansion for over 30 years. He frequently claimed that Mitchell's ghost visited him every spring and brought jonquils from her grave in Oakland Cemetery. He stated, "Margaret wanders through the house looking things over. She never talks." I can imagine since she died a year after losing the lawsuit, she may be biting her tongue to keep from telling him off.

Taylor became more eccentric and the mansion more dilapidated. He continued to live inside with no plumbing or electricity and only a partial roof until his death in 1981. Neighborhood kids referred to the mansion as "that haunted house."

An even weirder occupant stepped up to the plate next. A former neighbor, Dennis Walters, a historian and gun collector who worked at the Cyclorama, began claiming he had bought the house. Then he began to retract and say he "sort of" owned it. Finally his story was that he was "taking care of it for the real owner."

Walters had a problem "sticking to his story." His problems got worse when his wife caught him having an affair with their adopted teenage daughter, Wanda. He married the "daughter" and moved to Decatur. Shades of Woody Allan. The story became more Hollywood when his young wife informed him she was leaving him for another man. Walters completely snapped. He shot her to death and then killed himself.

The house passed first to Robert J. O'Donoghue, a Denny's restaurant manager, who actually began repairs but was stricken and died before he could do much. Then in 1994, Woodrow Mankin, an interior designer, held an exorcism on the grounds. He built a sort of efficiency apartment within the ruins. Mankin believed one particular mirror was cursed and he covered it with a black cloth. He died shortly after that of heart failure at age 37.

The next buyer was a real estate agent who was evicted in a foreclosure and had his possessions, including the "accursed" mirror still swathed in black, put on the curb by police. Finally the mansion came into the possession of the Preservation Center and has been restored to its former glory. It is now the center's headquarters.

There is another haunted home in the Atlanta area with ties to GWTW. The Holliday-Dorsey-Fife House, in Fayetteville, was built in 1855, by John Stiles Holliday, a local doctor and uncle of John Henry "Doc" Holliday, the gunfighter. The Hollidays were relatives of Margaret Mitchell's grandmother who lived with at the Holiday's home while she attended Fayetteville Academy. While Margaret Mitchell was researching GWTW, she visited Fayetteville and located many of the graves of her great-grandfather's family buried in the city's cemetery. This was the nucleus of the O'Hara clan. Scarlett O'Hara attended the fictional Fayetteville Female Academy.

It's not a big stretch to assume she based the characters of Melanie and Ashley on her distant cousins, Mattie Holliday and Mattie's first cousin and love of her life, John Henry "Doc" Holliday. As everyone familial with the famed gambler and gunfighter knows, He left home after he was not allowed to marry his cousin. She went into the convent and took the name Sister Melanie.

The icing on the cake is that it has a resident ghost. No, not Mitchell. The spirit at the Holiday-Dorsey-Fife House is believed to be "Manse" or "Manny," John Manson Dorsey, who was the flag bearer in the Fayette County Rifles, 107 local volunteers, the first Confederate troop from Fayetteville. He was wounded at Gettysburg. The home, once a museum is now closed.

Interesting, Mrs. Permelia Ware Holliday was one of the makers of the Confederate flag for his company. It was made partly in the Holiday-Dorsey-Fife House.

Another home with a much gentler history is The Wren's Nest, the home of Joel Chandler Harris, the creator of Uncle Remus. One of the stipulations Mrs. Harris made when the home was converted to a museum was that Joel's bedroom was to be untouched. It is just as it was when he died and it is rumored that he still visits the room from time to time.

Some visitors have heard a loud ringing noise. Others saw a tall figure of a woman walking toward a closet and glimpsed a man's face in a mirror. In 2008, the Wren's Nest staff captured audio of ghostly voices.

While there, drive on over to Jonesboro a few miles away and visit Margaret Mitchell Memorial Park. August 31 through September 1, 1864 Jonesboro was the site of the last battle before Atlanta fell to Sherman's firebugs. Nine historical markers in Jonesboro's Historic District help tell the story

Margaret Mitchell's great-grandfather, Philip Fitzgerald, lived in Jonesboro and it is commonly believed that Stately Oaks was the inspiration for Tara. It is an 1839 plantation home built by Whitmell Allen. It was located four miles north of Jonesboro, where Union soldiers camped on its grounds during the Battle of Jonesboro, until it was moved to its present location. It is now the headquarters of Historical Jonesboro/Clayton County Inc.

Past President and Historian Ted Key who doesn't normally believe in ghosts was quoted as saying, "many people in the plantation at night after closing have heard strange, heavy footsteps walk across the parlor and into the dining area but, when they came to investigate, no one was there."

He told a reporter for the local paper, Bill Baldowski, about some experiences he has had with the resident ghost. One night as he was leaving a board of directors meeting, he glanced up at the supposedly closed plantation house. He saw a "definite silhouette of a person that seemed to be looking out on the front lawn." Because the form was highlighted by a light located in the back of the plantation which shone through the dining room area, he couldn't see a face or details but was positive there was a person in the building. He rushed back to the meeting and got the key, and he and the members all searched inside but no one was there.

"Things have happened in this house that I simply can't explain," Key said.

He is not the only one to experience the paranormal here. Many others have heard the footsteps and some have caught a glimpse of a Confederate soldier

You may feel like you are living in GWTW in Jonesboro. Not only will you find Tara but, Ashley Wilkes plantation, Twelve Oaks, is believed to be based on the Crawford-Talmadge Plantation. General John Bell Hood's defeated army gathered there to regroup after the fall of Atlanta.

Warren House is another significant home of the period. This 1860 home was the most prominent landmark on the Jonesboro battlefield. First Confederate and then Union forces occupied it as their headquarters. It was a hospital and signatures of Union soldiers are carved in the walls of an upstairs room. Residents of the home have reported strange voices, noises and groans as if someone was in pain.

The Atlanta Ghost Hunters investigated Stately Oakes, Warren House and the Confederate Cemetery and found many unexplained phenomena. The strangest phenomena occurred at the Warren House. They heard a bouncing noise on the stairs that occurs at exactly 9:30 each night.

The Patrick R. Cleburne Cemetery is the final resting place of 600 to 1,000 unidentified Confederate soldiers killed during the Battle of Jonesboro. The unmarked headstones are laid out in the shape of the Confederate battle flag and there is a memorial in the center, and 12 cannon balls embedded in the entrance archway. The cemetery is located in downtown Jonesboro near the railroad tracks. Judging by the number of sightings of ghostly Confederate soldiers all over Jonesboro, many of the soldiers do not rest in peace. Perhaps they wish to be identified and their graves marked with their names.

On the second weekend in October, Jonesboro hosts its annual Fall Festival and Battle of Jonesboro Reenactment. I would pick that as being an extremely active time possibly second only to the actual battle dates.

Roswell, although a separate city, is part of the Atlanta metro area. When Roswell King, a surveyor from Darien, Georgia, first saw Vickery Creek in the 1830s he knew he had found a perfect home base. The creek was where he started his milling empire. Remnants of his mill remain today. You'll see an 1854 machine shop and a 1882 mill. The old dam and raceway are still there. There is a covered bridge leading across Vickery Creek. You can stroll along the creek and see markers telling about what was once there.

However in those days in the South, most building including this mill was done with enslaved laborers. A measles epidemic struck killing many of the workers. It is believed their spirits still roam this park after dark.

Bulloch Hall in Roswell has an interesting history that adds to its ghostly story. When Roswell King came with his family he invited a few friends, one of them, James Stephens Bulloch, partnered with the Kings in the cotton mill and factories. James Bulloch, wealthy before the move to Roswell, built Bulloch Hall in 1839 as a showplace of his wealth.

Its biggest story was the unlikely romance of a pretty southern belle and a young New York aristocrat. Martha "Middie" Bulloch was James' youngest daughter. She married Theodore "Thee" Roosevelt, Sr. on December 22, 1853. Few northerners attended the wedding perhaps foreseeing the coming war between North and South. Only the groom's parents, Cornelius Van Schaack "C.V.S." Roosevelt and his wife, Margaret, attended. Middie and Thee went to New York to live in a home gifted by Cornelius. It was there that their son, Theodore Roosevelt, was born.

Their second son, Elliot Bulloch Roosevelt, fathered Eleanor Roosevelt who became the wife of her cousin, our 32nd president, Franklin Roosevelt.

When the Civil War erupted, Middie's two brothers, Irvine and James, enlisted in Confederate forces. James was the Confederacy's highest-ranking secret-service agent in Great Britain and operated blockade runners. Thee paid a substitute to serve in the Union Army. Middie remained a staunch Confederate sympathizer throughout her life.

If James sounds a bit like the fictional Rhett Butler and Mittie like Scarlett, it may be no coincidence. Margaret Mitchell as a young reporter interviewed Mittie's good friend and last living bridesmaid,

Evelyn King Baker, then owner of Barrington Hall. Her story showed Mittie as a spirited girl who defied tradition.

When Mattie left to go north with Thee she left behind her life-long companion, the young slave Lavina.

Roswell Ghost Tours guide, Ben Glaizer, told about things that happen at the annual reenactment of Mittie's wedding. Candles often go out for no reason. Another thing that happens there is that people are often seen in the attic and the light is on when no one is there. There have been incidents where a rocking chair on Bulloch Hall's porch often rocks by itself. If a person sits in the chair people claim they feel someone staring right into their face. Some people have seen figures dressed in Civil War-era clothing in the second-floor windows when no living person is in the home.

Another story involves a teenage enslaved girl whose body was found in a well on the property. Whether she fell in accidentally or was murdered no one knows. Some say she likes to flicker the home's lights. Perhaps that disturbs Mittie's spirit who likes to read in the library at night.

Bulloch Hall has a reconstructed slave quarters dedicated to the role of African Americans in Roswell's history.

Another cemetery is very active. Oakland Cemetery founded in 1850, overlooks the city of Atlanta. It is the final resting place of many of Atlanta's most famous citizens like Bobby Jones, Margaret Mitchell, and Maynard Jackson. Its beautiful garden, sculpture and architecture draw visitors. But it has a darker story to tell if you are there at night. Visitors have heard a young woman calling out to her lover. People hear a voice calling a macabre roll call of the dead sol-diers buried in Oakland. The spooky thing is he gets answers.

This is the place where General John B. Hood stood helpless as General Sherman burned Atlanta and killed over 500 Confederates, wounding over 1,000 others. No suprise it has its share of haunting?

One tomb, called the Tomb of the Unknown is reputed to be the scene of most of the graveyard's ghostly activity. The cemetery offers tours in October.

When you enter the Fox Theater you feel as if you stepped into a scene from "Arabian Nights." The building was contracted in 1927 by the Yaarab Temple Order of Shriners. But after the stock market crash, they could not afford to pay the taxes, and it was foreclosed by the city. It bounced from owner to owner until 1974, when Southern Bell tried to buy it to tear down and construct a new headquarters. That desecration was prevented by a civic-minded group called Atlanta Landmarks Inc., which lobbied for the building's extensive restoration and placement on the National Register of Historic Places. Thanks to them, you can now view this treasure.

There may be something more in the building than its magnificent decor. People have reported seeing a Confederate Soldier there. Why a Confederate soldier when the Fox was not built until years after The War? Perhaps he died on the site the building was later erected.

The Fox had its own real Phantom. An elderly man named Joe Patten lived in the bowels of the theater until his death in 2016. The apartment which he was allowed to construct there reverted back to the theater. Joe knew the theater better than anyone else and watched over it like it was his own in life. Too soon to know but my bet is Joe's spirit is still there.

The Fox is not Atlanta's only theater with ghosts. Perhaps actors, who usually have quirky personalities which are more prone to the dramatic, encourage this epidemic. Who know? But everyone who had studied paranormal phenomena knows theaters are known hotspots for haunts.

Lakewood Amphitheatre, a few miles south of downtown, is the home of a musician's spirit. Supposedly the performer was shot onstage in 2002 and now haunts the seating area. You'll know if you encounter him by the cold hands around your neck.

For the most haunts, the New American Shakespeare Tavern takes the prize. They are filled with friendly shades from the past. According to Jeanette Meierhofer, former marketing manager, during a 1990s performance, actor Tony Brown who played Falstaff erupted from his dressing room and exclaimed that a boy dressed in Victorian-period costume appeared beside his dressing table.

Other actors have seen a female spirit and an old man. They are wearing 19th century garb. The actresses often find items misplaced or broken in their dressing rooms. Shadowy figures materialize at odd times on the catwalk above the tavern's stage. Voices are heard in empty corners of the theater and lights act up on their own.

Nightclubs that offer live concerts are just one step removed from a theater. Masquerade is such a place and true to form it has its own spirits. It was built in 1890 as the Excelsior Textile Mill. Working conditions were unsafe and many of the young female employees died in accidents. Many others died of tuberculosis brought on by the unhealthy working environment. Present day club customers have heard screams, footsteps and cold spots on the back stairs. Occasionally, the large amplifiers are turned over. Some people have seen the ghost of a tall man roaming around of the club.

One attraction in the Atlanta area literally towers over all others. Stone Mountain, the largest granite outcropping in the world with its Confederate heroes carved in giant scale, is riveting. It's eye-candy in the highest form. Jolie Varner, a local resident, says,. "It's beautiful. If you go up there and relax or see the sunset, it's so peaceful."

But things are not always peaceful on the mountain. Native Americans long respected the huge granite outcropping as a mystical healing place with supernatural powers.

The Antebellum Plantation at Stone Mountain Park has several places that are reputed to be haunted. At the Thornton House, a 1790s home of a well-to-do planter that has been moved to the site from Union Point , many people feel a presence at the top of the stairs, between the children's rooms. Sometimes it seems to follow visitors. Some have actually seen a young boy in his teens dressed in period clothing both in the house and staring at guests from an upstairs window. This is the oldest building in the complex.

At the Dickey House, a Tara-like Greek Revival mansion, several Confederate re-enactors have seen a woman in the top floor windows while camped on the grounds for a reenactment.

In the clapboard slave cabins people have reported feeling spirits. The park features "A Tour of Southern Ghosts," each fall where you wander the lantern-lit paths of the Antebellum Plantation grounds and can hear many interesting ghost stories. Beware, you may cross the line from make-believe to unreality and witness a real ghost here.

Of course there are many earthly delights at the park as well. The Crossroads section of the park is filled with shops and eateries. You can circle the park via its own train. The museum tells the history of this mystical mountain. You can ride The ducks, enjoy a performance at the Tall Tales of the South Theater, play golf or miniature golf or just lounge around a and watch a spectacular laser show. You can hike or take the SkyRide to the peak. From the top you can see all the way into downtown Atlanta and beyond. Doug Elrod, a SkyRide operator, sees the mountain as "one of the wonders of the world." He is right. This is one park that should not be missed.

Outside the park there are strange forces at work on the mountain. There is an old cemetery at the end of Main Street near the village of Stone Mountain. It predates the Civil War and is often filled with orbs at night. There are granite slabs between graves and people standing on these feel as if someone is pulling them off the stone.

Some mystics believe Stone Mountain is some sort of vortex which would explain the abundant phenomena there.

Six Flags over Georgia is different type of fun. It's bursting with life and excitement from March through October with all the typical theme park rides and attractions. Here too are some strange happenings. The ghost of an actor named Joe is known to hang around the balcony and backstage at the Crystal Pistol Music Hall. He is believed to be the spirit of a performer who died before going onstage. Maybe if he could ever perform on stage he would be able to move on. There is a legend of a little girl ghost who is seen near the entrance of the park. She will run away from you and when you try and follow, she disappears.

Of course there are lots of fun things to do in Atlanta not related to the paranormal. Atlanta's watery treasure, the Georgia Aquarium is located in the heart of downtown facing Centennial Olympic Park. Although when the Titanic Exhibit was there ghost hunters did find spirits. The park, an attraction in itself, acts as a plaza for not only the Aquarium but World of Coca-Cola, CNN Studio and Imagine It! Children's Museum of Atlanta.

With more 100,000 animals of 500 different species, Georgia Aquarium is the world's largest. Entered from the central atrium, the aquarium's five galleries, Georgia Explorer, River Scout, Ocean Voyager, Coldwater Quest and Tropical Diver, offer an in-depth look at different aquatic environments. The aquarium has the world's largest tank, holding more than 6 million gallons, making it almost as large as a football field.

This is the only aquarium in the United States that has whale sharks and a graceful manta ray. It's also home to two Beluga whales. Ms. Whalen explains how the whales arrived. "They were brought in to the loading dock just like apples or oranges. A gantry was then lowered and attached to a tarp to hold the whales and then raised and taken straight into the Ocean Voyager Exhibit."

Unfortunately there are no ghosts there unless you count the ghostly jelly fish or maybe a ghost crab.

Next door a different liquid is the main event. The new World of Coke-Cola is large enough to house 1,200 artifacts from around the world. It showcases the history of the country's favorite carbonated beverage."

One visitor, Donna Potter, remarked, "I never realized Coke has been a part of our history for so long."

A nostalgic tour of Coke-inspired pop-art and a 4-D movie combine to make this attraction fun for all ages. Everybody agrees the best part is the tasting. You can sample Coke products from all over the world.

Coke Ambassador, Joyce White states, "In 1956, the company raised the price of Coke-Cola from five cents to six cents. Everyone was outraged. Don't you wish you could still buy a coke for a nickel?"

At the other end of the park, CNN Studios offers an inside look into one of the world's busiest news studios. Bill McElhaney, CNN Tour director, explains, "People have no idea what goes on behinds the scene. The average reaction when they see the newsroom is a look of astonishment. Their eyes light up."

The Capital has been here for 130 year. Everything within is from Georgia. The entire fourth floor is a museum filled with artifacts of natural and cultural importance. The kids will gravitate to the two-headed cow and two-headed snake. Lady Freedom, who graces the top of the gold-plated dome, is a story all by herself. She is Georgia's version of the Statue of Liberty.

Zoo Atlanta's most unique display is its Panda exhibit. Not only will you find traditional pandas but the cutest red panda you'll ever see. The gorilla exhibit is something special but then all of the exhibits are awe-inspiring. Simone' Griffin, Zoo Atlanta's Public Relations Coordinator, describes it as, "Real live fun!"

The zoo is just one of several natural attractions in Atlanta. The Botanical Gardens is a treat for city-weary eyes. It's an island of floral beauty in a very polished urban area.

There is no telling what type of creature you may encounter in the Atlanta area.

Chapter 20 Gwinnett County,
Such a Spirited County

Gwinnett County was named for Button Gwinnett, one of Georgia's signers of the Declaration of Independence. Gwinnett never lived in the county and died before it was named in his honor. Located in the northeast part of Metro Atlanta, it has more ghost stories then any of its neighbor counties.

To tell these stories, The Lawrenceville GA Ghost Tours began in 2005. The town square which is built around its historic courthouse is filled with spirits. Cynthia Rintye, then Director of the Lawrenceville Georgia Ghost Tours, explained, "When I drop by the shops on the square to deliver brochures, again and again I am told about how their particular shop has activity; books flying off the shelves in the antique shop, a cold spot in the basement of the salon. There is a great deal of activity at a particular coffee house"

Cynthia was one of the original guides and has been director of the tour since 2008. She loves the stories and the charm of the area.

One of her favorite stories is about an unjustly executed slave whose spirit is still imprisoned. She reports the story thusly:

This story is about the historic jail. On an alley (called Calaboose Alley) just west of the courthouse square is this squat, nondescript building that people pass by every day. They do not realize that it is the historic jail, built in 1832. And on the Lawrenceville Ghost Tour, we go inside. Well, that is, if the ghost that resides there deems to let us in. But I'll get to that later.

The jail is built out of double blocks of solid granite that are doweled together for strength. It was actually used as a jail until 1940 - for over one hundred years! At some point, they added electricity, but they never added indoor plumbing.

The story that we tell in the jail comes from 1840 and it is about a slave by the name of Elleck. One day, Elleck's master comes after him in a fit of rage. Elleck tries to escape by going into his quarters. His master follows. Elleck scrambles up the little ladder to his sleeping loft but his master follows and draws his sword. Elleck tries to defend himself and his master ends up falling to the floor below. With his master dead at his feet, Elleck does not run; instead he goes to the sheriff and tells him that his master had been killed but that it was in self defense. Elleck is the only slave ever to be tried in Lawrenceville and the jury finds him guilty. He is sentenced to be hanged and brought back to the jail and locked into the cell on the right.

Not accepting this horrible miscarriage of justice, Elleck starts to chip his way though that granite wall. You can still see the large mark on the wall that shows the progress that he made. However, someone on the street hears a noise and alerts the sheriff. When the sheriff sees what Elleck has done to the jail, he is enraged. He chains Elleck to the floor by his wrists and ankles and leaves him there for three days. Elleck pleads to be allowed to sit in a more comfortable position, but his pleas are ignored. To pass the time Elleck sings to his beloved:

"Oh, Betsy will you meet me
Betsy will you meet me
Betsy will you meet me in heaven above"

On the fourth day, Elleck is taken from the jail to the gallows where he is hanged. But his spirit never has left the jail where he was so tightly bound for so long, and people still swear that they can hear him sing... "Betsy can you meet me in heaven above.

"Well, that's the story that has been handed down through the years. Now, I have never heard the ghost sing, but I have felt Elleck's presence in many ways, " Cynthia said.

Cynthia is not the only person who has felt Elleck's presence. In 2006, a team of paranormal investigators came to the jail and documented all sorts of activity. A picture taken in his cell revealed red orbs in an arc. One investigator felt an unseen presence touch her.

Cynthia's experiences exceed that. She tells of feeling the presence of something else when in that jail. She stated, "The feeling does not frighten me. Rather it makes me feel more alive."

She explained some of these experiences, "There were three guides that helped develop the tour in 2005. During this process each of us developed horrible insomnia. My insomnia broke the first night that we performed the tour.

"While the words of the song were handed down over the years, the melody had been lost, so it was up to us to create our own. I wanted mine to sound low and mournful; similar to the song sung in *Oh, Brother Where Art* Thou in the scene with the three gravediggers where George Clooney is just about to be hanged. But once I created this song, I could not get it out of my mind. Over and over and over, I kept hearing it, hour after hour, day after day after day. It would not go away for the longest time."

She explained her feelings while singing the song.

"When I have a tour group inside of the jail and am singing this song, there are times that I really feel filled by the presence of some-one else. If I get this light-headed feeling while I'm singing, I know that I've connected with the paranormal. One tour, I felt it strongly and after the song was done, I could tell that one lady felt it too. It disturbed her so much that she had to walk into the open doorway so she would no longer feel surrounded by the presence.

"Now, one October I told this story seventeen times. Seventeen times! It's hard to do the tour over and over and make sure that you are keeping it fresh. One time in the jail, I was singing and heard my voice sounding not deep and full as it usually does. Well, all of the sudden, I hear my voice deepen. I could feel that it came not from within me but from outside of me."

Even entering the old jail can be an experience. "Let's talk about getting into the jail," Cynthia said. "The door is metal and has this amazing key, like nothing you've ever seen before. And most of the time, it works easily. But there are times that the guides cannot open the door. All of the guides will talk about struggling and struggling and finally giving up but on the very next tour, the key turns with ease.

"One time I went to the jail before my tour to change the batteries in flashlight that we keep in there. I could not get the key to turn. I struggled and struggled and struggled for a good three minutes. Finally, I pleaded out loud, 'Please let me in!' I tried the key one more time and it turned with no problem."

Sometimes strange things happen to the guests on a tour. On one tour a group had two little dogs. "Now, according to our website, dogs are not allowed, but it was a small tour that night and the dogs were small enough to pick up if there was a problem," she said. "I wondered how they would react to the jail, but did not say anything to their owner. Once inside, they started growling (for the first time that night) and had to be taken outside."

The jail is not the only place you will find phantoms. One particularly busy weekend in October 2008, she was giving a tour. She recalled, "Now, on weekends in October, we may have seven tours using three different guides going out of an evening, so it is essential to keep on schedule. Well, this night, early in the tour, when I'm talking about the historic cemetery (which Patrick Burns of Ghost Hounds calls the 'most active' cemetery he has ever seen) the word 'jail' pops out of my mouth instead of 'cemetery'. A couple of stories later, it happened again; I mean to say one word, but instead the word 'jail' comes out of my mouth."

So, I'm thinking, "What's going to happen in the jail tonight?"

"At the half-way point of the tour (where Larry Flynt of Hustler was paralyzed), I look at my watch and am delighted that I am running five minutes ahead of schedule. I am never ahead of schedule; I am always fighting time. But that night, for the first time, I was running ahead.

"Next, we cross Crogan Street and head down Calaboose Alley to the jail. While we are in the jail we hear all sorts of sirens screaming very close to us. I make a joke that when the bombing begins that the jail is where we want to be because it will be the last thing in town left standing. I finish Elleck's story and the other story we tell in the jail. Now, I'm a little disappointed because nothing out of ordinary happens in the jail. But when I head back to Crogan Street, I first see a police car then another police car then a fire truck and an ambulance. Then I see the horrible accident that had taken place. A truck had plowed into a car so hard that the car was on its side. Had I been on schedule instead of running five minutes early, I would have been right at that intersection at the moment that that accident happened."

Cynthia remembered one other strange night, "I'm in the jail one night and have a large group of about 25. Now, there is one small cell that has an open door and two large cells that we see through the bars of the closed cell doors. Since it is pretty crowded, I stand in the little recessed area in front of one of the cell doors. As I'm telling, I do something that I have never done before; I casually place the palm of my left hand against one of those granite blocks of the cell wall. Suddenly, I am filled with almost unbearable sorrow. I struggle to keep my hand there for the duration of the story. When I take my hand off that wall, the feeling of being filled with sorrow stops as suddenly as it began."

The Courthouse has quite a history. The first courthouse, a simple log structure, was built in 1820 by Isham Williams elsewhere on land he owned. Then another log courthouse was constructed on Elisha Winn's land. The Elisha Winn House is preserved as a museum)

Then in 1824, that courthouse was replaced by a brick structure. After the war, members of the Ku Klux Klan burned down the courthouse on Sept. 10, 1871 in the hopes of destroying evidence of their crimes. Apparently the damaging paperwork was not in the courthouse and thus was saved. Hopefully, the Klan members were convicted of both bootlegging and arson.

The courthouse which replaced the burned one was completed in 1872 but had very poor construction and was torn down in 1884. Today's two-story courthouse was built in 1885 at a cost of the vast amount of $23,083. It is listed on the National Register of Historic Places. It was used as a courthouse until 1988 when the new Gwinnett Justice Center was completed. It now houses the Gwinnett Historical Society.

Another place that is filled with the dead, literally, is the historic cemetery right in the middle of Lawrenceville. Its wrought iron fence lends it a very peaceful air but its inhabitants include one Revolutionary war veteran named Nathan Spence who died in 1833 and many from the Civil War. It has a section where local slaves were buried. It's also the final resting place of Gwinnett County founders, William Maltbie and Elisha Winn and Lawrenceville's first mayor, John Clay Smith. Earliest burials date from the mid 1700s.

One of the most common specters seen here is a woman in white. She is seen walking along the center row of the cemetery between the trees.

Patrick Burns, Founder and Director of Ghost Hounds, visited the cemetery one night to check out some audio recording equipment. He asked if anyone was there to show themselves. Next thing he knew he was watching a woman in a white dress walking inside the cemetery gates. This was not too unusual in itself but the fact that she just walked back and forth was eerie. What cinched the sighting as supernatural was when the lady just disappeared.

Historic Ghost Watch and Investigation, based in Atlanta, investigated this cemetery also. Although they did not see the woman in white they did pick up a lot of paranormal activity. Some cameras would not work properly, EMF meters recorded evidence of a presence and one EVP was captured. One investigator heard footsteps in the same area where their psychic felt a "motherly" feeling.

The cemetery has had some very strange happenings. An article from the April 30, 1924 News Herald, Lawrenceville's local newspaper at that time, reported on the effects of a twister that tore through the area, "two skeletons were raised above the level of the ground and stood almost upright when uprooted by the storm."

Among more earthy strangeness, Gwinnett County is in the running for the weirdest. Take the 2005 case of the "Runaway Bride." Jennifer Wilbanks and John Mason were supposed to be married on April 30, 2005. Four days before the wedding Jennifer went missing from her Duluth, Georgia home and was the focus of a nationwide search. When she surfaced, a little bedraggled, three days later in Albuquerque, New Mexico her story was front page news and filled every TV news hour. Her claim was that she had been grabbed by a scruffy Hispanic man with bad teeth and his blond girlfriend and sexually assaulted and driven to New Mexico. It didn't take long for Gwinnett County police to pick a lot of holes in her strange story.

The media that had filled pages of print and hours of air time were left with only a 'fleeancée' with cold feet instead of a sensational crime story. Initially Jennifer was charged with a felony but this was watered down to a lesser charge which she satisfied with community service and probation. Apparently she no longer satisfied her former fiancé and he married another woman.

One local businessman, David Ryan, who owns Pappy's Peppers on the Lawrenceville Square, has began distributing a private label pepper sauce called Jennifer's Hightailin' Hot Sauce. It's a case of cold feet promoting many cases of hot stuff. And, oh yes, Pappy's Peppers also has its own resident haunt. It takes pleasure in moving a paint can when no one is there.

I guess like when they were living beings, spirits each have different tastes.

Lawrenceville has some real eccentrics in its phantom population.

Chapter 21 Coweta County, More than Murder

Perhaps the first thing that comes to mind when you mention Coweta County is *The Murder in Coweta County*. It's been the subject of a book and movie starring Johnny Cash as Sheriff Lamar Potts, June Carter Cash as Mayhayley, the Oracle, and Andy Griffith as John Wallace. If you hadn't heard that story, it's the classic tale of a rich man who thinks money earns the right to get away with murder. Add in one bought-and-paid-for sheriff in neighboring Heard County, one sharecropper who defies his wealthy landlord, one honest sheriff of Coweta County where the murder was actually committed and one self-styled "Oracle of the Ages" who "sees" where the body is buried and doesn't mind making a few bucks informing on her wealthy "friend."

The first I heard of this Oracle of the Ages was from Josh Fisher, Director of Operation at Dunaway Gardens and son of its resurrector, Jennifer Bigham. When I asked him about any ghost stories connected with the Gardens, he replied, "We don't like to play up that aspect."

He did admit that the ghost hunter groups have been there because part of the gardens sit atop a large granite outcropping, an extension of the bedrock that creates nearby Stone Mountain, long considered by Native Americans as s sacred healing place. The gardens are so relaxing it is easy to understand that this may be sacred ground.

The original gardens grew out of a timeless love story. Hetty Jane Dunaway was one of the East Coast's finest actresses during live theater's golden years of the "Roaring Twenties." She fell in love with and married prominent Atlanta booking agent, Wayne Sewell. When Wayne moved his base from Atlanta to his family's ancestral plantation in Coweta County, Hetty was daunted by the prospect of living in the middle of nowhere. He promised her she could make the home and grounds into a theatrical center. Hetty went about it with a vengeance. She transformed the acres into a garden filled with springs, pools, rock outcroppings and an outdoor amphitheater. She built Honeymoon House for lodging and the Blue Bonnet Tea Room for dining.

Celebrities and soon-to-be-celebrities were drawn to the beauty of the picturesque gardens. Walt and Roy Disney enjoyed many a meal at the Tea Room. Sarah Ophelia Colley, better known by her stage name, Minnie Pearl, fresh from graduation at Ward-Belmont College, began her career there as head instructor at the drama school. Tallulah Bankhead visited often.

After Hetty's death in 1961, the gardens deteriorated. The Tea Room was the victim of arson. The rock walls crumbled. The sun-loving plants were overshadowed by large shade trees. Kudzu enveloped the site. It appeared beyond restoration.

Then a modern-day Hetty appeared in the person of Jennifer Bigham. She saw potential hidden beneath the ruin. But Josh pointed out even Jennifer didn't see the whole picture. She wanted it as a family getaway. Then she, her family and 20 workers began the slow restoration, some days covering only feet of excavation. They would probe the earth with metal rods and determine by the sound what lay beneath the ground. As the rock outcropping, stone walls and walks, the original amphitheater and the huge hollowed rock swimming pool emerged, she realized this was too big for just one family to cherish. Hetty's dream had to be shared with the world.

Today, Dunaway Gardens is temporarily closed but will be reopening soon. ena Clark and her business partner, Lynn Eden, purchased the property in 2021 and plan to return Dunaway Gardens to its original purpose, adding a restaurant, theater and spa and expect to reopen in late 2024. They plan to add sound stages and a recording studio nearby to accommodate filming in the county. They will also have a spa and event center they want to focus on the beautiful outdoors. Through all the construction, Hetty is still watching over her dream, she is a happy spirit.

One of the celebrities who visited the Gardens in its heyday was a strange physic who called herself the Oracle of the Ages. Amanda Mayhayley Lancaster had been born "under a veil," at birth, her face was covered with a thin membrane. Old legends claim any child born thusly will have the gift of "second sight" or clairvoyance as we refer to it today. This gift made Mayhayley a wealthy woman if not a happy one. She never married and dressed flamboyantly often wearing a man's World War 1 hat and an army coat. She was missing her left eye and sometimes inserted a red marble in the empty socket. Still seekers flocked to her with unanswered questions.

At one point she was at Dunaway Gardens telling fortunes. Wayne was not happy with this strange looking psychic hanging around and he asked her to leave. She offered to tell his fortune first. Predicting an automobile accident where he would break his arm driving to his old barn.

When things came to pass as Mayhayley predicted, Wayne invited her back to tell fortunes at the Gardens.

This self-proclaimed Oracle of the Ages proved her gift in the famed murder trial when she was able to tell Sheriff Lamar Potts where to look for the body of the sharecropper murdered by wealthy John Wallace. Apparently Wallace had been visiting her for years and considered her a friend. He did not know she often worked as a police informant.

There is no indication that Mayhayley still roams the Gardens but her burial place in neighboring Heard County is rumored to be active. People still visit her grave seeking advice. They often leave money, usually a dollar and ten cents. In life, she charged that for her services. She always said, "A dollar for me and ten cents for my dogs."

Dunaway Gardens has another link with the world of the paranormal. This one not so benign. Cedar Creek flows along the garden boundary. Just down Roscoe Road is a bridge. In the 1930s, the original bridge was the scene of an accident that took the life of a woman and her child. People visiting the bridge at night have seen a apparition of a misty female shape, experienced sudden cold spots and hear her screaming. The bridge is called "Screaming Bridge.

Elizabeth Beers, operator of Tours with Elizabeth, tells of another country road with phantoms. "This happened when my husband and I were courting. We were driving into town on a county road and saw a man who was standing in the road. As one we both turned to look then he passed through the car and we felt a cold chill. He just dissolved. I saw him wearing overalls while my fiancé saw him as looking like Christ."

When I asked her for the name of the road, she replied, "Mount Carmel Road."

What makes that particularly interesting is that Chattahoochee Bend State Park, on that same road, is haunted by spirits of Native Americans. People have heard native drums and sounds of voices crying in the night. Could it have been one of these spirits they saw?

Elizabeth is also on the board of the Newnan-Coweta Historical Society. Their showplace museum is The Male Academy. She tells of an interesting trunk the society acquired. "A lady called to ask if we wanted a trunk that has a little girl spirit attached to it. Of course, we said yes and I went with a friend who had a station wagon to pick the trunk up. When we arrived, the lady told us the little girl had been waiting all afternoon. We loaded the trunk in the station wagon. We could feel her presence but as we drove to the museum she gradually faded away"

The Male Academy originally was a private boys' school in the 1880s. It became obsolete in 1888 with the advent of the public school system. Today, it is filled with artifacts related to Newnan's history from pioneers like the Smiths who traveled from Virginia to settle here, to the Civil War, and an Alan Jackson Room depicting highlights in the life of Newnan's most famous singer.

Music is always important in Georgia. The three-story Reese Opera House, later housing the Bank of Coweta on the ground floor facing the town square, opened in January 1883. Although it was called an "opera house," few musical troupes made it to what was then the frontier. More often the featured acts were touring lecturers, local pageants, psychics and magicians and dancing bears. For the Reese Opera House grand opening, "the world's greatest comedian," John Thompson, who would perform his glorious comedy, *Around the World,* described as "A Roar of Laughter in Three Acts."

It seems that Thompson did not perform on Jan. 5. Perhaps he was chased off too many other stages with overripe tomatoes and decided to take acting lessons instead.

Twenty-two years earlier, no one was laughing or planning any pleasure trips. The War Between the States had broken out and Georgia was soon engulfed by guns and fire. By the summer of 1864, Sherman's troops were laying waste to a large swath of Georgia. Sherman sent out General Stoneman and Brigadier General Edward McCook to the south to disrupt railway travel and food supplies.

McCook met Fighting Joe Wheeler's cavalry near Browns Mill. McCook believing himself surrounded by Confederates was forced to retreat leaving behind his wounded and dead.

Even before the Battle of Brown's Mill, Newnan had so many hospitals set up it was called "The Hospital City." The Atlanta & West Point Railroad was used to transport the wounded into Newnan for treatment. There was even a brief skirmish at the depot. The fact that both Union and Confederate wounded were treated at these hospitals may account for Newnan being spared the fate of so many Georgia towns, the torch. Without a doubt may of these restless spirits still roam Newnan.

Both Confederate and Federal dead were originally buried in Newnan's Oak Hill Cemetery. Later the Yankees were removed and reinterred in Marietta National Cemetery. Oak Hill Cemetery is worth a visit because of its historic value. The cemetery dates back to with the earliest marked graves being 1840. Two Georgia governors, two Revolutionary War soldiers, and 269 Confederate soldiers lie within its confines.

The most renowned grave is for William Thomas Overby, a member of Mosby's Rangers. Overby was captured and hanged because he refused to divulge the location of his unit. Overby was originally buried in Virginia but in 1997 he was reinterred at Oak Hill Cemetery. This second funeral was a spectacular occasion. His body was transported to Oak Hill via a horse-drawn caisson in authentic Confederate style. A procession wended its way from the courthouse to the cemetery.

At the gravesite, former Georgia Gov. Lester Maddox spoke. About 300 people took part in the ceremony. Another gravesite you may want to visit is that of Sheriff Lamar Potts. He and his wife are buried here with small plain stones to mark the graves. He was a simple unassuming man in life and his burial place reflects that.

One of the most unique interments was of John Keith's arm. He lost it in a sawmill accident. After his death, his body was buried in the same lot beneath a marker with an engraved arm. Elizabeth Beers, an expert on Newnan history, has developed a cemetery walk that will interest any history-minded visitor.

One of the homes possibly used as a hospital was the St. John-Banks House. Built two years before the war, it was the home of a merchant family, the Davises. It passed down through the years and various remodeling and emerged as Something Special. Literally. It was owned by Mike Meyers who reopened the home as Something Special Events Center in 1997. Later, it passed on to Ashley Keeley who continues offering special event services while preserving a piece of the local history. It's now Something Special at Lillian Gardens. While the exterior property has retained its southern antebellum charm, the interior has been renovated to reflect modern Victorian elegance.

Mike was an easygoing guy with a long history in the hospitality field so this is a natural fit for him. He is also a master gardener and justly proud of his gardens and home, as well he should be. His restoration of the home and servants quarters won him the Restoration Award from Newnan-Coweta Historical Society in 2005. Then in 2006, Something Special was named Best Events Facility for the southern arch by *Lifestyle magazine*.

There is one other thing special about this magnificent old home. It has an abundance of ghostly inhabitants. Mike said he "doesn't believe in that sort of thing but..."

Soon after he moved in things started to happen. Strange things. Things like what happened to a sheetrock installer, Buford, that drove him to tell Mike he refused to work in the old house alone. Buford experienced a cold breath on the back of his neck and the feeling of being watched first in the birthing room and, then after the phenomena made him unwilling to work there, in the dressing room across the hall. When Mike got back, an excited Buford informed him, "You've got haints up there. That's right haints up there."

You notice I mentioned a "birthing room?" Not the usual thing in houses of any era. The reason for it is that the daughter of the second owners, Virginia Banks, married Doctor St. John. The good doctor would deliver babies in a special room right at the top of the stairs. This room seems to be one of the psychic hotspots in the house.

Another thing that gave Mike a hint of these unearthly inhabitants was his early efforts at decorating. He explained, "When you first buy a big old house a lot of time you don't have the right accessories to decorate with. I went to Wal-Mart and bought some plastic faux stained glass to hang in the side windows and some cheap plastic framed mirrors and inexpensive pictures to hang on the walls. Well, they kept on falling off the walls and out of the windows. I figured the spirits didn't like my Wal-Mart taste in decorating. But funny thing, once the City passed the truck ordinance prohibiting logging trucks from going up and down Greenville St., things stopped falling off the walls."

Mike told me his overnight guests heard footsteps going up the attic stairs around 11:00 to 11:30 at night. He admitted, "I never hear anything and if I do, I just roll over and figure there must be squirrels in the attic again. When you live in a big old house by yourself, your mind has a way of working things out. Denial is a wonderful thing."

Several years ago the activities at Something Special alerted the Georgia Ghost Society that something was going on outside the norm. Mike recalls, "They set up motion detectors, sound and video equipment, took pictures and stayed for about three or four hours. It was very entertaining to hear the motion detector go off when ever anything alive or dead went up the attic stairs. They got pictures with orbs in the parlor and in my bedroom. Children's faces looking out the windows of the servant quarters out back."

Even more informative was the information from the group's physic. She said that there had been a multiple birth upstairs in the birthing room and the babies didn't survive. She could still hear them crying. She told Mike that the 3rd floor was a portal for the spirits to pass through from one world to another. She said that someone likes to sit up there in the dormer overlooking the back-yard. Mike wonders, "Could that be the sounds my guest hear going up the stairs?"

I bet the spirits still visit the new owners?

It's not just antebellum homes that have spirits. The Casa Bella Bed and Breakfast was built around 1911 for Dan and Carrie Dent Manget, one of the owners of the Manget Brothers Cotton Exchange and Manget Brannon grocery chain. Today it is owned by Ron and Patty Gironda.

Patty has experienced some strange phenomena. She first was contacted by an apparition of a woman who appeared at her window in Florida while still unable to sell that house. Then when they were in Atlanta, the same woman came to her in a dream. She asked Patty to open the window and let her and her friends in. A group seemed to enter the room then. The woman told her "Get up let's dance." Which she took to mean things were worth celebrating.

Next morning when Patty woke up, the formerly closed bedroom window was now open. Sure enough, two days later, the Florida house sold leaving Patty and her husband free to move on.

In the new home, Patty began to miss her spirits especially the one she called "her lady." then in a dream, she saw the woman again. She told Patty, "We are with you. We are in the walls."

The first signs that the spirits had truly followed Patty were that she started seeing a spirit cat. He would walk across a bed and you could see the indents of paw prints. She began seeing a man appearing and disappearing upstairs. Other guests began reporting seeing the man and the cat. Some guests felt it was a dog but Patty is sure it was a cat.

The house originally had some tragedies happen over the years but gradually as the spirits roamed the beautifully restored mansion, guests began to remark on the peaceful, serene feeling they experience at Casa Bella. Whether or not you experience a visit from one of the inn's spirits, you know you will be coddled and pampered. And fed oh so well. Did I mention Patty also hosts a local weekly cooking show on cable television called *Home At Last!*?

It wasn't only white families in Newnan that occupied homes where their spirits would remain. The Caswell House which is now the headquarters and slave museum for the African American Alliance of Coweta County may still shelter some of the original residents, Ruby Caswell and her brother Hoyt.

The house was moved from its original location on East Broad Street a few years ago and sits next to an old slave cemetery. The cemetery is believed to be filled with orbs. Some may not be benevolent. Rumors abounded of demonic ceremonies that once took place in the old shotgun house and adjourning burial grounds in the 1980s.

However, Aunt Ruby, as Mrs. Caswell was called, is a protective spirit and she fights to cleanse the house of any remnants of evil. She is proud of the home's new use as a museum. In life, she loved kids and now it is not unusual for families with children to find them playing with a person they will tell you is Aunt Ruby. The museum, which is one of the few in Georgia, provides exhibits on African-American history, genealogies, and architecture. It provides help to families seeking to trace their roots.

Ever get tired of living in the 21st century? Want to go back to another era. Visit Senoia on the south-eastern end of Coweta County. The town was established by settlers from South Carolina who wanted to establish an agricultural Utopia. The town of Senoia was founded in 1860. The most interesting thing about the area is that the original settlers for the most part remained on the settled lands and determined to preserve their settlement as it was in the beginning. Naturally, some newer homes and businesses crept in but for the most part Senoia is just as it was around the turn of the 20th century. Most of the downtown section was and is owned by descendants of the original families. For this reason it is a prime area for period movies. *Fried Green Tomatoes, Driving Miss Daisy, The War, Andersonville*, and others have been filmed there.

Scott Tigchelaar, former president of River Wood Studio, bought into the town's drive to maintain its roots because it is much easier to shoot a movie there. Scott explained, "If we need a scene in the 1800s we cover the street with red clay. If we want a more turn-of-the-century look, we use the street as it is. Nothing there is out of place for the times. We wanted to preserve the quaintness of Senoia."

Scott feels people are tired of plastic businesses and want more individuality in shops and businesses. As he phrases it, "We're 25 miles and 100 years from Atlanta."

Southern Living agrees with him. So much so that they built one of their "Idea House" in Senoia. Kristen Payne, director Southern Living Homes Group when the home was built, at a gathering at Maguire's Irish Pub in Senoia said. "With the growing attention on small town life and family-oriented, walkable communities, we set our sights on finding a historic town under revitalization. This town is blending the best of today with the nostalgia of yesterday. It's why we chose this location to tell our story with this year's Idea House."

Browsing the downtown shops is a real treat. It is such an eclectic blend of historical architecture and fun shopping. It's possible you may run into some old haunts that the shops have collected over the last century. The building housing Cydney's Alley, a shop filled with interesting "junktiques" is 111 years old and was a doctor's office at one point in its long history.

Liz Barnett, the shop owner, told me of an interesting experience. "I had a man come in one day and tell me his baby sister was buried outside on the corner of the property. He said his mother had some sort of trouble and the doctor delivered the baby, it died and the doctor buried the little body there. He also showed me where the top of his finger had been chopped off and the doctor had sewed it up without pain meds."

Maybe that is the reason Liz had strange things happen in her shop. She told me that often the radio will be off when she leaves but when she opens in the morning, it will be blasting away. Usually on a different station. Well, we all know how children love to twist dials!

She said, several of the other shops had had unexplained pneumonia happen in their shops as well. Kristie, who owns You're Invited next door, has had things jump off the wall especially when she is talking about the ghost. Pat, who owns Steel Magnolias, feels her place is haunted as well

The old Buggy Shop Museum is a great place to soak up the town's history. And look for spirits. Mrs. Bagerly who owns it has had some "ghost busters" come in and investigate. They determined it was a little girl ghost

Thought we finished the GWTW links in Atlanta? No way. A Senoia bed and breakfast, The Veranda, played host to Margaret Mitchell while she was researching GWTW. At that time, Confederate soldiers held their yearly reunions at The Veranda so it was a natural place for her to glean some insight by speaking to actual participants in the war she wrote about so eloquently.

This 1906 Greek Revival mansion was originally the Holberg Hotel. Some of the other celebrities who stayed under its gracious roof are Elijah Wood, Kathy Bates, Jessica Tandy, Newt Gingrich and another politician, William Jennings Bryan (of the Scopes Trial fame) who stayed here in 1908 while running for President. If it looks familial to you it may be because *Broken Bridges* starring Burt

Reynolds, Toby Keith, Willie Nelson, Kelly Preston and a host of other stars was filmed at The Veranda in 2006.

The Veranda, owned by Rick and Laura Reynolds, was named 1990 Inn of the Year on Pamela Lanier's Inn of the Year Honor Roll. The Veranda was named one of the ten top places to stay in Georgia in the Better Homes and Gardens Magazine's April, 2013, and has received the Certificate of Excellence from Trip Advisor for several years in a row. Try it out for yourself. You won't be disappointed.

There are several legends as to how Senoia got its name. The most credible is that it was named for Senoya, the mother of Chief William McIntosh, the Creek chief who signed Treaty of Indian Springs giving the white man rights to this part of Georgia. Most of the Creeks did not approve of the treaty but McIntosh felt that if they did not sign, the land would be taken anyway. He paid with his life for that signing much like Major Ridge did with the Cherokees.

Angry Creek warriors led by a brave named Menewa, attacked McIntosh at his plantation in Carroll County, Georgia, killed and scalped him and burned the plantation to the ground.

There is a legend that McIntosh buried the gold he received for signing the treaty but it has never been found. Perhaps you could be the one to unearth the buried Indian gold.

By the way, if you want to pass for a local in Senoia, drop the "A." Only tourists say Seh-noy-yuh," Of course, due to southern good manners, no one will say anything, but everyone will know you are not a "local."

Chapter 22

Troup County, Over Hills and Dales

Troup County is best known for two things; beautiful LaGrange College and the serene waters of West Point Lake. West Point Lake is unique in that in 1975, West Point Dam and Lake were developed for flood control, hydroelectric power, fish and wildlife development, and recreational use. Recreation was not an afterthought here. There are 26,000 aquatic acres just waiting for your boat, jet sky, kayak or whatever other type of water fun you have in mind.

For the fisherman, it's heaven. The lake is considered one of the best largemouth bass lakes in the country, partly due to species of hybrid bass found there that often weigh in at the 10-pound range. There are hundreds of miles of shoreline for camping, picnicking and wildlife watching. You will find osprey, bald eagles, deer, bobcats, deer, dove, quail, turkey, wood ducks and dozens of species of songbirds. When we were there we spotted a huge osprey nest with babies and both parents in attendance. It's not unusual to find eagles soaring above the lake.

There are guide services to take you fishing or out in pontoon boats to explore the lake. In fact the only thing missing is a resident ghost.

LaGrange College makes up for that lack with one of the sweetest ghost stories ever. It's the oldest college in the state charted for the higher education of women and its ghost story revolves partly around its oldest building, Smith Hall, constructed in 1860. It's a beautiful building of handmade brick formed from native clay and is on the National Register of Historic Places. Today it houses offices, classrooms and seminar rooms but it has seen its share of tragic events.

The college was chartered on Dec. 26, 1831 as LaGrange Female Academy. It was a peaceful setting where many beautiful southern young ladies were educated. Then came the war that stole the peace from so many Georgia places–and people.

Well before Sherman and other generals advanced across Georgia, homes, businesses and college halls became makeshift hospitals to treat the wounded Confederates who were everywhere staining Georgia's red clay an even darker red. Since September of 1863, Smith Hall was the building at LaGrange College devoted to caring for the wounded boys in gray. Many of the students had returned to their homes and the few who remained enrolled at the college must have been horror stricken as the nearby Battle of Brown's Mill filled the hospitals first in Newnan and then overflowed to LaGrange. One young student in particular knew her brother was fighting nearby and must have confined in her friends how afraid she was for him.

When the young lieutenant felt the ball penetrate his flesh, he knew he wanted to head for LaGrange instead of the closer Newnan. There were better doctors in LaGrange and his sister was a student in the college and would surely nurse him better than a stranger. Yet, when he stumbled from his horse at LaGrange College, it was not his sister he first saw. A beautiful young lady with soulful eyes helped him into Smith Hall and staunched the bleeding wound. He fell deeply in love for the first time in his life.

After the bullet was removed from his shoulder, the young lieutenant's wound did not heal as rapidly as he hoped. At first he worried that his lovely Lorena would abandon him but she came to visit him faithfully. She must have been heartbroken as she watched her brave soldier worsen and gradually die.

Even in death, the lieutenant still seeks his first and only love. Students at Smith Hall have reported feeling a presence and seeing the form of a Confederate soldier softly calling "Lorena. Lorena."

His lady love would most likely have been staying at Bellevue Plantation while Smith Hall was being used for a hospital. The Hill family graciously offered its hospitality to the out-of-town ladies attending the colleges in town.

Today, the beautifully restored Greek Revival mansion built in the 1850s for Benjamin Harvey Hill. The Confederate president visited Bellevue often, since Hill, a senator for the United States and the Confederacy, was one of Jefferson Davis's best friends. The home is open for tours.

It is a classic example of the most graceful style of antebellum home designed for entertainment and gracious living. It was once the centerpiece of a 400 acre plantation reached via a driveway of flowering crepe myrtle and flanked by four large magnolia trees.

As many of the stately old Southern homes, there are things happening there that defies scientific explanation. When one walks up or down the stairs, one occasionally smells a faint fragrance that doesn't emanate in the present, as if some ghostly lady's perfume was lingering in the air. The other is that the small steps used to get onto the high bed in the "groom's room" upstairs, are often found relocated from where they were left.

The floors are of course very sound, they have steel reinforcement beams put in during one renovation, so the fact that these steps move is unexplained. Unexplained perhaps? But when one considers the tragedies this mansion witnessed as the most devastating war America had ever undergone tore apart hearts and homes across Georgia, it becomes understandable.

Another ghost legend relates to a pair of lovers. The clock tower in LaGrange is famous as a replica of the Campanile of St. Mark's Square in Venice, Italy. Legend says it is visited by a headless woman's ghost and her young lover. They are believed to appear after dark on moonless nights. Wonder if it could be the same ghosts?

Like many southern cities, LaGrange was left almost defenseless when all of her able-bodied men went off to fight for the Confederacy. LaGrange was one that did something unusual about that situation. Carol Cain of the LaGrange Historical Society in character as Nancy Morgan explained. "We woman were left here defenseless. So Mary Heard and I got together and decided to do something about it."

What Morgan and Heard did was organize a company of women volunteers called the Nancy Harts after the famous Georgia heroine who killed and captured British invaders in the Revolution. Never mind that this was unheard of in that era. Forty ladies answered the call and drilled and practiced their marksmanship diligently. The guns that were left in the city were old muskets and flintlocks so decrepit that a comment was made as to "whether the muzzle or the breech was more dangerous."

The war was actually over several days before the Nancy Harts saw action. A troop of Wilson's Raiders led by Colonel Oscar H. LaGrange, whose name was not connected to the city name, marched towards the town with the intent of destroying rail lines. The colonel, who had several confederate prisoners along, was confounded when his approach to what he deemed to be "defenseless" LaGrange was blocked by 40 women brandishing guns and prepared to fight for their city. LaGrange, being a gentleman promised that if the group would disarm, no homes or peaceful citizens would be harmed.

The grateful ladies invited LaGrange to dinner and he allowed the local prisoners to visit their families. True to his work, no homes were harmed. Doing better than many male units, the Nancy Harts had prevailed in their only confrontation, without firing a single shot.

LaGrange's history goes back to the Revolutionary war but one location in town will take you farther back. Explorations in Antiquity Center, a unique attraction about anthropological finds in the Holy Land, has guides dressed in biblical costumes to explain life in that time frame. You can enjoy a "Biblical Meal" served in a realistic setting. Be prepared, you eat as people then did with no silverware. It was a lot of fun and really delicious.

One of the most graceful homes and gardens you can visit in LaGrange is Hills and Dales, the former residence of Fuller Earle Callaway Sr., the textile magnate, and his wife, Ida, and later his son Fuller Callaway Jr's. and his wife Alice. He built the grand Italian villa in the midst of Ferrell Gardens, a formal boxwood garden that dates back to 1832.

The garden was nurtured by Sarah Coleman Ferrell. Mrs. Ferrell welcomed local children into her gardens and many children of the time had fond memories of that tranquil setting. One youngster who remembered playing there was in a position to preserve the setting when Mrs. Ferrell died in 1903. Fuller Callaway bought the entire property and built his mansion on the site of Mrs. Ferrell's former home. Since then two generations of the Callaway wives have continued Sarah Ferrell's masterpiece. They have done a magnificent job. Today, the formal boxwood garden is among the best preserved 19th century gardens in the Southeastern United States.

While you are on the square, there is an interesting custom regarding the famous Lafayette stature and fountain there. During the Revolution, he remarked that the local countryside reminded him of his home, LaGrange. The stature is a replica of the Lafayette statue in LePuy, France.

The story is told that when he left to fight in the Creek Indian War of 1836, Col. Julius C. Alford tossed a coin into a well near the courthouse in downtown LaGrange, made a wish and commented, "Here you go, Lafayette." All of his men and their sweethearts and wives did likewise.

They believed that the more coins that were tossed into the well on the square, the better a chance of their wish coming true. Alford had learned of this French custom from the Marquis de Lafayette, hence the phrase, "Here you go, Lafayette."

After the courthouse burned in 1936, a fountain was erected and later the statue of Lafayette was added to the fountain, the phrase that Alford coined, "Here you go, Lafayette," took on a different meaning.

The idea is that a person will take a coin and stand back-to-back with the statue of Lafayette in the downtown fountain, toss it over his shoulder and make a wish. Then a second coin is tossed by the visitor standing face-to-face with the statue. One wish that will come true is a pleasant visit in LaGrange and all of Troup County.

This photo was taken at Marietta Museum of History seconds and a step away from the front cover image. It was a slide not a digital. I don't develop slides and could not have altered it. I did not see any difference in the two photos until I got them back from the developer

Snodgrass Cabin at Chickamauga

Gordon Lee Mansion. See the figure in the upper right window? It could be a reflection but it looks like a woman in antebellum dress.

Marietta Museum of History

Weird smoke ring at Battle of Resaca Reenactment.
This was one of the battles leading to the Battle of Atlanta.

Section 5 Classic South

This was the Georgia of the earliest days. Here you find Revolutionary War stories mingled with Civil War ones. It is a land of traditional plantations and some of the oldest sites, and ghosts, in the state.

Chapter 23 Augusta, Golf and Ghosts

Augusta is best known as the home of The Augusta National Golf Club, site of the prestigious Masters Golf Tournament. Augusta, known as the "Garden City," is Georgia's second-oldest and second-largest city. The Augusta Museum of History is a good place to start understanding the city. Ezekiel Harris House Museum also comes under the museum's umbrella.

Built in 1797, the Ezekiel Harris house was an isolated house in the country on a dirt road. It was then surrounded by his 323 ½ acres. The Smithsonian Guide to Historic America called it "the finest eighteenth-century house surviving in Georgia..." Since then, much of his original land was sold so that now the home sits in the middle of the Harrisburg neighborhood. While you will hear stories of the ghosts of 13 patriots hanged by the British, that story is untrue. While no doubt there may be some other phantoms here, it's not the 13 soldiers who were hanged at Mackay's Trading Post.

To fathom all its ghostly legends it helps to understand the city that was the backdrop of so many tragic stories. Connie Kersey, Augusta ghost expert, has this to say. "As far as I know, there are no less than 21 haunted places in Augusta. Some of these stories have been documented. Others I know because they have been passed down through my family."

Naturally cemeteries are one of the most likely places to hunt for ghosts. In two of Augusta's cemeteries, you will find a variety of spirits. Not all of them are at rest. Magnolia Cemetery is a blend of many burial grounds. It has five Jewish sections and one Greek as well as the Christian burial areas. The earliest interments began in 1818 so there are many Revolutionary War and Civil War figures residing in this cemetery. Over 300 Civil War graves both Federal and Confederate are here. There are seven Confederate Generals including Brigadier General Alexander Porter, who shelled the Union troops before Pickett's charge at Gettysburg.

The most commonly seen phantom is not a soldier but a man in a top hat and a trench coat. He will only be visible for a moment as he disappears as soon as you spot him. There are other strange manifestations here too. People see lights reflecting off tombstones but there is no way the light could penetrate the solid brick walls of the cemetery to be seen where they are spotted. I haven't been able to find any explanation for the gentleman or the lights.

Saint Paul's Episcopal Church is the site of the oldest church and cemetery in Augusta. The current church was built in 1918 and is the fourth structure on the site. The first was built in 1750 as part of the original Fort Augusta complex. The cemetery around the church was used from colonial days through 1816. It is the final resting place of many notable Georgians including signer of the Constitution, William Few. As might be expected in a place where so much history took place, it has its phantoms. Photos taken there may turn up with a few orbs on them.

At the Cedar Grove Cemetery, the city's first "colored" grave yard, there is a more sinister phantom. The Resurrection Man was a middle-aged black man named Gradison Harris who used to work for the Old Medical College of Georgia. His job was to dig up bodies to supply the medical students with cadavers to dissect. Since Cedar Grove was a poor black cemetery where lots of slaves were buried in unmarked graces it was prize territory. Harris's spirit has been seen walking along the headstones of those he disrespected. The spirits of the disinterred dead are found prowling the cemetery at night. Perhaps seeking a final resting place where they will not be disturbed.

The Old Medical College of Georgia also is very uneasy. It was the first medical school in Georgia, completed by 1835. During the Civil War, it was used as a Confederate hospital, another sure fire place to find a few restless spirits hanging around. As to whether the spirits result from butchered soldiers, many of whom died due to lack of sanitary practices common to the era, or from disturbed rest of deceased slaves, is not know but there are some unearthly presences in the old building. Moans emanate from the third floor where doctors used to perform autopsies. The basement, where they would rebury the bodies after dissection, is also haunted. Probably both floors saw use during its stint as a war hospital. Today, it's a popular wedding and event center.

Another of the most active sites is the old federal arsenal. Dating back to the 1800's, it saw use during the War Between the States. There is also a cemetery here. When Freeman Walker, mayor of Augusta and a U.S. senator, sold seventy-two acres of his land to the government for an arsenal in 1826 he retained an acre within the boundaries of that land for a family cemetery. He and his descendants are buried there today.

One of those descendants is Maj. Gen. William H.T. Walker. Walker was an up and coming U.S. Army officer when the War Between the States erupted. He resigned his commission and joined the Confederate Army. After succession, Commandant Arnold Elzey, commanding officer at the arsenal was forced to relinquish the property. He insisted on surrendering his sword to Walker, a former classmate at West Point. Then Elzey returned his soldiers to Washington, resigned his commission in the United States Army and promptly enlisted in the Confederate Army.

During the war, Major General Walker was wounded in the Battle of Atlanta and died from that wound. He is buried in that cemetery located at the northwest end of the Augusta State University.

Augusta State University, is one of the most haunted sites in the city. One of the professors was walking to his car one day and saw a man dressed in a long gray military coat with the yellow sash of a Confederate officer. He thought little of it and assumed it was someone dressed up for a play on campus. Then it occurred to him. There were no plays going on that night. He looked back and the figure had vanished. Could it be that General Walker is still patrolling his land?

Bellevue House, built in 1815, is one of the oldest buildings on the campus and in the entire city. Part of the original arsenal land, it was Freeman Walker's summer home. In 1861, it was home to John Galt and his family. He had two daughters, Emily and Lucy. Emily became engaged to a soldier who was going off to fight in the Civil War. Following a common custom of the period, she engraved her name and the date on a bedroom window with her diamond engagement ring. Shortly afterwards, she argued with her fiancé about him going away to the war. He insisted on doing the honorable –read stupid– thing and was killed in battle. Emily in despair hurled herself to her death from an upstairs window in Bellevue.

Workers have heard a man and woman arguing late at night at Bellevue. When the building is searched for the intruders no one is ever found. Other things like the phone system going haywire and a television that turns itself off and on. During Bellevue Hall's last renovation, the etched window was removed and put in storage. The building now is used for student counseling and testing and the powers that be decided Emily should not be influencing the students who visit there.

The building next door to Bellevue is Benet House, used as the admissions' office. Many of the workers in that building have heard footsteps, found items mysteriously rearranged and seen gray images in a mirror. Often when alone in the building, staff members hear doors slamming as if by an angry person. Even stranger is the chair that rocks by itself. And then there is the haunted closet in an upstairs room, frequently a sound like hangers rattling is heard but there will be no hangers when the closet is opened. It is believed that two ghosts inhabit the closet. Most employees avoid the basement of the house, which contains an entrance to a closed-off brick tunnel from the time the place was used part of the arsenal.

Many of the historic homes in Augusta have been converted to modern uses. The Nicholas Ware House built in 1816, is now the Gertrude Herbert Institute of art. Once it was a rich man's obsession. Ware was mayor of Augusta and then a U. S. Senator. He invested $40,000 in building his gracious Federal style home. Because of the vast (for its time) expense, the house was referred to as "Ware's Folly."

Perhaps after lavishing so much wealth on his home, Ware is loath to abandon it to the artists. People in the home will sometimes hear footsteps, most often coming from the former nursery upstairs. The doorbell will often ring although there is no one there. It has been checked for electrical problems and gets a clean bill of health yet as soon as the electricians leave it begins its ringing again. Past residents as well as present visitors have sensed a presence in the hallway. One employee even felt someone brush against her face. This presence seems to be jovial and welcoming, perhaps Nicholas Ware greeting guests.

Another interesting explanation for a presence, possible along with Ware, are the human bones found in the first floor walls during a renovation in 1935. When the news was released a young woman who had lived there as a child came forward with an explanation for the bones. As a child digging in the garden, she had found them and took her newfound treasure up to her favorite play spot in the attic.

Later, knowing her mother would be displeased with her about the digging, she dropped them into a hole in the attic floor. The garden was not the normal place to bury a person. Could the bones have been those of an unwanted infant murdered and buried there by some long-ago young woman?

Sibley Mill is located on the site of a former Confederate Powder Works. It was the only permanent structure completed by the Confederacy. It was built on a portion of the old United States Arsenal site between the Canal and Savannah River and at the time was the second largest gunpowder factory in the world. After the war, it was dismantled and only a single chimney left standing as a memorial. This Obelisk Chimney was designated to "...remain a monument to the Confederacy should the powder works pass away." It still stands today near the bank of the Augusta Canal.

In 1880, Josiah Sibley commissioned a mill on the property. Sibley Mill was modeled after the English House of Parliament. In 1906, many people worked at the mill, weaving cloth to earn a living. One of those women, Maude Williams, had a bit of drama going on in her otherwise drab life. She was having an affair with a married man, Arthur Glover. Maude decided to end the affair but Arthur would not let it end that way. He stormed into the mill one afternoon with a gun clutched in his hand and shot Maude to death in front of her bewildered co-workers.

Arthur received swift justice. He was sentenced and hanged quickly. But the story doesn't end there. After the tragedy, workers would come into a supposedly empty mill and see Maude quietly weaving at her machine. Old friends would run screaming from the room but often new workers who did not know the story would try and talk to the ghostly weaver.

Care to share your room with a convivial spirit? Try the Partridge Inn. It began life in 1816 as the two-story home of Daniel and Elizabeth Meigs. By1908 Augusta had become a hot resort city, New York hotelier Morris Partridge bought the home, which was then called Three Oaks, for his personal residence and a small hotel. From then on it was unstoppable. It played host to notables ranging from President Harding to modern day names like Charlton Heston, Dennis Quaid, Bob Dylan, Crystal Gayle, Reba McIntyre and others.

After Mr. Partridge's death in 1947, the inn began to decay until another entrepreneur, Sam Waller, purchased the historic landmark and began restoration but by the 1980s the building was so bad it was awaiting the wrecking ball. Once again fate intervened. The community rose up in its defense and found investors to salvage the historic treasure.

By 1983 it was renovated and reopening in 1987. The next owners, an Atlanta investment company Walton Way LLC, poured more into a multimillion-dollar renovation that was completed a year later.

All of the renovations have not rid the hotel of its oldest guest, Emily. That story dates back to 1866 When Emily, reputedly the prettiest girl in Augusta, was in the bridal suite dressing for her wedding. The lavish wedding reception was prepared and the guests were in place. All that was missing was the groom. He had recently returned from the war and was due to arrive at the Partridge Inn at any moment. However as the young soldier rode into town, some locals mistook him for a man wanted for treason. They informed the sheriff who shot him. He fell from his horse and died in the street. Emily was devastated. She refused to take off her wedding dress for weeks. She never married and died at the age of 86 but those who knew her say she had never recovered from the loss of her fiancé.

Many guests and employees at The Partridge Inn claim to have seen a beautiful girl with long chestnut hair in white wedding gown roaming the hall.

A more recent spirit whose home is now preserved is Woodrow Wilson, who lived in Augusta from 1858 to 1870 while his father was pastor of the First Presbyterian Church. The home then was the church's parsonage. It has been restored by Historic Augusta, Inc. The home has 14 rooms and is furnished period correct to the decade of the 1860s when the Wilsons lived there.

It was not only whites who contributed to the history of Augusta. Even before the Civil War, black citizens strove to overcome the legal and economic yoke placed on their shoulders. One such person is honored with her own house museum. The Lucy Craft Laney Museum of Black History honors Ms. Lucy Craft Laney.

Born in Macon, Georgia on April 13, 1854, the seventh of ten children born to Rev. and Mrs. David Laney, Lucy, in violation of existing laws, was taught to read by the time she was four by Ms. Campbell, her owner's sister. Lucy's father was a Presbyterian minister and a talented carpenter who used his skill to purchase his family's freedom.

In 1869, Lucy entered the first class of Atlanta University and graduated 1873. She began her teaching career and started Augusta's first school for Black children. She believed that the only way for Blacks to be successful in America was through education. During her life she was honored by countless awards and died on October 23, 1933.

Green in Augusta means more than the color of its famous golf jacket. The top green spot in Augusta is the Augusta Canal, and one of Georgia's National Heritage Sites. It was built in 1845 to produce power long before alternative energy sources were important.

It is nation's only industrial power canal still in use for its original purpose. But it offers so much more: history, recreation and unique experiences along miles of towpath, trail and waterway. You can travel along the canal on foot or bicycle. You can canoe or kayak on it or take a guided tour aboard a replica canal cargo boat. You can fish from the banks or watch wildlife.

You can pick up a free self-guided tour map to this state treasure where natural, cultural, historic and recreational resources come together in a unique landscape.

The Augusta Canal Interpretive Center at Enterprise Mill, once a working mill fueled by the energy of the canal, brings you face to face with the people who built the canal. You can learn about the progress, problems and promise of this century-and-a-half watery treasure.

There is a wonderful trail from the canal gates to the Augusta Riverwalk. The Riverwalk is one of Augusta's main downtown attractions located directly on the beautiful Savannah River. Many festivals and events are held here. It has a unique ghost story.

In 1838, a young lady who worked at a local tavern became involved with a business man who visited Augusta often. The lady discovered she was pregnant and begged her lover to marry her. He refused saying he already had a wife and children back home. The devastated young woman ran from the tavern out onto a train trestle that crossed where one of the Riverwalk bridges are located today. She threw herself into the Savanna River and drowned. Her spirit is still seen there searching for her unfaithful lover.

Another green spot in Augusta is Pendleton King Park. The park originally was a plantation belonging to the Bugg family. It was purchased by John Pendleton King before his marriage in 1842. In the early 1900s the plantation manor burned and was never rebuilt.

Today the grounds where the plantation once was is a 64-acre bird sanctuary filled with pine forests, sand ridges, and marshes. Its gardens are a thing of beauty.

You will find all type of recreation there: playgrounds, an 18-hole disc golf course, tennis courts, a workout course, nature trails for walking and cycling, picnicking areas and a Bark Park for your best friend.

There is one other feature in the park; the Bugg family cemetery. It's surrounded by a brick wall and well maintained. One of its residents often shows itself to visitors as a white figure darting among the trees.

If you see a profusely blooming camellia bush where the old mansion once stood, beware, the legend is that this bush would be covered in blooms when one of the King family was about to die.

Of course the most famous ghost story in Augusta is the the "haunted pillar" which was one of the city's most recognized landmarks. The legend says if you try to move or touch the pillar, you will die.

This pillar was all that remained of the Market, two large sheds where residents came to buy meat and produce, that once occupied the center of Broad Street from 1830 until 1878. The sheds were called the Upper and Lower Markets,

The story is that a traveling minister came to town in the late 1800s and demanded he be allowed to preach at the market. For whatever reason, he was not allowed and he cursed the market and the entire town. He placed his hand on that pillar and prophesized that a great wind would destroy all of the market except the one pillar. He farther stated that any-one who tried to remove it or even touch the remaining pillar would die.

When disaster in the form of a tornado struck on Feb. 8, 1878, people remembered the old preacher and gave credulous to his curse. When the twister had passed, the entire market was leveled. It was totally destroyed except for one pillar which was left standing. It was the exact pillar the preacher had touched.

Augustans have kept that pillar although they have moved it several times. When the city council decided to rebuild the Market, the pillar was moved to the corner of Fifth and Broad. Later, two workmen who attempted to move the pillar were struck by lightning and died. Suppos-edly a bulldozer operator died of a heart attack when his machine made contact with the pillar. According to the police, traffic accidents seem to occur at the intersection where the pillar is. Of course, maybe it is because drivers are looking at that one pillar and wondering what it is doing there in the middle do the intersection. The pillar has been struck by lightning twice and been hit by an out-of-control car at least once.

Whether there is any truth to the haunting story about the pillar or not, locals did love their pillar. On December 12, 1996, the Haunted Pillar received its own historical marker. Unfortunately, The pillar was crashed into and destroyed by car on Dec. 17, 2016. Augusta said then that the pillar would be rebuilt, but so far it hasn't been.

Woodrow Wilson's boyhood home

Arsenal Museum

The Partridge Inn

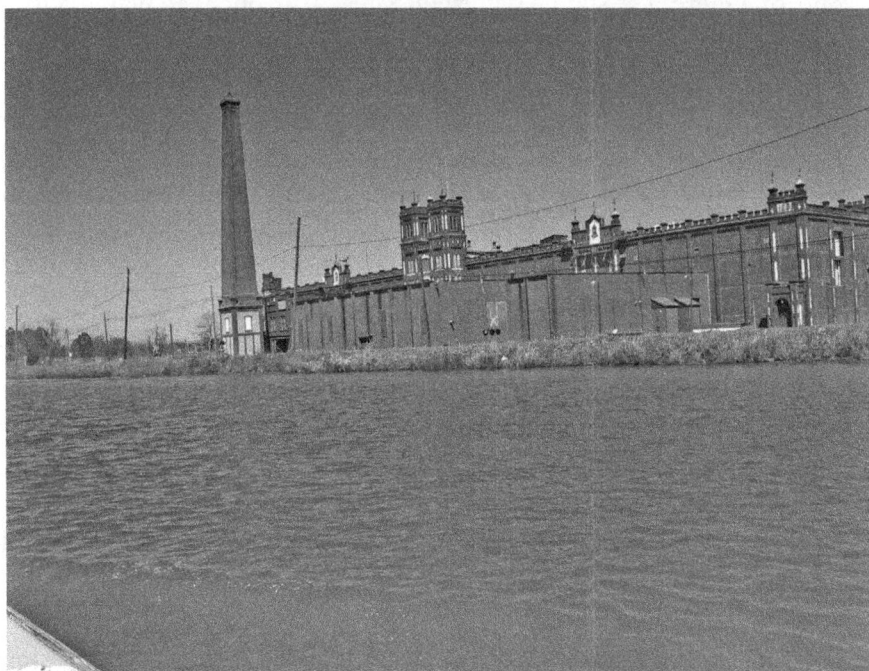

The Sibley Mill once the Confederate Powder Works

Section 6 Cherokee Sites

Long before the white man set foot here, Georgia was home to the Cherokee. They had their own legends and ghost stories. One of their most enduring beliefs was in the Nunne'hi, or immortals, who lived throughout the highlands of the Cherokee nation. These spirit people were invisible except when they wanted to be seen. When they did manifest themselves, they appeared to physically resemble the Cherokee. Generally, they were friendly and frequently helped people were in need. They resembled the Cherokee in their habits as well. They loved music and dancing. In short, they were much like the ghosts and spirits we find so interesting.

Chapter 24 New Echota, Hope and Betrayal

Today, New Echota is a ghost town. No one lives there anymore. It's one of Georgia's State Historical Sites. But once, it was a vibrant community, the capital of the proud Cherokee Nation. By 1825, the Cherokees had established a form of government that was modeled after the United States government. This was the site of their Supreme Court, Council House, a town square and perhaps most importantly, The Phoenix, the only native American newspaper printed in a native language. This was the seat of government for a highly civilized, literate people.

By 1835, New Echota was abandoned, it's citizens imprisoned and then banished to the wilds of Oklahoma. Over 4,000 men women and children died before the Cherokee reached their barren new home. A few hundred managed to evade the Georgia Militia and remained hiding in the woods. These few comprise the ancestors of the Eastern Band of Cherokees living in North Carolina today.

The reason behind this tale of man's inhumanity to man is simple, greed. Gold had been discovered on the Indian lands. The state of Georgia wanted it. Andrew Jackson was president and he hated all Indians. In spite of the fact that Cherokees had fought with him in the Creek War, he wanted them removed at all costs.

One Cherokee, Junaluska, saved Jackson's life at the Battle of Horseshoe Bend. Jackson proved to be a hero with feet of clay.

When Junaluska came to Washington and asked for an audience to plead against his people's exile, Jackson refused to see him.

Even in the face of the Supreme Court's upholding the Cherokee claim to their land, Jackson plotted removal of the same people our government had once promised "You shall remain in your ancient land as long as the grass grows and the water runs." The Trail of Tears is a red stain of infamy on the history of a people who had pledged "liberty and justice for all."

Not all white men upheld the persecution of an innocent people. Samuel Worcester was a minister who had come to New Echota not only to preach the gospel but to help in the establishment of the Cherokee newspaper. The Cherokees called him "The Messenger."

As Georgia Governor Gilmer pushed harder for Indian removal, he passed laws prohibiting whites from living on Indian land without obtaining a license from the state. Worcester and several other ministers nor only refused to get the license but met at New Echota to sign a resolution against it as undermining the authority of the Cherokee Nation which had been upheld by Chief Justice John Marshall of the Supreme Court.

Governor Gilmer had Worcester arrested and imprisoned. The Supreme Court upheld the signers but the governor continued to hold them prisoner. When Worcester was released the following year, he left for Oklahoma to prepare for the relocation of the Cherokee nation.

Today, Samuel Worcester's home, the only building original to the land, stands far to the back of the historic site. It is a place troubled by the evil that occurred around it. There are tales that a Cherokee was murdered in the house in the 1830's.

Even without that act of violence the crimes perpetrated against the Cherokees on this site could account for the troubled feeling one experience within the house. Whatever the reasons, newspaper accounts as far back as 1889 report ghostly manifestations in the simple two story white farmhouse.

Although the death of the Indian is only rumored, two deaths are proven. In the 1900's the house was used as an apartment house. Two card players got into a dispute over the fairness of a game of chance and killed one another in the downstairs area of the house.

Visitors have heard dragging chains, disembodies footsteps and seen the unearthly figure of a short, thin man. One park employee told me that people frequently report seeing ghostly images in or near the house.

The uneasy feeling you will experience within the house is completely at odds with the furnishings of a typical rural Georgia home in the early 19th century. A loom, and other weaving implements, an old-fashioned cook stove and other everyday items attest to the fact that this was once a happy home shared by Samuel and Ann Worcester before greed and betrayal left its aura on the lonely house.

I visited the park on a day there were few visitors. When I reached the Worchester house, I was the only one in it. I had a feeling of someone staring at my back the entire time I was inside.

As you wander the site, many of the buildings are steeped in an aura of melancholy. Chief Vann's Tavern is another original building which was mover to its present site. Chief Vann was a prosperous plantation owner and businessman before the removal.

So much treachery and evil occurred here. The reconstructed *Phoenix* Office is a highlight of the park. The *Cherokee Phoenix* began in 1828 as a means of uniting the Cherokee Nation by keeping the far-flung people informed of the latest happenings and laws. The editor, Elias Boudinot, became a member of the "Treaty" party led by Major Ridge and his son John.

The "Treaty" party felt the tribe's only hope of survival as a nation was to accede to Georgia's demands and move to Oklahoma. The Principal Chief, John Ross, opposed removal. The paper ran out of funds and ceased operation in 1834. When John Ross attempted to move the press in the dead of night to a safer location in Tennessee, the Georgia militia and Elias' own brother, Stand Watie, captured the press, stomped the soft lead type into the red Georgia clay and burned the original building. They had effectively silenced the voice of the Cherokee Nation.

As you peer into the tiny office, the importance of freedom of the press comes to mind. Remember it was only three years after the destruction of the Phoenix that the Cherokee people were rounded up, herded into stockades for five months and then marched over a thousand miles in the dead of winter with inadequate food and clothing prodded onward by men inflamed with racial hatred.

The means to remove the Native Americans came about when Boudinot, Ridge, and his son John signed the Treaty of New Echota in December 1835. Major Ridge stated after he signed the treaty, "I have just signed my death warrant."

Indeed that was true. Within six months, the three men were brutally slain by fellow Cherokees. The crime of selling tribal land without the permission of the Supreme Council was ruled treason, punishable by death.

Perhaps there is another ghost that stalks this tiny place, the spirit of the slain Cherokee Nation.

Chapter 25 Adairsville, Rome, and Northeast Georgia

The two most common sources of ghost stories are lost love or murder. Barnsley Gardens includes both – a love too strong for death to destroy and fratricide resulting from two strong-willed brothers' battle of wills to possess the magnificent estate.

It has spirits that have been recorded through the decades. It has stately ruins that bear witness to Southern history's most turbulent times. The resort boasts a garden over a century and a half old planted by a spirit who still lingers to care for it. The floorboards of the old ruin have a bloodstain that will not wipe out. The story is poignant and tragic.

The Barnsley story, as well as the history of Adairsville, begins with Godfrey Barnsley, an Englishman who moved to Savannah as a penniless youth of 18. There he made his fortune as a cotton broker. There, too, he met the love of his life, Julia Scarborough, the daughter of a wealthy merchant and shipbuilder. He and Julia were married on Christmas Eve 1828. They soon began a family and by 1841 had six children. On the surface, it looked like a fairy tale life. But the fates were lying in wait.

By 1841, Julia's health was in decline. Godfrey decided to move his family to the healthier climate of north Georgia. His discriminating eye was caught by a beautiful parcel of land in the small village of Adairsville. In particular, an acorn-shaped hill on the 10,000 acres was his choice of the perfect place to build his beloved Julia a home worthy of their love.

An old Indian shaman who worked for him warned Godfrey not to build on this particular site; he told him the site was sacred to the Cherokee and anyone who tried to live there would be cursed. But Godfrey was a sophisticated man and ignored the old Indian. He began the construction of his beautiful mansion there.

He chose an Italian Villa style with 24 rooms. There would be hot and cold running water, unheard of in his day. The marble for the mantel and the tiles for the verandas were imported. Everything was to be the finest workmanship money could buy. He designed the gardens in the style of Andrew Jackson Downing and filled it with every kind of rose he could find. His Julia deserved the best.

Fickle fortune who had smiled on Godfrey for so long now turned away. His infant son died. Before the home could be completed, Julia passed away. Devastated, Godfrey lost all desire for the home that had been his passion. He threw himself into his business and on his infrequent trips home, he sat among the untended roses in the garden he had hoped to share with his beloved.

Then in a letter that is preserved by the estate, he told of "seeing" Julia in the garden. She spoke gently to him and told him it was her wish that he get on with his life and finish the home she was so proud of as a legacy for their children.

Godfrey was imbued with new spirit. Work began again on the mansion. But fate continued to withhold her favor. His oldest daughter, Anna, married and left to live in England. The second daughter died in the house in 1858. Then the Civil War began. Godfrey's fortune was in the cotton he brokered, and now that was no longer sellable. It rotted in New Orleans warehouses.

In 1862, his oldest son, Howard, who had become a ship's captain, was killed by Chinese pirates while sailing in the Orient. Barnsley's other two sons, George and Lucian, enlisted in the Confederate military.

His daughter, Julia, had married Confederate Army Captain James Peter Baltzelle who had insisted his wife seek refuge in Savannah.

Still Godfrey was obsessed with finishing the castle. He accumulated art and furnishings from Europe for his home. When the War finally came to Woodlands, Union troops found Godfrey alone with his treasures and his still-incomplete mansion. The day was May 18, 1864. A friend of Godfrey, Colonel Robert G. Earle of the Second Alabama Light Cavalry, rode to Woodlands to warn Barnsley of Sherman's troops' approach and was shot down within sight of the house. He was buried there at Woodlands and still remains in the garden perhaps in spirit as well.

Charles Wright Willis, 103rd Illinois infantry, wrote this account of the event in his book Army Life of an Illinois Soldier:

> May 18, 1864. Our cavalry had a sharp fight here this p.m. and on one of the gravel walks in the beautiful garden lies a Rebel colonel, shot in five places. He must have been a noble-looking

man; looks 50 years old, and has fine form and features. Think
his name is Irwin. There must be a hundred varieties of the rose
in bloom here and the most splendid specimens of cactus.

The Federal officer commanding the troops, Gen. McPherson, for-
bade looting of the unfinished mansion but his orders were blatantly
disregarded. Godfrey's costly furnishings were destroyed; Italian
statuary was smashed in a search for hidden gold; what could not be
consumed or carried away, was broken and smashed.

By the war's end, Godfrey was almost destroyed financially. He
moved to New Orleans to try and salvage something of his brokerage.

George and Lucian refused to sign the oath of allegiance to the
Union and immigrated to South America where their descendants
live to this day. Godfrey left his son-in-law, James Baltzelle, and
daughter Julia to manage Woodlands. Julia was a strong woman who
some say Margaret Mitchell modeled her famous Scarlett after. She
led the servants out into the fields and woods and searched out wild
edible plants to keep them from starvation.

Baltzelle started a timber business but was killed in 1868 by a fall-
ing tree. Julia and her young daughter fled to New Orleans to join
Godfrey. Julia later met and married a German ship captain named
Charles Henry Von Schwartz.

After Godfrey died a broken man in 1873, Julia returned his body
to Woodlands where her new husband also died.

Adelaide, Godfrey's second daughter, grew up at Woodlands and
married a chemist named A. A. Saylor. Saylor too fell prey to the
Barnsley curse and died while their two sons, Harry and Preston,
were very young.

Times grew dark for the family. A tornado in 1906 destroyed the
roof of the main house and forced the Saylors to take refuge in the
only intact part of the home, the kitchen wing.

The two boys grew very different as they matured. Preston used
his body to earn a living and became a nationally known boxer under
the name K. O. Dugan.

Harry became somewhat of a schemer and got involved with a
group of men who wished to divide up Woodlands and sell it to
developers. Harry had remained at home while Preston traveled to
rings around the country. The brothers fought bitterly over what was

best for them and their mother. Harry, influenced by his cronies, induced their mother to sign a mortgage on Woodlands. He had Preston committed to an insane asylum supposedly because he had become unbalanced due to blows to his head suffered in the ring.

The power struggle came to a head in 1935 when Preston, finally released from the asylum, shot and killed Harry in the small kitchen wing where he and Adelaide still lived. Preston chased his brother down and kept firing until Harry fell and died in their mother's arms. I could almost feel the trauma when I looked at the bloodstain that is permanently embedded in the dark wood of the floor. Many say Harry's spirit is still there as well.

Preston turned himself in and was sent to prison. The governor who knew much of the circumstances surrounding the murder pardoned Preston after he had served less than seven years, but it was too late for Woodlands.

Adelaide had struggled valiantly to keep the mortgage paid, but when she died in 1942 the estate and what she had not sold piecemeal of its furnishings were sold at auction for a fraction of their value. Preston did not get out of prison until a few months later, and by then all was gone. The property was used for farming and the once magnificent home left to the encroaching kudzu.

It would seem that Godfrey's dream was finished. But fate again turned her head and smiled. In 1988, Prince Hubertus Fugger and his wife Princess Alexandra, of Bavaria, purchased Woodlands, which was now called Barnsley Gardens. Clent Coker, a neighbor who had grown up obsessed with the Barnsley story and was unwilling to see such a historic treasure lost, went to the prince and told him of the history behind the ruins. The prince agreed that the estate had to be restored and its history honored. Between them, that has been done.

Clent continued the research he began a boy, interviewing the elderly residents of Woodlands and preserving the Barnsleys' story in his book, *Barnsley Gardens at Woodlands: The Illustrious Dream.* He passed away in 2022 but was the historian for Barnsley Gardens during his lifetime.

The Prince brought in gardeners to salvage the gardens and restore them to their former glory. He build cottages to match the historic feel of the old castle and turned the ruins into a showplace.

Present management does not play up the supernatural elements of their resort, yet they cannot deny them. Stories of apparitions dot the long Barnsley history and persist today around the ruins.

Godfrey's statements about seeing and speaking with his dead wife in the gardens are well-documented by his letters. He was not the only one to report seeing Julia there. Julia Barnsley Saylor, her granddaughter, told of having seen her grandmother in the gardens so frequently that she came to view it as natural. Mrs. Saylor had another paranormal experience that she documented. The night her Uncle George died in Brazil, he appeared to her at Woodlands.

Would Godfrey's life been different if he had heeded the words of that old Indian and built his home in any other spot than that acorn-shaped hill? Like a Greek tragedy, the one decision made with hubris shapes the inevitable future.

How the Rice House came to be at Barnsley Gardens is an interesting story. It started life in 1854 as a log farmhouse in Rome, Georgia, home of Fleming Rice and his family. It survived a Civil war battle in 1864. The bullet holes still scar the front exterior wall.

During Barnsley Garden's ownership by Prince Fugger, Clent Coker told the prince about the historic building that was doomed to destruction. Instead of letting it meet its fate, the prince bought it, had it cut in sections, loaded on trucks and moved the few miles to Barnsley Gardens in 1994. There it was restored and now houses the fine dining facility of the resort. It is a nice balance for the other larger restaurant at Barnsley Gardens, Woodlands Grill. Rice House serves contemporary Southern dishes and is only open two nights a week, whereas Woodlands is more of a steakhouse and is open seven days.

Rice House does have one thing most other restaurants don't offer. Visitors have reported hearing doors opening and closing and a man in a suit and top hat has been seen occasionally. He is reported to sit and stare, then disappear.

In Cartersville, you can explore the West at Booth Western Art Museum without ever leaving the South. From exhibits by the artists that explored the real life early west to depictions of the Hollywood version of the wild and woolly West, you will find them here in Georgia's second-largest museum.

There are sections devoted to the Presidents and the Civil War. There is a theater for showing the museum-related film *The American West* as well as other films, a reference library for Western American art, culture and history, Civil War history, United States presidential history, and local history related to the art collections.

It's lots of fun to ride the glass elevator operated with real weights – one of only two in the country. If you meet Jim Dunham, Director of Special Projects, ask him to show his artistry with a gun. When we visited, he put on a faster-than-lightning exhibit of fancy gun handling. In fact, Jim taught many of Hollywood's fastest-guns-in the-West how to perfect that fast draw. If you search the credits in many westerns, he will be listed.

Just off I-75 near Cartersville are the remains of an ancient culture. On this 54-acre site are all that remains of what was once a thriving village: six earthen mounds, a plaza, village area, borrow pits and a defensive ditch.

More than 500 years ago, Native Americans performed elaborate religious ceremonies atop a 63-foot flat-topped earthen knoll. They buried their priest/chiefs in handmade costumes accompanied by items they would need in their after-lives.

The Etowah Mounds, now a Georgia State Park, is the most intact Mississippian Culture site in the southeastern United States.

Even though less than 90 percent of this site has been excavated, we are learning a lot about the people who came before us. The park is open Tuesday through Saturday during normal daylight hours and on Sunday afternoons. They offers candlelight tours of the mounds at certain times of year. That would be a wonderful way to search for the spirits that must be still lingering in this sacred spot.

Another Native American site in the area is located in Rome. The Chieftains Museum tells the story of Major Ridge, the leader and principle signer of the Treaty of New Echota. Ridge struggled to adapt to the white man's ways while still remaining true to his Cherokee heritage, an impossible task in his time.

The main building in the museum complex, Ridge's family home, was originally a two-story dogtrot-style log cabin that was added to as the family became more prosperous. Today, it's a National Historic Landmark. It's located on the banks of the Oostanaula River, where Ridge and his family were ferryboat masters, store operators and slave-owning planters. The museum contains exhibits describing Ridge's life and times and some history of the Cherokee people.

It contains something else. Nancy Ridge, Major's 17 year old daughter died during childbirth there in 1820. Her baby survived a few months.

Many people have seen or heard Nancy roaming the halls of her former home and her baby crying. It is said she only appears to women. One woman who had seen and heard Nancy and the baby is Debbie Brown, who passed away in 2013 but was previously the program manager of Chieftain's Museum.

Nancy died on the second floor of her home now the museum. "I thought as long as I stay down in my office and she stayed upstairs, we would be fine," Debbie said. "But of course, she didn't."

The meeting occurred when Debbie was closing up the museum with her daughter. Both women heard rapid footsteps running inside the unoccupied museum.

Southern Paranormal Investigators did a search and got audio recordings of Nancy "answering" when they called her and videos that appears to be faces and shadows in the windows of the museum.

Myrtle Hill Cemetery in Rome got its name because a plant called "trailing Myrtle" grew wild all over the hill. Myrtle Hill Cemetery is registered as a Historical Landmark and it also has some residents that still roam at night.

There are stories of a Confederate soldier and people hearing eerie footsteps when no one else is around.

Some of the famous people buried there are Ellen Louise Axson Wilson, the wife of President Woodrow Wilson who died while he was in office. There are two of Rome's founders at the top of the hill. Colonel Daniel R. Mitchell and Colonel Zachariah B Hargrove.

Veteran's Plaza is the location of the Tomb of the Known Soldier, Private Charles Graves. Like the Tomb of the Unknown Soldier in Washington, his grave is dedicated to all the soldiers killed in WWI. There are two Confederate monuments recently relocated to Myrtle Hill. The cemetery contains over 368 Confederate and Union soldiers including 75 Unknown Confederates and two Unknown Union Soldiers that lost their lives in Civil War battles near Rome.

The Historic DeSoto Theatre in Rome, Georgia is haunted by a a child named Ruby. Ruby lived in Rome in the 1930's and loved to visit the theater. She would ride the trolley there and would spend the day binge watching films. One day when Ruby exited the trolley she was struck by a car. She lay still as a crowd gathered around her. Then she came to and seemed fine. She was given a ticket to the theatre and as usual sat in the balcony and watched movies all day. That night as the theater was closing, she didn't come down. An usher found Ruby dead in her seat.

DeSoto closed down as a movie theater in 1982 when it could no longer compete with TV. The Rome Little Theater took over and began performing there.

Actors and directors know Ruby is still there. They have experienced pranks that Ruby plays. There are times when costumes or props disappear and then return in strange places they would never have been put by their living users. One actor saw a young girl dressed in white with a face that looked doll-like dancing in the theater.

Ruby seems to have drawn some friends to the theater as well. An older man's shadow is seen there and there are two resident ghosts, nicknamed Statler and Waldorf after the Muppet duo, who are often heard whispering in the empty theater.

Turning to more intellectual spirits, Visit Berry College. Martha Berry was born in 1865 into a well-to-do family and was well educated. At a young age, she realized that not all children received the kind of education she did. In fact, she was appalled to discover that many poor children did not even learn to read the Bible. She was sitting on the steps of a small log cabin built as a playhouse one Sunday reading a Bible. Some of the local children came by, and she began reading them some Bible stories. The children had never heard anything like this, and when she invited them back next week, she told them to bring their brothers and sisters.

Next week the children returned with not only brothers and sisters but "babies and dogs." Her cabin became a "beehive of humanity."

This was actually the birth of Berry College. She began driving to three different locations in the area to teach the mountain children. In 1902 she opened her first school, the Boys Industrial School. In 1909 that school was followed by the Martha Berry School for Girls.

Berry College has grown to a 28,000-acre campus, the largest campus in the nation. Attendance averages more than 1,800 undergraduates.

Along with being a remarkable university, Berry College has become one of northwest Georgia's most popular tourist attractions. Art connoisseurs are drawn to the Martha Berry Museum to view the fine collection of art there.

Nature lovers are ecstatic about the gardens, Sundial Garden, Goldfish Garden, Sunken Garden and Formal Garden as well as the Wildflower Meadow and two nature trails, Fernery Nature Trial and Hillside Trail. They have to visit the Catfish Pond and Bridal Walk.

History buffs enjoy touring Oak Hill, the mansion where Berry grew up. The Greek Revival mansion is furnished as it was when Martha Berry lived in it and managed her rapidly growing school. There are many other historical buildings on the campus.

Martha Freeman was Berry's beloved servant and companion throughout her life. Freeman's home is preserved as it was during her lifetime. It was constructed as a schoolhouse for the Berry children and later converted as a home for "Aunt Martha."

The original cabin, the Roosevelt Cabin, now used as a museum dedicated to Martha Berry, an old mill house, a carriage house containing several of the vintage automobiles presented to Martha Berry by her friend Henry Ford, and several old churches are a history lover's fantasy.

Practically the entire campus is a ghost hunter's dream. One of the kindest spirits found on the campus is Martha Freeman. Rebecca Roberts, our guide, told me about the experiences of several students who stayed in Martha Freeman's cabin. "Instead of installing a security, we relied on students to protect Oak Hill, and many of the girls who stayed in this cabin swore they felt someone sit on the side of their bed or tuck them in, but when they looked, there was no one there."

One of the most common stories that recur about Berry College is of a little boy. I spoke to a former student of the college, and she recalled an experience in the office when she saw a small boy approach her and then disappear. The child was dressed in rough clothing as a mountain child might have worn in the late 19th century. Rebecca confirmed that there have been several instances of students witnessing the sighting of this little boy.

The ruins and cemetery of the old Mountain Springs Church are another spot where strange things occur. People have claimed to hear music from the church and footsteps and crying from the graveyard.

There is a wooded road that runs between the main campus of Berry College and the new mountain campus. Before the mountain campus was built, this was a popular spot for students to go at night to neck. There is a legend on campus that one couple had made use of the seclusion for a bit of heavy petting back in the 1940s.

Afterwards, the couple argued, and the girl demanded to get out and walk home. Angry, the boy let her out and drove off. After driving a little ways he cooled off and returned to find his girlfriend. In his haste, he felt the car strike something and believed it was a deer. But when he got out the car to check, he found he had struck and killed his girlfriend. The story goes that if you go to the spot on the road where the girl was killed and say, "Green lady, green lady, green lady," a pale green light will appear in the trees.

Another legend about a dead student revolves around the tower between two girls' dorms in the Ford area, East and West Mary. The story relates that a student at Berry hanged herself in the tower and the body was not discovered for days. Although the door is kept locked nowadays, if you stand outside it you can feel an unearthly cold seeping through and if you continue to stand outside it you can hear her crying as she did before taking her life.

Another phantom is in better spirits; he is usually seen by the old watermill and is dressed in a costume from the mid-19th century. He walks around and may glare at you but not say anything. He then disappears when you look back at him.

Fortunately, Berry College has been around for more than a century and is not going to disappear, so make it a stop on your next Georgia visit.

Worchester House at New Echota

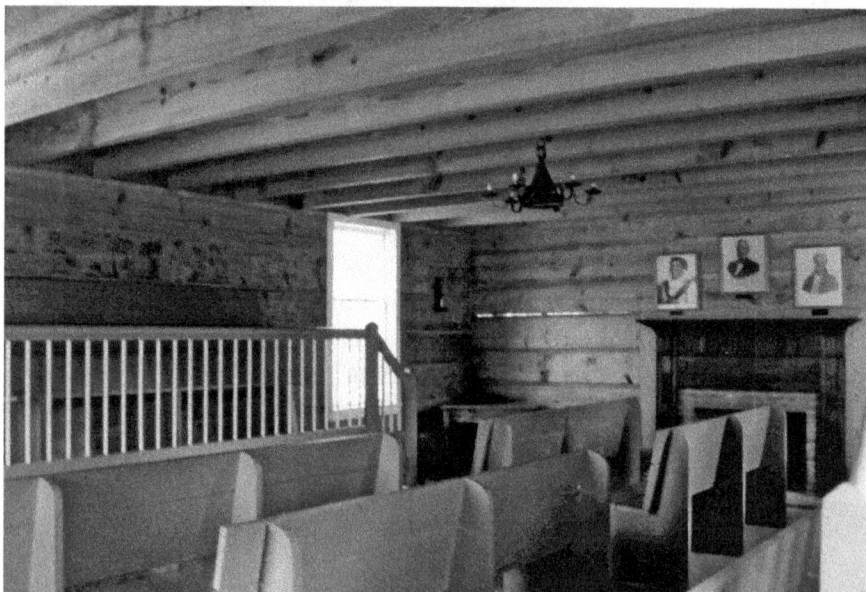

Council House at New Echota

Barnsley Castle

Stagecoach at Booth Museum

Old Mill at Berry College

Chieftain Museum

Weird tombstone almost swallowed by a tree at Myrtle Hill Cemetery

Section 7 Georgia's Mountains

The rugged peaks of the Appalachians created a barrier only a few of the hardier settlers wanted to breach. Even the rocky foothills were settled only by the hardiest of the white men. For the most part they lived in peace with their Cherokee neighbors until "Gold Fever" brought a new type of settler to Georgia's last frontier.

Chapter 26 Dalton, Turfting and Tunnels

In 1855, Benjamin Franklin Prater built his mill on Coahulla Creek near Dalton, Georgia. He built it to last with state of the art equipment and last it did. It served surrounding farmers for over a century and withstood encampments of both Confederate and Union troops.

Today, it is the site for the Prater's Mill County Fair. Although the grounds are open year-round for picnicking, fishing and canoeing, the mill and surrounding buildings, the Cotton Gin, the Old Country Store and Westbrook Barn are open to the public during the fall festival held annually in October. The Mill is preserved in working order and during the festival you can buy cornmeal or flour and watch it being ground as your ancestors might have done over a century ago.

The festival has over 200 exhibitors. Crafters and artists display quilting, tole painting, candle making and many of the old skills that were part of every family's lifestyle. There is so much going on you are pulled in all directions.

Allow lots of time to satisfy your curiosity. Blacksmiths create forged iron work on a portable forge that was used in the 1800 on isolated farms to shoe horses or repair farm implements. An authentic mooonshiner will demonstrate the workings of an old moonshine still. Numerous potters throw clay pots or vases. The time I attended, Rickie Ellis, from Hossin' Around Carving School, showed us how his grandfather created a beautiful carousal horse.

The entertainment is non-stop The Center Stage located on the main fairground, the Store Stage across the road and all around the festival someone is performing. The acts are top notch. Groups like New Day Gospel Singers, Choo-Choo Cloggers, Simply Blest and many others give you an idea of the style. Storytellers, jugglers and wandering bands abound.

Of course, you will want to wander through the old mill and watch the millers grind corn. Part of the charm is the "genealogical graffiti." B. F. Prater's signature is on one of the beams. Former millers and customers scrawled their names and dates on the walls and steps of the mill.

There is even more from the past awaiting you there. Murray County Paranormal Investigations has conducted investigations there and found one thing that happened multiple times. There is a little boy. He has interacted with at least three teenage girls when the society is doing tours of the mill. Each time the girl is between the ages of 14-17 and sitting in one particular rocking chair. Each girl when she looked up the steps and saw the same little boy standing there. Once, he stepped down and took the girl's hand. No one knows who the little boy is, but many people have seen him.

Dewayne Patterson with Murray County Paranormal Investigations said, "We never tell the tours coming through about anything that has ever happened in the past."

Peacock Alley offers a glimpse of the cottage industry that put Dalton on the map as the "Carpet Capital of The World," hand tufted chenille bed spreads are made right there and hung on clothes lines as they once lined the local highways from Atlanta to Chattanooga. The local ladies way of garnering a bit of the tourist money that passed by daily. It was one step from spreads to carpets, now the main industry of the area.

Aside from hosting one of the best North Georgia festivals, Praters' mill has an interesting legend. Varnell, where the mill is located, was at one time called Varnell's Station. It was a stage coach stop. There is a story that a coach headed for Ringgold from Varnell's Station never arrived. It is believed the coach got lost in an unusually heavy fog and was driven into a sinkhole called The Blue Hole. The Blue Hole is located on what used to be the old Federal Road between Varnell's Station and Ringgold. Some say that at times horses can be heard protesting forward prodding by the coach driver.

Located north of Dalton, Georgia lies an unnamed, almost forgotten cemetery. The cemetery dates to the Civil War era and was the burial place of many slaves. It is known as the "old black cemetery."

Its graves are rarely visited by the living, but those adventuresome souls who do come to the graveyard have reported sighting a misty figure in the darkness. Several witnesses have described it as a man of medium height wearing a hooded cloak. The phantom is reported to have a bloodless white face and eyes that glow red in the night.

Many of the new homes built near the cemetery experience unusual poltergeist type activities.

While you are in the mood for cemeteries, be sure to visit the Dalton's West Hill Cemetery at night. If you park your car and put it in neutral, you will be mysteriously pushed uphill. This cemetery is the final resting place of many famous people.

Dalton's founder of the bedspread and textile industry, Catherine Evans Whitener is interred there. Two sports figures are buried there. Henry "Suitcase" Simpson was one of the earliest African-Americans to join the Negro Baseball League. Simpson, who called Dalton home, was considered the best defensive right fielder in the league. The other is champion motorcyclist and Hall of Famer Dale Singleton. Another "resident" of the graveyard is Anthony Johnson Showalter, composer, music teacher and publisher most famous for writing *Leaning on the Everlasting Arms*, one of the most popular gospel songs of the 20th century.

Many of those resting there lived in the 19th century. General Duff Green, a native Kentuckian who fought in the war of 1812, was a member of President Andrew Jackson's "kitchen cabinet," and a former owner of both a newspaper in Washington, DC and the United States Telegraph company lies there.

The Civil War era section of the cemetery has 421 Confederate graves and a commemorative wall listing the names of both Confederate and Union soldiers buried there. Architectural features include a Gothic-inspired stone chapel, a reproduction Civil War cannon and a number of exemplary obelisks, pedestals and angels, as well as a statue known as the Lone Sentinel.

Many of Dalton's historic homes were hospital sites or commanders' headquarters due to their proximity to important Civil War battles. The city is now actively restoring its cultural heritage. A new museum was built on the site of the Tunnel Hill Battlefield.

Construction on The Wink Theater began in 1939 with the grand opening taking place in '41. It closed due to its deteriorating condition in 1980 and was remodeled in July 2002, after four years of renovation; the Wink was briefly back in show business. It hosted live concerts, classic movies and local live theater productions.

But it once again changed hands. It is now occupied by Rock Bridge Community Church so there are no more shows; although they do rent it out upon occasion. But is there another kind of unearthly production going on in the Wink? Local legends have told of a black man being killed during the construction of the theater. Supposedly, he is buried beneath the theater. That may explain the cold spots and strange noises heard in the theater.

Connie Hall-Scott, the owner of Dalton's Ghost Tour, has a lot to tell about the ghosts at the Wink. And she has the credentials to tell it. Her father was the man who renovated the historic theater. Connie herself worked there for a little over a year as a director. During that time she heard many stories of ghosts from the patrons. Today, her ghost tour starts right across the street from the Wink.

One story was told to Connie by a former janitor at the theater. His father at that time was the managing director and came home and reported some unexplained happenings. He would hear the sound of footsteps on stairs once used by African-American patrons. One night he heard the sound of large containers that were used to store film being dragged up and down the stairs but when he investigated he found nothing.

His son who was an unbeliever soon became converted. The young man worked as a projection operator and janitor at the theater. He was often alone in the theater into the wee hours of the morning. On one occasion, he was sweeping the empty aisles late at night. He had some music playing loudly to fill up the cavernous space. Suddenly the music lowered and he heard what sounded like a large man with big clumsy feet running towards him. He was afraid to turn but equally unwilling to meet his fate without seeing what approached. In an instant, the music returned to its set volume and when he turned he saw no one.

On another occasion, this time in broad daylight, he left the projection room for a few minutes to sit in a nearby seat. He then heard what sounded like someone inside the projection room bashing a metal stool on the walls. When he returned to the projection room, everything was just as he had left it.

When Connie begins to tell about the Wink, many others have experiences to add. Women, in particular have had sightings in the ladies' restroom on the second floor. This spirit often shows herself to young girls. Some ladies experience breathlessness in the bathroom or the sensation of being watched.

Many of the people affiliated with The Wink over the years start out skeptical but someone–or something– that lingers in the old theater convinces them that something out of the ordinary happens when the light dim and the curtain falls.

Railroad enthusiasts will want to visit the Dalton Freight Depot Visitor Center, downtown. It's been renovated and is open Monday through Saturday 9AM to 5PM. Dalton is a railfan's hotspot with 50 to 55 trains passing through daily. It is the only place in Georgia besides Atlanta where two different rails lines converge and run side by side: CSX and Norfolk-Southern. There is a viewing platform which offers a wonderful place to photograph the locomotives.

The railroad passes over a supposedly haunted spot here. A Cherokee chief named Young Bird originally built one of the county's earliest homes. He and his wife occupied a log cabin in what later came to be called Hamilton Springs. Young Bird's farm was prosperous with twenty-two acres in cultivation and two large stables. Horses were his passion. He was killed by a fall from one of his thoroughbreds in the late 1830's and buried on the property. His wife was probably sent on the Trail of Tears soon after.

The house was then occupied by John Hamilton while his home, the first brick house in Dalton, was being constructed. Hamilton was a civil engineer for the Western and Atlantic, the railroad line which built their iron road directly across Chief Young Bird's grave.

The Crown Cotton Mill was built on the former Indian property in 1884. But neither the huge cotton mill, the imposing brick house nor the railway itself could stop Chief Young Bird's soul from returning to harass those who encroach upon his final resting place.

The Hamilton House is open by appointment. It offers a history of Whitfield County; the Tufted Bedspread Museum, The Civil War Room, Crown Cotton Mill Hall and many other historic artifacts.

While you are in Dalton, enjoy spirits of a different kind. Stop in at Dalton Distillery. Raymond Butler, who passed away in 2021, who was the distillery's master distiller had been involved in making moonshine since he was six. Now his son and grandson manage the distillery. Raymond's Reserve is named in his honor. You can tour the distillery and buy a bottle of the only sunflower spirits in the world, TazaRay, made using Raymond's family recipe from malted sunflower seeds and corn. I wouldn't be surprised if Raymond's spirit is still lingering to look after the distillery.

Tunnel Hill is a small community just outside of Dalton. The tunnel was built in 1850, the first south of the Mason-Dixon Line. The Clisby-Austin House located nearby was used as a hospital as well as General Sherman's headquarters while he planned the siege of Atlanta. Today it is privately owned but you can view the exterior from behind a small picket fence.

One interesting story about the house is that of General John Bell Hood's leg. The General was wounded and had his leg amputated. He was sent to the Clisby-Austin House to recuperate. The leg was sent with him in case he died it could be buried with him. However he lived and the leg is buried alone in the family cemetery. Perhaps his leg gets restless and seeks the missing body, who knows?

This is the scene of a huge Civil War re-enactment each September. It's a wonderful way to relive those historical days. The tunnel area was the scene of much fighting during the Civil War. Perhaps that is the reason that re-enactors have frequently witnessed ghostly soldiers in and near the tunnel. Ken Sumner, Captain of the 35th Tennessee Infantry Reenactment Group when I met him, has had some hair-raising experiences. He said, "I had personally experiences many unexplainable phenomena and was in hopes that we could determine it had been either natural occurrences, my imagination, or actual activity of a paranormal nature."

On March 16, 2002, Ken met with some researchers from the Foundation for Paranormal Research at the battleground site. Their efforts were rewarded early on. In the early morning hours, they recorded what appeared to be a young man saying "See, see" or "Can't see" or "Sleep sleep" or "Can't sleep."

Shortly after this, Ken was able to "converse" with an entity by means of his Field Strength Meter. This is a device that detects unusually high amounts of electromagnetic energy. He explains what occurred.

This meter began emitting a most peculiar tonal pattern, almost as singing and I was called to listen. When I entered it seemed to me an attempt to communicate through this device (as modulating the signal would be the easiest way for a weak entity to convey information). Additionally, my past employment in Communication and Control Signaling made me more aware of this modulation. Not knowing that this had never been done with the group and thinking they were in communications, I began a series of questions to see if this entity if it was such and not just stray electrical phenomena, would try to communicate. 'He' or 'It' or 'They' indeed wished to communicate.

My questions in this peculiar situation tended to be aimed at determining if this was a soldier from 1860's or not, or if a pattern could be determined. It appeared that several (perhaps 3) were in the tent. The questions began with 'are you a soldier? Answer 1 beep for NO and 2 for YES' (reason being that 2 beeps to me would indicate something trying to answer yes and not just a fluke beep). The answer came following a ramping up of the field sense audio tones from the meter (and these in almost a sing-song) followed by 2 beeps. The contact lasted for over an hour and could have gone longer except for need of a break, with an increasing feeling that more information was contained in the ramping up tonal quality, as well as the answer beeps. I attempted to determine the soldiers name and came up with a last name of Yancy, either Tom (or Thomas) or William.

In breaking, I asked 'Tom' if he'd like to go sit by the fire and have a cup of coffee with me, and he indicated 'Yes' with 2 beeps. On leaving the tent, I distinctly felt something follow me out. I poured his coffee in my Civil War type cup and drank my own in a borrowed cup.

In the course of the "conversion," Ken determined that there were 23 separate spirits there. At least two of them were malevolent.

Two of the other investigators saw the image of a Confederate soldier in his gray uniform when a lightning flash illuminated the field. Ken was aware of a presence he calls "My Sentry" and alerted the group photographer when the spirit was present. The photographer took a photo, which showed a large orb where Ken said "My Sentry" was standing.

Ken Sumner and many others continue to have experiences here with many spirits of Confederate soldiers. He has found that these occur more often on very cold nights. Perhaps this has to do with the fact that Civil War General Patrick Cleburne, known as "Stonewall of the West," and his soldiers camped there during one of the coldest winters ever, 1863 to 1864. Naturally the weather took its toll on the poorly supplied Confederates. Add to that the five to seven clashes that took place at Tunnel Hill, where hundreds of Union troops and an unknown number of Confederates gave their all.

When you think of the tremendous loss of lives, most of them young men in their prime, it is not surprising that the once blood soaked fields still harbor the restless spirits of these soldiers.

If you find yourself in the vicinity of the Mitchell Bridge heading towards Chatsworth at night, beware. You could be chased by a headless horseman, the spirit of a wealthy man who buried his money somewhere and did not live long enough to retrieve it. He was decapitated and buried in a nearby cemetery. He doesn't want to harm you. He just wants to tell you where the money is.

Three historical groups are predominant in Whitfield history; the Cherokee, the Confederates and the Union Soldiers. All represented a bloody segment of Georgia history so perhaps there are many more restless spirits waiting to be discovered here.

Chapter 27 Dahlonega, America's First Gold Rush

Gold! Since the beginning of time the quest for the precious metal has led men a merry chase. It brings out the best in mankind and the worst. It has opened new frontier. The settling of the American West owes much to the California Gold Rush of 1849.

Nearly three centuries earlier, Hernando De Soto had ranged halfway around the world searching for El Dorado, the fabled seven cities of gold in northwestern Georgia. Strangely enough, that was the site of the first American Gold Rush.

Twenty years before Sutter's Mill, the Appalachian foothills of northwest Georgia rang with the excited shouts of successful prospectors.

It all began in 1828 when Benjamin Parks was out deer hunting and kicked at a rock. The rock was a gold nugget and the rush was on. Before it ended, thirty three million dollars of the purest gold ever mined in the United States was taken from the ground and the city of Dahlonega was born.

Word of Mr. Parks golden pebble spread like wildfire. Prospectors, fired by the dream of instant riches, flocked to the area. They originally settled mainly in an area about six miles south of present day Dahlonega around the William Dean cabin. The settlement was first informally called Deans but when Nathaniel Nuckolls provided a tavern for their entertainment, the grateful miners changed the name to Nuckollsville. In spite of the name, the miners were generally law abiding and only one murder was ever committed in the town.

John C. Calhoun, later to become vice president, was a mine owner in the area. He favored a more dignified name for the town. His friend Dr. Croft suggested Aureola meaning "shining like gold." In 1833, the citizens adopted a slightly different version, Auraria, meaning "gold mine or gold region."

By this time, the thriving city was locked in battle with its neighbor to the north for the right to be Lumpkin County Seat. Dahlonega was the victor. The courthouse was built in 1836. Auraria's final death knell was sounded in 1838 when the nation's first branch mint opened in Dahlonega. Today all that remains of Auraria are a few old ruins. Woodie's grocery located on Auraria Road, off highway 52 was the last to go. Kate Woody. The last of the family to own the store, ran it for over 45 year. She kept it open until 1997. Someone bought it from the Woody family recently so maybe he or she will renovate this almost forgotten piece of history.

When gold was discovered in California most of the prospectors who had not found their fortune in Georgia headed west. Gold still continued to be extracted from deep beneath Georgians red clay until early in the twentieth century when the government fixed the price of gold at $35 per ounce. Although rich veins still lay beneath the earth, it was no longer profitable to mine it. In 1958 and again in 1980, gold donated by the citizens of Lumpkin County was sent to Atlanta to cover the capitol dome with some of the purest ore in the country.

Dahlonega's gold still lies buried deep within its hills but it reaps another rich bounty. Today, Dahlonega mines the golden tide of tourism.

The old county courthouse, built in 1836, still stands. It is the fourth oldest courthouse still in existence and the state's second most visited museum. It houses the Dahlonega Gold Museum and tells the history of Lumpkin County from the gold rush days until the present. Its exhibits and film give you an exciting glimpse of a turbulent era. With such a heritage, it's only natural that there would be some restless spirits still hanging around.

To find evidence of them you need look no farther than the courthouse wall. There is a framed photo taken by an amateur photographer, Madeline Anthony, at the Mount Hope Cemetery. Ms. Anthony was cleaning up the cemetery grounds with another church member on a spring day in 1953. She shot several snapshots of their handiwork to show the church committee. She had them developed and printed and had the developer enlarge the one he considered the best. When she looked at the finished print, there, among the gravestones, were the images of several people dressed in old-fashioned clothing.

Since no one had been there when she took the photo, she confronted the studio that had developed the prints. The person who developed them had no idea where they could have come from but he had no inclination or motive to play this kind of trick. He assured her he had neither the money, time nor skill necessary to superimpose this many other images on the negative. His assessment was that she had truly captured spirits from the past. Look at the photo and decide for yourself.

The Dahlonega Inn formerly the Historic Worley House Bed and Breakfast Inn has an unusual and well-authenticated story. The inn was built in 1845, and was once the home of William Jasper Worley and his family. When the War between the States broke out, William Worley enlisted in the Confederate Army and was elected Captain of Company D of the 1st Georgia State Line Regiment.

After the war during the late 1800s, Captain Worley was clerk of the court in Dahlonega. The captain was the owner of the Buford Gazette. In that era, children passed into adulthood much earlier. So when he sent his son, Claude, to Buford to manage the newspaper it was not unusual. Claude was 14 and ready to step into young manhood. It was a quirk of fate that decreed that the promising boy would never live to fulfill his potential.

In Buford, young Claude stayed at a private home and was friends with two local boys. As part of his job he would get the mail from the train that passed nearby. The three teens went to the station one day to do that. What happened next is uncertain. Perhaps "boys will be boys" then as they are now and the three dared one another to risk crossing the tracks as the train approached.

Whatever the reason, two of the youngsters emerged unhurt. Claude did not. He was struck by the train and died. Claude's body was returned home to his grieving parents and was buried in Mount Hope cemetery. The child's mother, Victoria, never recovered from the loss of her son. She went into deep mourning and remained thus for the rest of her life. She would often sit by her son's gravesite for hours

The next owners, Frances and Bill Mauldin, restored the home to its 1800's roots and operated it as a bed and breakfast. In 1999, Frances brought in a professional photographer to take photos of the home for use in an advertising brochure. She picked a few to use and the rest of the photos were stored for several years then when she got them out to study, she noticed something strange.

One of the bedroom pictures had an unusual blur. Not just a ruined photo, the picture had a misty impression of a young boy lying in the bed. There is a picture of young Claude Worley on display in the house and it bears a striking resemblance to the ghostly photo. Frances sent the picture to a firm that specializes in authentication pictures. They found that this picture could not have been altered.

She does not wish to use the photograph as an advertising gimmick out of respect for the dead child's family.

Right from the beginning of the restoration, odd things began to happen in the home. If anyone in the house engaged in an argument, the front door would open by itself. One of the bathroom windows continues to opens by itself. During the renovation, they were allowed to install storm windows but had to keep the original windows in place. One of the old windows would raise by itself, but the new storm window stayed down.

Mark and Darcy Pitman are the current owners. They purchased the Worley homestead in 2023 and are maintaining the colonial charm but updated with modern amenities and technology.

The visitor's center is on the square and is a good place to gather brochures and information. The square, which is registered as a National Historic District, offers many small shops ranging from art and antiques to jewelry and native crafts. If you only stop in one store, make it the Dahlonega General Store. It's a step back in time to the old country store and then some. Its nickel cups of coffee should be inducement enough.

The Holly Theater is another must see. You can see a live stage performance or a performance by someone that is no longer alive. Many unearthly occurrences are observed in the theater. Usually after it is closed and mortal theatergoers have returned home, glowing, white clad figures float past the etched glass windows. During performances, you may feel a sudden cold spot or catch a glimpse of a misty shape on stage. Sometimes the building's lights flicker unexplainably.

Randall Holly Brannon built the theater in 1947. It closed in the 70s and began a downward spiral until 1992. Some private citizens banded together and purchased it as a community theater. After renovation, it reopened for live shows in 1994 and for movies in 1995.

The community is justly proud of the theater and knows of nothing in its history that would explain the phenomena. It is believed that a house stood on the site in the mid 1800s. Perhaps some dark happening in that earlier structure has remained on the site.

Since the gold rush was such an important part of the town's history, you need to visit one or more of the mines.

Crisson Gold Mine offer's you the chance to watch a 113 year old stamp mill crush the ore out of gold bearing quartz. There are only two original working stamp mills in the eastern United States and this is the only one in Georgia.

Consolidated Gold Mine offers you another view of mining. This one is deep in the ground. The shaft where you enter was once buried under a small mountain. Between 1845 and 1880, the mountain was blasted away to expose the ore. That was not done with explosives as you might think but with huge water hoses by a process called hydraulic mining.

When all of the loose material was washed away, then the hard rock mining began. After testing for the best locations, tunnels were blasted into the rock with dynamite so that the miners could get to the quartz that contained the precious mineral. In 1901, the largest gold containing quartz vein in the world was discovered here. It measured over twenty-two feet thick.

The most obvious feature you see when you go underground is the Glory Hole. The Glory Hole is the place where all the major veins converged. As they dug it out the result was an immense skylight opening from the bowels of the earth to a view of clear blue sky. As you stand here on the rock floor of the first level, you are 300 feet beneath the surface and 140 feet below the water table.

There were three levels in the original mine but no one has been into the bottom tunnel for over a hundred years. It is believed to be over a mile long and a thousand feet deep. When the price of gold dropped in 1906, the miners left the mine as it was tools and all.

To keep intruders out, they dynamited the entrance. This was where the water was being pumped out, so all the water and debris that washed down the open glory hole rapidly filled the mine. Over 4,000 tons of debris had to be removed to open the top tunnel. Excavations are still being done in the lower tunnels.The original machinery is still there and, wonder of wonders, most of it still works. Your tour guides are actual miners so they give a very technically accurate and highly informed tour.Both mines have a gold panning area where you can experience the actual thrill of panning your own gold.

Dahlonega sits on the edge of the Appalachian Mountains, so the fall leaf show is gorgeous but the scenery is breathtaking all year.

Hiking, horseback riding, and canoeing on the white water rivers are all popular pastimes here.

No trip to North Georgia is complete without a visit to Amicalola Falls State Park. The park offers camping, cabins, a luxurious lodge and restaurants as well as other park amenities. Amicalola is the Cherokee word meaning "tumbling waters." That's certainly an appropriate word for these 729-foot falls, the highest in Georgia.

Over a century ago, the Cherokee braves would journey up the mountain on a vision quest. To them the falls were sacred. When the white man came, the beauty of the area impressed them. Today, you can vacation at an impressive stone lodge built atop the mountain.

But while you enjoy the view from the dining room, keep a sharp eye on the kitchen. It's here that the spirits manifest their displeasure at anyone disturbing the serenity of the mountain. Should any of the kitchen staff began to squabble, they may become a target for a flying pot or pan. The utensils often fly across the room from a hook on the wall when no one is near them. The staff has often experienced patches of icy air in the otherwise steamy kitchen. The only explanation is that the Indian spirits do not want their sacred mountain defiled.

Aside from the otherworldly phenomena, Dahlonega is a great place to visit if you like festivals, this area abounds. Dahlonega has Bear on the Square and World Championship Gold Panning Competition the third weekend in April, Wildflower Festival of the Arts the third weekend in May, Bluegrass Festival in June, Family Day, Celebration of July fourth, Sidewalk Sale Charity Festival in August, Gold Rush Days third weekend in October, and Old Fashioned Christmas every weekend in December.

Amicalola State Park also has frequent festivals and events to promote the mountain culture. Appalachian Pioneer Trading Days are a celebration of the old ways.

Foxfire/Civil War Days introduce you to an earlier way of life with everything from military drills to ladies fashion shows. This event is usually held in the beginning of November. To celebrate more modern ways, Dahlonega launched its first annual independent film festival in 2001.

Whether you leave with a nugget of gold or a head full of information you are sure to have fun acquiring it in Dahlonega.

Chapter 28 Helen, The Town That Led Two Lives

In 1968, the town of Helen was dying. Little was left in the remote mountain community except a few drab old concrete buildings and a few diehard citizens determined to save their hometown. They hit on a unique solution.

Helen had begun life with a promising start. During the Georgia Gold Rush of 1828, the precious metal was discovered nearby at Dukes Creek. Then when the gold fever died down, the settlers realized they had another resource, timber. The Byrd-Matthews Lumber Company and the Gainesville and Northwestern Railroad came to town in 1913. The town was officially named Helen after the daughter of a railroad surveyor. The lumber was depleted by 1931 and people began to drift away.

One of the local residents was an artist named John Kollock, who had spent some years in Germany. He and the other residents realized the one thing they had in abundance was a beautiful mountain setting. They decided to recreate their town with a Bavarian flavor.

Today, Helen's downtown is completely renovated as an Alpine village. Chalets filled with craft shops and cobblestone streets blossom with bright flowers. Unique shops and restaurants play host to millions of visitors every year. Mountain crafts such as pottery are found side by side with Bavarian glass blowers. In addition to the shopping found in the village, Alpine Outlet Mall offers direct from factory savings.

Another natural boon to Helen's success story is the Chattahoochee River which flows through the town. Several of the restaurants, like Paul's, are located on its bank and offer dining over the water. The fast flowing river provides an opportunity for tubing. There are several tubing outfitters who will provide you with tubes and shuttle service. Since the water is extremely shallow, it is safe for any age tuber.

If you want to stay close to the river, try the Riverbend Motel and Cabins. There are rumors that it is haunted by children. At night you can hear kids running down the halls, knocking on doors and laughing.

The favorite festival in Helen is the Octoberfest, held annually from mid-September into November. Another of their annual activities is Fasching, a German Mardi Gras, held in February and an outdoor Christmas market and winter festival.

The area also provides horse drawn carriage tours, horseback riding, an amusement park with rides and miniature golf, a golf course and hot air balloon rides. Of course, they provide both public and private campgrounds that can accommodate anything from the smallest pup tent to the largest motor coach.

A mile south of Helen, Narcoohee Village is home to some fun shopping. Habersham Winery and tasting room offers a supply of Georgia wines and Nora Mill is one of the few remaining water powered grist mills still in operation

Concerts and dramatic performances are offered frequently in the Santee-Nacoochee Arts and Community Center. In fact, Santee-Nacoochee has been named one of the 100 Best Small Arts Towns in America. It's History Museum is housed in the community center and preserves much of the area history. They perform plays related to the history of the valley called Headwaters. Sautee Center has a folk pottery museum strictly devoted to folk pottery.

The Old Sautee Store/Museum is the oldest continually operating store in White County. It dates back to 1873 when it was also the post office. The museum part houses the largest collection of old store memorabilia likely to be found anywhere in Georgia.

Near here you will find the Nacoochee Indian Mound. Marked by a round, white gazebo, the mound is the burial place of ancient Indians. Legend claims it is the final resting place for two star crossed Indian lovers, Sautee and Nacoochee belonged to warring tribes. Saute, a brave of the Chickasaw tribe and Nacoochee, daughter of a Cherokee chief, met and fell in love. They secretly met one night and ran away to nearby Yonah Mountain where they enjoyed a few idyllic days together. Then they had to pay the piper. They confronted Nachoochee's father, Chief Wahoo, and suggested creating peace between the two nations. He would not consider such a thing and instead ordered Sautee thrown from the high cliffs of Yonah Mountain. Nacoochee broke free from her father's braves who held her captive and leaped from the cliff to join her lover. As she smashed into the ground at the base of the cliff, the dying Santee dragged his broken body to join her and the star-crossed locked in a fatal embrace.

Chief Wahoo was devastated by the death of his daughter and at last repented. He buried the lovers, together there on the banks of the Chattahoochee River in a burial mound.

Their spirits are together forever and roam this area. The Smithsonian Institute excavated the area in 1914 and found that it once held over 300 dwellings.

Many visitors don't realize that the site of the gazebo is part of Hardman Farm. The magnificent Italianate home was built in 1870 by Captain James Nichols. It was the home of Anna Ruby Nichols, the namesake of nearby Anna Ruby Falls.

You can tour the old milking barn was that operated from 1910 until the mid-1920s, the spring house, and former horse barn. The tree-lined road leading from the Visitor Center to the house was once part of the historic Unicoi Turnpike, a 200-mile road that went from Toccoa to western North Carolina and eastern Tennessee. It was originally a buffalo trail, then a Native American trading route. Today, there is the Helen to Hardman Heritage Trail along the river between the old farmstead and Helen.

Across the road from the mounds is Crescent Hill Baptist Church. It's a pre-Civil War church built by slave labor. Many people visiting it especially at night experience an overpowering scent of roses.

Continuing down Highway 255 N a few miles, there is an old covered bridge. It's called the Stovall Mill Covered Bridge. The first bridge was built in the early 1800s, but washed away in floodwaters n the early 1890s and replaced in 1895. This is the bridge still standing today. You may have seen it in the 1951 movie "*I'd Climb The Highest Mountain*" starring Susan Hayward. There is a ghostly legend that predates the bridge. The story is that an old enslaved woman threw her baby into the river, drowning it, probably so it would not grow up as a slave. Supposedly, if you stand inside the bridge at night you will hear the spirit of the baby crying. Another story says you can hear a horse-drawn carriage driving across the bridge. No idea of where that part of the story comes from. Perhaps someone who died in an accident before or after crossing the bridge.

The bridge spans Chickamauga Creek near the old Stovall House, now The Stovall House Bed and Breakfast with a ghost or two of its own. The home was built by Moses Harshaw known locally as "the meanest man who ever lived." According to one online genealogy site, his tombstone reads, "Died and Gone to Hell."

He was known to treat his slaves horribly. Possibly the reason the poor woman threw her baby in the creek. Drowning was better than being owned by Moses. When one of his slave grew old or was unproductive, Moses took him to Lynch Mountain and pushed him over a cliff to dispose of him. Some stories said Moses would make a slave he wanted to dispose of dig his own grave then would shoot the slave as he stood over the hole.

Moses refused to let his slaves ride in a wagon. He would put a halter around the slave's neck and drag him behind the wagon so that he to run to keep up.

A tragedy occurred once while he was out of town. His young daughter died. In those days of pre-embalming and pre-refrigeration, bodies needed to be buried quickly. His wife, Nancy, bought a dress for dead baby's burial outfit. She paid $10 at the local store. When Moses returned and learned of the purchase, he was so irate that he had the dead baby dug up so he could see the dress he felt was exorbitantly priced. Nancy divorced him.

Not only was Moses a cruel miser, he was charged with manslaughter several times but as a lawyer, he was able to get the charges thrown out.

Ham Schwartz, the former owner, says he feels the little dead girl is still present. She seems to be protective of her former home. He feels there is another spirit of a former owner who also looks after the historic home and its residents.

The William Stovall family, who give the historic house its name, were the owners of the house from 1893 to the late 1940's. They were the ones who built the mill and were in residence for the longest. When the Stovalls sold it to ex-navy doctor, Austin Walter, people in the valley now had much needed medical care and a true country doctor to look out for them. Apparently Dr. Walter has never stopped looking out for his people.

After Ham Schwartz bought the home one of his employees had an interesting experience. Several people were working in the kitchen. One of the women went out to unload some supplies from the car and fell and cut her wrist on a broken bottle. Another woman working with her tried to stop the bleeding with a tourniquet on the wrist but it did not seem to be helping. Then a fair haired man behind her spoke up and told her to move the tourniquet farther up the arm. The woman did so and the bleeding stopped. At that point another employee came in and watched her actions. "Why did you move the tourniquet?" he asked.

"Because the blond haired man standing behind me told me to," the woman replied.

'What man? There is no one there," he stated.

As Ham explained, Dr. Walter seems to still be acting as a guardian angel for the people at his old home. He told me of another case where a doctor was on the receiving end of the same type of phenomena. The doctor had been out of town for about a month and when he returned, he was called out to visit a sick patient. He took a different route because the weather was stormy. He was driving his buggy towards a bridge over a river when he saw a familiar figure waving him to a stop. He recognized a former patient he had worked hard with to patch up a badly broken leg. But the man was acting strange. He didn't respond to the doctors greetings. Perplexed, the doctor got out of the buggy and walked a few steps forward where he saw the bridge he was soon to cross. It was now washed away by the storm. Had he continued he would have fell to his death.

When he returned to his office the next day, he told his partner about the incident with the former patient. The partner looked at him with a strange expression on his face. "That's impossible. That man died while you were out of town. I signed his death certificate." he explained.

In December of 2018, Schwartz sold it to Jeff Sidwell and Erin Fight who maintained as a peaceful bed and breakfast and events center.

Have an urge to get back to nature? That's easily satisfied in this area, too. The Dukes Creek Waterfall is a series of cascading falls, one of which falls a breathtaking 300 feet. It's located off Richard

Russell Scenic Highway, Hwy 348 which runs between Hwy 180 and Hwy 75A about 3 miles west of Helen. This highway is worth a trip just for its scenic vistas. Raven Cliff Falls is located off here. Another popular falls in the area is Anna Ruby Falls located northeast of Helen near the entrance to Unicoi State Park on Hwy 356.

Unicoi is a large diverse park offering camping, cabins, lodge, craft shop and restaurant as well as normal park activities. They offer planned programs and activities, such as a day set aside to celebrate the old Appalachian crafts. The lodge there is one of the area's top lodgings. That it exists today is largely due to one woman, Amilee Chastain Graves who was known as the "First Lady of the Mountains." Amilee was a woman ahead of her time. She was a newspaper publisher, a mayor, and a visionary who worked tirelessly to make the northeast Georgia Mountains a better place to live.

Born on November 18, 1910 in Winder, Georgia, she went on to graduate from Berry College in 1929. After her marriage to Charles Taylor Graves, they both ran a small Clarksville Georgia newspaper. In 1950, Amilee was elected as mayor of Clarkesville, the first woman to hold an elected office in Habersham County and one of the first female mayors in Georgia.

Amilee 's most prized contribution to Georgia was her role in the planning and construction of the lodge and conference center at Unicoi State Park. She was chairman of the North Georgia Mountains Authority and worked for ten years to obtain funding for the center.

Amilee's daughter Lynne noted, "I believe Unicoi was one of mother's most fulfilling projects. The completion of that facility was one of the highlights of her life."

The conference center was named for Amilee and her portrait still hangs over the main fireplace in the lodge's great room. Amilee passed away November 3, 1983 and was buried in Clarkesville. But her soul remains with her beloved park lodge. Night crew workers have reported many strange occurrences which they attribute to Amilee. They believe her spirit is still looking after her favorite park.

Also nearby, three miles west of Helen on Hwy 75A, is Smithgall Woods Dukes Creek Conservation Area. This opened in 1994 and is the only one like it in the state as far as I was able to find out. It provides eighteen miles of road, five miles of trails, and four miles of creek bank. It allows hiking, biking, and catch and release fishing and is closed to public vehicular traffic. Van tours are provided free at specific times. Call to check the times. It provides education on conservation and has some interesting display on the subject as well as a disabled hawk they are rehabilitating. They offer frequent activities dealing with nature such as a class on distinguishing edible from poisonous mushrooms and herbal information. They have a convention center for businesses or groups who want to conduct their conventions in a natural setting and the elegant Lodge at Smithgall Woods for an overnight mountain retreat. The park requires a state park pass or a small daily fee for admittance and its tours and activities are free.

If you like to shop or do almost anything else, Helen and the surrounding area can satisfy your vacation needs. Oh, by the way if you like to pretend you're visiting the Alps and climb mountains, they can provide lots of those, too.

Chapter 29 Jasper and Ellijay, Marble and Apples

Legends tell that an Irish stonecutter, Henry Fitzsimmons, evicted from a stagecoach in Pickins County for imbibing too freely from his jug of moonshine, recognized a fine marble outcropping along the road. The pink marble torn from the red clay of Pickins County became famous around the world. Jasper Marble Festival recalls the days when "Colonel Sam," one of Georgia Marble's more colorful presidents, ruled the county with an iron hand

Sam Tate was a domineering man in life. He wanted things done his way. He made a fortune on the pink marble his company mined. He built a magnificent mansion to showcase his product. Today Sam's lavish home is a bed and breakfast. Tate House was begun in 1923 under Sam's personal supervision. It took over four years to complete but it was a masterpiece. Sam, his brother, Luke, and sister, Florentine, moved into the palatial residence in 1926. Sam demanded total control of everything he touched; his home, his employees and even the county. He dictated his employee's personal morals forbidding any behavior he deemed inappropriate. Perhaps that is why it's no surprise that he refused to leave his home after death. It's more of a mystery why his sister is still hanging around the mansion,

Col. Sam must have been upset after the last living Tate family member left the home sometime after 1955. The neglected palace fell into disrepair. It was a favorite hangout of the town's young people who wanted a place to sneak some forbidden pleasures and give themselves the thrill of a good scare.

Things began looking up for the mansion in 1974 when Ann Laird discovered it. Ann moved her family from Arizona and with their help began the massive restoration project. She furnished with gracious antiques and the Laird family used it as their home as well as a lavish bed and breakfast. The back area looking out on a pleasant patio was refurbished into a bar to host weddings and parties. The entire family knew they still shared the home with the original owner and his sister but they respected each other so it worked out okay.

Occasionally the otherworld inhabitants startled one of the guests. Ms. Laird's daughter, Cindy Navarro, told me of a guest who was attending a wedding held there. The lady confined that she didn't believe in any of "that nonsense." However, when she came out of her room for breakfast the next morning she was rather agitated. When asked why, she admitted "I had left my panty hose lying on the floor last night. Of course, I locked my door. But when I woke up this morning someone had picked up the panty hose and rinsed them in the basin."

Her hostess just shrugged "I told her it was probably Miss Flora."

She recounted another incident she witnessed. "Someone stole a large gilt framed portrait of Col. Sam. I don't know how they got such a huge thing out but they did. We had offered a reward for its return. Anyway, I was tending the bar a few days after and I saw Col. Sam pacing up and down in the back patio. He looked pretty agitated. I think he was upset about the theft of his picture."

Then in January 2001, the estate once again changed hands. It was purchased by Holbrook Properties, LP. Lois Holbrook and Marsha Mann continue the restoration of the mansion and gardens. It is now used as a venue for weddings, receptions and special events

The highlight of the year is the Marble festival held in October each year. The public is allowed to tour the largest open pit marble quarries in the world during the Annual Georgia Marble Festival. Be sure to make a reservation since the tours are limited and fill up fast. Also make sure you visit the Marble Museum for a look at both the history and art of marble.

While downtown, you want to tour the Old Jail. From 1906 until 1980, it served to house inmates on the top floor and the sheriff and his family on the bottom. Murray County Paranormal Investigations recently did an investigation and found paranormal activity at the Old Pickens County Jail and the Quinton-Kirby Cabin that is located next to the jail.

Next door to the jail, you can view how a less affluent citizen lived in Pickins County in the nineteenth century. Tom Quinton reconstructed the log home from the original logs used in the frontier cabin of Stephen and Mary Mann Kirby who are both buried in the little cemetery next to the church in Jasper.

Pickens County Master Gardeners designed and maintain the heritage garden at the cabin and will sell you some seeds if you want a unique living memory of the place.

In the northern region of Gilmer County near Ellijay there is a section called Whitepath. There is a small marker telling you this was once the home of the Cherokee Indian Chief Whitepath. He was born in 1761 near Ellijay and grew up in a cabin that once stood here. In 1814 he helped General Andrew Jackson defeat the Creeks at the Battle of Horseshoe Bend. White Path opposed his people adopting white ways and felt they should remain true to the traditional ways. When Jackson passed the Indian Removal Act, he joined Chief John Ross to travel to Washington and denounced the removal treaty signed by Major Ridge and his followers as void. Of course Jackson would not give in. In the fall of 1838 White Path, then 77 years old, left on the Trail of Tears and died en-route at Hopkinsville, Kentucky.

It is said he cursed any future owners of his land. Later a hotel was built on the land. It was the scene of several murders and suicides. It burned down in the early 20th century. People passing near the site report hearing screams and moans. It is said Chief Whitepath still roams his land at night.

A great way to get away from modern hustle and bustle is to go glamping at Elatse'Yi, a Cherokee word meaning "verdant, green earth." I stayed a few days in a geodesic dome in a large private site on their six-acre farm among woods with chickens, goats, and a great Pyrenees for neighbors.

The large dome sat on a fenced wooden dock and was furnished with a double bed and two singles spread about the room. Tables, desk, stocked bookcases, a telescope for star gazing and rugs on the wooden floors made for a comfortable experience. I had a private outdoor bathroom and shower as well as a deep soaking tub and a canopied picnic table and chairs. There is a well-stocked cowboy kitchen.

It's near man-made 3200-acre Carters Lake, a perfect place for kayaking or fishing. Many believe there are spirits lurking around the lake. Some have seen a man in a ball cap and jeans. Others have reported seeing a little blond-haired girl playing and then disappearing. Perhaps some of the Cherokee who once owned this land still remain.

While not exactly a ghost there is another mysterious presence here. Bigfoot has been seen often in these mountains. Expedition Bigfoot is not a hokey-scary spot. It is a real-life investigative research hub. Owner, David Bakara, stated, "I have seen two of them." He was referring to when he and his wife Melinda spotted the creatures on a research expedition in Florida using a thermal imaging camera. The BRAT, an ATV set up for researching Bigfoot, is on display.

The museum is filled with one of the largest collection of artifacts like footprints, handprints, butt print, hair sample, and feces sample from bigfoot. The videos give a background of factual sightings. There are newspaper accounts. Headphones let you listen to recorded "conversations" of bigfoots vocalizations. Believer or non-believer, you will enjoy this museum.

Ellijay is filled with agri-tourism places like wineries, farms, and orchards. R and A Orchard is a third generation orchard owned by Jennifer and Andy Futch. They are open year round and offer home-grown apples, peaches, blackberries, corn, strawberries and other produce in the roadside market as well as a small restaurant serving home-style meals and the best peach ice cream ever. They offer seasonal tours and u-pick opportunities in the orchard.

Other agri-tourism options include Engelheim Winery, Cartecay Winery, Fainting Goat Vineyards, Mountain Valley Farm, and more. Ellijay hosts the Apple Festival in October.

When it comes to dining you have a lot of choices. Music and dining go together here. The night I dined at Cantaberry, Matty Croxton was performing. He was equally as good as the Tomato Basil Soup, Chicken Salad, Philly Cheesesteak sandwich. The desserts there are to die for. Cantaberry is located on the square and has inside or patio dining.

Since I love outdoor dining in nice weather, Back Porch Bistro was another favorite. Salads are scrumptious. Again music was playing. The singer/guitarist inside said there would be a group of musicians arriving to play within the hour but I had to more on. So much more to see.

Mountain Town Coffee at Hemlock Bazaar is a perfect choice for breakfast. Aside from great food, it has good wifi. You can dine inside or in the outside back patio. There are many other choices that no matter your favorite food, you will find it here.

The many antique shops transport you to different eras. Just off the square in Ellijay I browsed at Main Street Antiques, Antiques on North Main, Antiques Outback, and Black Bear in East Ellijay.

Chapter 30 Blairsville, Hiawassee and Blue Ridge, Cherokee Homeland

Once it was part of the land of the Cherokees. They roamed at will in its green valley and brought forth abundant crops from it red clay soil. In spring, they watched the white Dogwood flower in its bridal splendor. In summer, they shared the multitude of wild fruit and nuts-blackberries, wild strawberries, black walnuts-with the black bear and the raccoons.

When the leaves on the surrounding mountains turned every shade from vivid yellow to flaming orange to scarlet red, they knew soon it would be winter, a time of stark beauty and bone chilling cold. White snow would lie on the ground. The leafless trees would cast a sharp shadow on the earth. The crystal columns of ice would climb the steep cliffs. And always there was music in the mountains. The babble of a rushing stream, the moan of the wind, and the song of the people blessed this beauty.

The early settlers began arriving in numbers after 1828, spurred by the gold found nearby; they stayed to farm the land. They brought their dulcimers, fiddles, and banjos, and sang of their mountain life. Sadly, the beginning of a way of life for the settlers chronicled the end for the Cherokees. Most were exiled to Oklahoma via the infamous Trail of Tears. Fortunately, a few remained behind and many more returned when they were able.

Now, the Cherokee lifestyle has been wiped from their old mountain home but traces of their heritage have been indelibly stamped on the land. It remains at places like Blood Mountain.

Located near the Union Lumpkin County line, it is the highest point on the Georgia Appalachian Trail at 4,458 feet. It was revered by the Cherokee as the home of the Nunne'hi, or Immortals, the Spirit People, who lived in the highlands of Cherokee Country.

Perhaps more than the legendary spirit people still linger atop Blood Mountain. It was here the Cherokee and the Creek clashed in a ferocious battle before the white man vanquished both. The battle was so fierce the mountains were colored red with the blood of the many warriors who died here.

Another persistent legend is that when the Cherokee were sent on the Trail of Tears, Blood Mountain was where they buried the gold they could not carry with them. Did they believe the spirits of the slain warriors and the Nunne'hi would guard it until they could return? The Cherokee have never returned to these mountains and the treasure has never been found.

Are the Nunne'hi still guarding the treasure? One piece of evidence says they might. On the upper branch of Nottely River, which flows out of Blood Mountain, there is a hole in the ground, like a small well which emits an unexplained warm vapor that heats the air all around. It makes a nice warming place for hikers and wanders, but don't stay near it too long, because the Nunne'hi are said to still linger there.

The Cherokee left behind other dead besides the warriors. One story concerns Trahlyta's Grave at Marker Number 093-3 on Highway 19 between Dahlonega and Blairsville, you will see a pile of stones in the road where Highway 60 intersects. The pile grows each year. It marks the grave of a Cherokee princess, Trahlyta. Her tribe, lived on Cedar Mountain just to the north. Supposedly, they had learned the secret of the magic springs that granted them eternal youth, from the Witch of Cedar Mountain. A rejected suitor, Wahsega, kidnapped Trahlyta. He took her far away and, deprived of the magic waters, she lost her beauty and her youth. After her death, a repentant Wahsega sorrowfully returned her body to be buried near her home and the magic springs. Custom arose among the Indians and later the white settlers to drop stones, one for each passerby, on her grave for good luck. The magic springs, now called Porter Springs, still flows 3/4 mile northeast of her grave.

Georgia's highest mountain is located in Union County. Brasstown Bald looms 4,784 feet above sea level. It provides a panoramic 360 degree view of four states. The visitor center at the summit houses exhibits about early settlers and Indians. A video presentation presents the four seasons of Brasstown Bald.

It is a fabulous spot to view the changing leaves in fall, but equally spectacular in other seasons. Picnic areas and hiking trails are located on the mountainside. For those who cannot or will not walk the steep trail to the top, a shuttle is available. The mountain, too, still retains traces of the Cherokee. They called it Enotah. Their mythology tells two stories about the mountain. One tells of a flood that killed all people except the ones that landed on the top of this great mountain in a huge canoe. The Great Spirit cleared the land and provided them with crops to survive.

Another story explains the creation of the balds. Bald mountain peaks are a phenomenon that occurs only in the Southern Appalachians. Science had long argued over why certain mountain top between 2,000 and 6,000 feet will not support tree growth. The Cherokee have an explanation. Perhaps theirs is as good as any. The myth goes that in the early days, the villages of the Cherokee were attacked by a monster called Ulagu. This giant hornet like creature would swoop down on the villages and carry off a child. The Indians tracked him to an inaccessible cave on the mountain's peak. The Indians prayed to the Holy Spirit and he sent lightning to shear away the tops of the mountains thus exposing the Ulagu so the warriors could kill him

Another site is found in Union County that may not relate to the Indian spirits but certainly are a lasting memento of their presence in these mountains is Track Rock Petroglyphs.

Located at Track Rock Gap, these six table-sized soapstone boulders, containing hundreds of symbols, carved or pecked into the surfaces, may predate the Cherokee. They may be the remains of an earlier mound building culture that existed here. In fact, the Cherokee name for the gap is Datsu'nalsagun'yi, "where there are tracks." The boulders are formed from soapstone, or steatite, a naturally occurring metamorphic rock common to the Georgia Mountains. Scientists say they could date as far back as 8,000 BC.

One of the common threads in all the mountain communities is the music. Mountain music is still alive and well here. Any weekend from spring through fall you will hear dulcimers and banjos and fiddles playing the old songs.

On Saturday, from Memorial Day through the middle of September, Vogel State Park presents a concert by different area musicians. The concerts are free however donations are requested for the musicians. Mountain Music Festival is a popular music/arts and crafts festival held at Vogel in September. Cabins and camping spots at the park are booked many months ahead for the festival. Vogel also has swimming and fishing in Lake Trahlyta. Just north of the park there is an overview for the waterfall. Vogel is the second oldest state park in Georgia, built in the 1930's.

Another popular spot for concerts is the old Blairsville Court House, currently housing the Historical Society and a museum telling the early history of the county. Concerts take place every Friday night from the first Friday of May through the end of October. 7:00 p.m. Many of the musicians go into the history of the songs and instruments. The courthouse, which is over 100 years old, has been painstakingly renovated and is complete including the clock tower. It is located on the square in Blairsville. Many people believe there are multi-presences in the old courthouse; perhaps criminals or maybe some innocent people who were tried and convicted there.

Back when I lived in Blairsville in the early 2000s, I sold whatever I could find at garage sales and junk shops. My business was housed in a little shop I rented from "Pappy" off Hwy 19 along the Nottely River in an area called Owltown. Pappy's Country Store anchored the mall. There were a bunch of other small shop owners like myself that sold various items. There was a restaurant run by one of Pappy's family members, his son I believe. You had to go to either Fannin or Towns county if you wanted anything stronger than iced tea.

Today Blairsville is home to a genuine distillery. The roots reach far back in mountain lore. Jack "Mimm" was an Appalachian moonshiner from the depression era up to his death in1969. His grandkids called him "Grandaddy Mimm." His product was legendary and only he and a few others knew the recipes. His grandson, country musician, Tommy Townsend, was able to locate the old recipes and has opened Grandaddy Mimm's Distillery just off the square. It hosts concerts and offers tours and tastings.

Another place that has changed and grown since I left Blairsville is my former cabin. Today, it is part of Paradise Hills, Winery Resort & Spa. When I sold my little cabin to Robert and Ilke Lander, they had a few cabins and a beautiful view of the mountains. Today, it has blossomed into an amazing winery, resort and spa. I can vouch for the hard work and kindness of the Landers and am glad to see them prosper.

The mountains that sheltered the settlers also isolated them so that their way of life remained the same long after the rest of the country had become homogenized. Progress came as it will, and in the 1900's, roads were cut into the gaps in the mountains making even Union County, the most mountainous spot, accessible to the rest of the world. Even then access was still difficult. The early Fords were fed their gas via gravity. The steep grade of the mountains prevented the gas from flowing into the engines. Enterprising drivers learned to back their vehicles up the mountains and tie a log to the car on the way down so their brakes wouldn't burn out. Fortunately, modern automobiles can cross the now paved mountain roads with no problem.

Today, the North Georgia Mountains is a popular destination for visitors from all over the world. They are drawn to the culture, the scenery and the spectacular autumn colors. Cabins, bed and breakfasts and campgrounds have sprung up to accommodate them.

Although modern facilities such as dozens of excellent restaurants, groceries, and shops are available, the soul of its early settlers, and the even earlier Cherokee, still is alive and well here. The changes came slowly to the mountains and it was during this period of change that a tragic and talented figure arose.

Byron Herbert Reece was born September 14, 1917 in Union County. The cabin at the base of Blood Mountain in which Hub, as he was called, was born is long gone but a recreation exists at The Byron Herbert Reece Farm and Heritage Center. In Reece's time, Union County depended on farming as its main source of revenue. Today, tourism is prevalent. Visitors have discovered the beauty of the Appalachian Mountains that Reece loved.

His farm home portrays early 20th century farm life in the North Georgia Mountains. It was not an easy life and Reece was always ambivalent about the farming that paid the bills, but took time from his writing. Both his parents contracted tuberculosis and died from it, which put the running of the farm on Reece's shoulder from a young age. Much of his poetry deals with planting and growing crops and the seasons. The visitor's center is the home Reece helped build for his parents. Inside there are artifacts from the home and a large picture of Reece sitting with his frail-looking mother while his father stood facing them in front of the fireplace.

Going outside you see Reece's writing studio, Mulberry Hall, a humble, red-frame building he built with his own hands. Inside there is a lifelike mannequin of Reece writing. As you walk the path there are stone circles with his poems engraved on a center stone. You visit a corncrib, chicken house, smokehouse, springhouse and petting farm with typical farm animals. In the restored barn, you can watch a video about Reece's life. The Farm hosts concerts frequently.

Lake Trahlyta, a man-made lake built with the coming of the Tennessee Valley Authority–and electricity–in the early 1940's, has swallowed some of his earlier traces. But he has left behind some of the most beautiful and haunting poetry of the twentieth century. And, at the Young Harris College Campus, perhaps something of his spirit still remains.

Torn between the past and the present, Hub Reece struggled to maintain the family farm, write four volumes of poetry and two novels and deal with deadly tuberculoses that struck his entire family. Although he never graduated from college, he was hired at Young Harris as a professor. He commuted back and forth between the college dorm where he lived and the family farm he continued to work despite his own disintegrating health.

Disillusioned with the changes coming to his beloved mountains and ravaged by his fatal disease, 'Hub" finished grading his students final papers, put a Mozart record on his player and fatally shot himself through his diseased lung with a 32 caliber pistol. It was on June 3, 1958, just a few months before his forty-first birthday. Hub's story, along with the saga of the mountain peoples' collision with the modern world, is kept alive with the help of the Byron Herbert Reese Society and lots of local labor at the Byron Herbert Reece Farm and Heritage Center on U.S. 129 just north of Vogel State Park.

Whispers tell that Byron Herbert Reese's spirit still walks the campus where he chose to depart this life. One story in circulation is that of several young male students in the late 1960s who decided to sneak into the room where Hub had died and hold a séance. The building was destined to be demolished. Whether in an effort to remove the presence or for economic reasons, who knows. The young men crept into the building in the dead of night through a window. They proceeded to call up the spirit of the dead poet. Suddenly loud footsteps were heard in the hall outside the locked door of the room. The footsteps stopped at the door and the terrified students witnessed the knob turn and the door bend slightly inward. They left the room through the same window they had entered but at a much swifter pace.

The destruction of the suicide building did little to dissipate Hub's spirit. Students today still attempt to sneak into Clegg Hall to find Hub. It is so common it has been given the nickname of "Clegging." Students also report that the water in some of the dorm rooms will turn on by itself sometimes. Is Hub still watching over the mountains he loved in life?

The old way of life that Hub loved is still preserved in the many area festivals. The last three weekends in October, which just happen to be the time the leaves are their most colorful, are devoted to the Sorghum Festival in Blairsville. The Sorghum festival is a celebration of the old ways. It features contests of log splitting, rock throwing, pole climbing, biscuit eating and of course Sorghum grinding and cooking. Local artisans display their wares and mountain music forms a happy background.

Towns County is not left out in the festival department. It hosts the biggest in the area. The Georgia Mountain Festival is held at The Georgia Mountain Fairgrounds on the banks of Lake Chatuge. The advantage is that the permanent buildings like the pioneer village give the fair an authentic touch. These old buildings, like the old one room schoolhouse and the log cabin, lend to the feeling you have stepped into another time. And that's what the festival is all about, recreating the mountain culture of the early Appalachian settlers.

There are ongoing demonstrations of Appalachian life such as the log splitting, blacksmithing, soap and candle making. An authentic water mill grinds meal you can purchase. Antique farm implements, many on loan from local families, are on display. One popular exhibit I enjoyed was Making Moonshine, presented by Mr. Luther Mull. He took us through each step of the process with an expertise that makes you wonder. He explains his intimate knowledge with the phrase "or so I've been told."

In addition to a trip into yesterday, you are treated to an extensive group of artists and craftspersons, lots of food booths, a complete carnival midway and lots of animal acts.

The adjacent Anderson Music Hall, where some of Nashville's best Grand Ole Opry performers have appeared, hosts two professional music shows daily during the summer fair while The Georgia State Fiddler's Convention is held in the fall during the Georgia Mountain Fall Festival. The highlight of the festival is their annual competition for "Georgia Mountain Fiddle King."

Towns County square has a gazebo that hosts musicians on the weekend. It too has unique shops and galleries nearby.

Water fun is also a popular pastime here. Lake Nottely provides a 4,180 body of water for fishing, boating or swimming. Lake Winifred Scott is another popular lake. Nottely River provides an opportunity for tubing, fishing, or wading. Another popular pastime is visiting the county's many waterfalls. Desoto Falls, Helton, and Dukes Creek Falls are the major ones but there are countless tiny falls located throughout the national forest. The many wildlife areas are great places to visit if you want to spot some bears, deer or other native animals. Just remember that bears are wild and should not be fed.

Hiking is also popular. The granddaddy of all trails, the Appalachian Trail crosses Union County at Neals' Gap. Mountain Crossings at Walasi-Yi Center, located there, is an outfitter, hostel and general gathering place for hikers. The owner, Winton Porter, wrote a great book highlighting stories and people he's met on the trail and at the shop through the years. It's called *Just Passin' Thru*. He also has a Boot Museum at the shop. Look up and you will see a plethora of well-worn hiking boots when you walk into the shop. You might call it a custom-fitted museum.

In Fannin County, the Cherokee believe the Little People, or fairies left behind tangible proof of their existence. The Fairy Crosses are found here. These twined staurolite crystals look like small crosses. They have been revered by the Cherokee and prized by collectors. People as diverse as Theodore Roosevelt, Charles Lindbergh and Thomas Edison have owned the stones. They occur in Fannin County in abundance. Your best chance of finding one is around the Mineral Bluff Area just after a rain. The Chamber of Commerce can give you more detailed information if you want to hunt for one. L. A. McKinney, a rock hound who has been hunting rocks most of his life says, "Georgia's staurolite is the best in this country. Maybe in the world."

There are two legends about the origin of the crosses. One tells of the Little People. Two thousand years ago when they heard of the Crucifixion of Jesus, they wept and each tear was changed into the mysterious crystals when it touched the earth.

The newer story is that they were formed by the tears of the Cherokee when they were driven from their homeland.

Three major festivals showcase local arts and crafts in Blue Ridge; Arts in the Park, held on Memorial Day weekend, Annual Mountain Harvest Fair, held on the third and fourth weekends of October, Holiday Art Show and Sale, in November and December.

Blue Ridge offers musicians many outlets for their artistry. Saturday nights, you will find music in the small park next to the depot. In fact you will usually find musicians aboard the train on Saturdays as well. Many fine local groups such as the Dowden Sisters and Butternut Creek introduce you to the music of the Appalachian settlers. Dulcimers and banjoes play true American Folk Music. The ballads of the mountains will make you laugh and cry.

Another unique attraction that is reminiscent of the "Good Old Days" is the Blue Ridge Scenic Railway. Riding the rails has always had an air or romance and adventure to it. In today's hustle bustle world, the railway has almost become a part of our lost past. Almost, but not quite. In Blue Ridge, Georgia, at the gateway to the Appalachians, it is alive and well.

The history of the railroad and Blue Ridge are irrevocably tied together. In 1887, the Marietta and North Georgia Railroad picked this spot for the area hub and the town of Blue Ridge was incorporated. It quickly became a boomtown as a result of the great iron road. Investors and tourists flocked there for many of the same reasons they do today, inspirational mountain views and a healthy laid back lifestyle. The boom, like all booms ended but Blue Ridge persisted.

Today, the old section around the depot has become a haven for artist and antique shops. Many of the buildings, like the depot, are on the National Historic Register. The Blue Ridge Scenic Railway is one of only two Georgia excursion train.

If you are interested in seeing some of the preserved history visit the Baugh House on West First Street. Built in 1890 by James Bough for his bride, Mary Giesler, this two story Federal style home was constructed of bricks from James' brickyard in Mineral Bluff. The home and grounds have been painstakingly restored by the Fannin County Heritage Foundation, Inc. and offer a glimpse into the life of an upper middle class family at the turn of the century.

If you want to search for some haunts of our own Blue Ridge Ghost Tours is the way to go.

For the visitor who likes more traditional pursuits, the Butternut Creek Golf Course in Blairsville and the Brasstown Valley Resort in Young Harris provides a championship eighteen-hole course with some of the best scenery around. Brasstown Valley Resort is a complete resort with a restaurant, gift shop, pub, spa, equestrian center, nature trails and star gazing observatory. It is one of the few places you can get an alcoholic beverage. Brasstown Valley Resort has some interesting exhibits on the Native American and early settler artifacts dug up during the excavation process while the resort was being built.

The first weekend in October, the tiny hamlet of Suches in the southwestern corner of the county, plays host to the Indian Summer Festival held in the historic Woody Gap School. Built in 1940 as a WPA project, Georgia's smallest school has been in continuous use for over seventy years but is still preserved much as it was originally built.

There is one problem visitors to North Georgia Mountains have to contend with after a visit. The mountains will weave their magic on you and draw you back again and again.

Etowah Mounds

Tunnel Hill That light sure looks eerie.

Worley B and B

Mine tour in Dahlonega

Downtown Helen

Exhibit at Brasstown Bald

Author Bio:

Kathleen Walls is the author of *Georgia's Ghostly Getaways, Finding Florida's Phantoms, Hosts with Ghost, Last Step, Man Hunt- The Eric Rudolph Story, Kudzu, Tax Sale Tactics Hosts With Ghosts: Haunted Historic Hotels in the Southeast and Wild About Florida, Under a Bloody Flag* and *Under a Black Flag, Missing—Gone but not Forgotten*, is a fictionalized version of a true abduction that occurred near her home in Florida in 2009 and has never been solved. Her latest work is American Music:Born in the USA, a history of American music. All published by Global Authors Publications (GAP). Kathleen is the publisher/owner of GAP. Several of her books are now audio books and most are also ebooks.

She is also a successful travel writer/photographer who has been published in numerous publications as well as her own online travel magazine, American Roads (www.americanroads.net) and several online tour guides.

She is a member of International Food Wine and Travel Writers Association (IFWTWA).

Her dual B.A. in Anthropology and Sociology from the University of Central Florida gives her a good insight into human behavior which is very helpful in writing realistic novels. You can visit her website at http://katywalls.com/

www.ingramcontent.com/pod-product-compliance
Lightning Source LLC
Chambersburg PA
CBHW060015100426
42740CB00010B/1492